A GOOD LIFE
WASTED

A GOOD LIFE
WASTED

OR

TWENTY YEARS AS A FISHING GUIDE

Dave Ames

The Lyons Press
Guilford, Connecticut
An imprint of The Globe Pequot Press

The Lyons Press is an imprint of The Globe Pequot Press.

10 9 8 7 6 5 4 3 2

Printed in the United States of America.

Designed by Lisa Reneson

ISBN 1-58574-631-2

Library of Congress Cataloging-in-Publication Data is available on file.

CONTENTS

Harry Morgan's Bridge

WITH ALL MY STRINGY FINGERS and all my splayed toes I still can't count the number of millionaires who have wished out loud that they could be me. This is surprising in its own right; what's *really* surprising is that these otherwise intelligent people have seen how I live. It wasn't always like this. I wasn't always such an icon of underachievement to the overemployed. I had a real job once, working as a hydrologist for the Lodge Grass National Forest in the urban hinterlands of Montana.

The federal building where I punched the clock, five stories of smoked glass and faceless red brick in downtown Cow Coulee, was the tallest building for four hundred miles in any direction. Jimmy Carter was president, the hostages were in Iran, and a revolutionary invention, the microchip, had just burst onto the scene.

My job was quantifying the effects of clear-cutting on stream quality. Compliments of Uncle Sam, I had the use of one of the first personal computers ever assembled. The battleship-gray Hewlett-Packard cost twenty thousand then, rattled like loose rivets on a torn wing, and occupied every square inch of a four-by-eight-foot table. The processor box alone could hold a picnic lunch and the beer cooler, too. A spaghetti of brightly colored cables was provided to link the drab boxes, but whoever wrote the instructions didn't know how it went together, either. And there weren't any programs. What you did instead was write long strings of code that boiled down to zeros and ones and eventually came to be known as software.

That first day on the job, a size-twelve foot through the door, I was so proud. Six months earlier I'd been dancing knock-kneed and naked at a Rolling Stones concert; now I wore long pants that weren't jeans for the first time ever. My shoulder-length hair was black as the tires on my new van, and I was in on the ground floor of the computer industry, the same as Bill Gates and Steve Jobs. I completed the reams of paperwork requisite to enlisting in the brotherhood of the federal bureaucracy, basking in the office hum, feeling like I'd finally grown up.

I had a desk. I had a secretary. I had a paycheck. I had health insurance, life insurance, a retirement plan. I even had paid days off, starting in six months.

Six months?

It was an interminable amount of time to spend indoors. And nobody ever said anything about cubicles. Or the stale, recycled gas that passed for air. It must have contained some oxygen since nobody died, but there couldn't have been enough to go around. I was so logy after a day's work, I became increasingly certain they'd laced the coffee with Novocain. That way nobody could escape. A week was more stupefying than opium. At the end of a month it was all I could do just to form complete sentences, and beginning anew each morning I had to force myself not to watch the thin hands on the big round wall clock.

The first designated cubicle release was the ten o'clock coffee break. I arrived at eight, and those first two hours of perpetual office twilight passed with agonizing slowness if I watched each minute tick by. Rules are stringent in the federal workplace. You're not required to accomplish anything but you do have to sit there, and since I couldn't walk around until ten I tried not to look at the clock until ten.

It was a game I played with varying degrees of success through the winter, and then came that first gorgeous spring day. Robins ate dried chokecherries in the bushes, and later that morning the Rocky Mountains were due for a total eclipse of the sun. The circle of the moon was going to exactly block out the circle of the sun, the kind of once-in-a-lifetime celestial miracle that surely spawned religions.

And I'd be watching from the asphalt oil slicks on the parking lot out back.

The chair squeaked as I leaned back at my desk, thinking how to describe in bits and bytes what happens to rivers when rain falls where trees once lived. I squirmed to find room for my bony knees between the sharp-edged runners on the metal drawer that wouldn't open. I flipped the three red toggle switches; the microprocessor whizzed, clicked, roared, and buzzed as it fell to sorting files.

That noise; loud, constant, annoying, it could get to you if you let it. Toilet paper tickled in my ears as I stared at the flickering green digits on the computer screen. Logging roads generated more sediment than current models predicted, so the numbers would have to be changed according to soil type. An eternity passed. What noise? Then, just to be on the safe side, I let another eternity go by. After a third eternity I finally looked at the clock.

It was fourteen minutes past eight.

My chin dropped to my chest. I was numb as I did the calculations.

An hour and forty-six minutes until the ten o'clock coffee break. Three hours until the eclipse. Nine hours until quitting time and thirty-three hours to the weekend, which meant, let's see—only eighty thousand hours to go before I could retire.

I looked back up at the clock, the thin red second hand was stuck on the six.

3

"NO-O-O!" I screamed. "NO-O-O!"

Now they describe this behavior in government employees as "Going Postal" and people duck, but back then there wasn't a word for it. Nobody knew I was dangerous, teetering on the brink of schizophrenic rage. Blinking heads popped up above cubicle walls like balding gophers in a prairie of yellow felt. I felt not just crazy but untethered as I took the steps in the concrete stairwell four at a time, past the red neon EXIT sign, sprinting for my white Chevy van.

I had to hold my right hand with my left just to get the key in the ignition, then ran the only stoplight in the county as I roared down Main Street. I turned hard left at the courthouse onto Bridge Street, skidding to a stop on the gravel in front of a splintered wooden false-front store, Joe's Hardware and Supply.

Joe was behind the counter, black grime under his fingernails as he whistled.

"That's some cut you got there," he said. "What happened? Did your wrench slip?"

My knuckles were skinned to the bone where I'd punched the office clock through the Sheetrock wall and into the next room on my way out. Blood trickled onto the check I wrote for a pair of number fourteen glass welding goggles and a box of Band-Aids.

"It sure did," I replied.

The pavement ended at the edge of town. An hour of gravel road to the west I stopped at the rounded top of the tallest in a line of scraggly prairie foothills. Surrounded by thirty miles of view, I sorted through the camping equipment in the back of the van. Humans see light at color equivalents up to about six thousand degrees; the sun burns at forty million degrees. A direct look at the fire that fuels our solar system, even when that fire is all but covered by the moon, and it's enough to blind you. It's bad genetic planning, I know, but there you have it. Welding glasses filter out the harmful ultraviolet. Joe's black goggles made me look like a World War I fighter pilot as I lay back in a chaise lounge, sipping a beer.

It grew noticeably colder as the black round moon oozed crescent by crescent across the round sun. When only a final curling torchlike wisp of light remained, the moon's shadow bull-rushed in from the east at two hundred miles a minute with an audible roar. The black shadow ate up thirty miles of olive sagebrush in seven seconds. In that last instant it was dark as twilight. Crickets chirped; birds sought out their nests. The sun's corona showed as a glimmering red halo around a black hole in the sky, an astronomical coincidence that even in the scale of the cosmos is a tad unusual.

The symmetry, the order; it means something, it has to.

I was born Baptist but they don't dance. In college Einstein had his way with me. In search of meaning, I formed a congregation of one in the Church of the Reduced Humanist. It's a simple faith: Reduce the world to its fundamental order, then everything else follows according to the Laws of Science, everything except Free Will.

Science explains everything yet determines nothing. Understand the electrons, you'll understand electricity. Understand quarks, you'll understand why some people leave the toilet seat up and some people don't. Understand the building blocks, you'll understand the building, and if you understand the building you have a lot better chance of finding the right room. If I could just understand the forces that render eclipses inevitable, then maybe I could make sense of what I'd just done.

My first real job, and I'd blown it.

What kind of dismal excuse for a white, Anglo-Saxon, Protestant male was I, anyway?

I needed a goal, a purpose, a direction in my life, so I set out to fish every mile of blue-ribbon trout water in Montana. Money would be a problem, but then it always is. Adhering to an abstract regimen would help build the character I so obviously lacked, therefore I resolved to fish Montana in alphabetical order.

To get it out of the way I promptly blew everything I had, then moved into my van. In a month I was down to my last nine dollars, not counting the change in the glove compartment. I'd bypassed zip codes entirely, but abstract regimen continued to elude me. In choosing waters I followed not the alphabet but the hatch of the giant orange salmonfly. Five rivers later I'd made it only as far as the A in Apikuni.

Pronounce it A as in *Apple* and rhyme it with *loony: Appe-koony*. It's a Blackfoot Indian word that loosely translates to "rotten buffalo robe," which loosely translates into "antique tuna casserole." Apikuni is a lot more than just a spoiled skin. It's a color. Blackfoot words often do double duty, and Apikuni is alive. It's growing. Apikuni is the color of life, a thousand shades of green, and that's where the river takes its name.

Turquoise springs of glacial flour bubble through the pine-green forest where the flow starts high in the limestone mountains on the east slope of the Rockies. The river tumbles ice-cold and blue-green through the rapids to the alkali foothills, where it slows to the color of spinach. The calcium-rich water is clear and clean; it's the fertilized river that's green, the reflection of a jungle of aquatic plants meandering along the bottom of the river in a leafy green underwater slash through the dry brown hills.

More plants equals more bugs equals more trout, and the Apikuni offers the best dry-fly fishing in at least the solar system—perhaps the galaxy. From the steep, undercut riverbanks you'll see mule deer, elk, eagles, the occasional grizzly bear. It's Blackfoot Indian country, a spiritual place where legend has it that Napi (rhymes with *happy*) tried to get some sleep after a hard day of making Human Beings.

Napi had a restless night wondering if he'd made a mistake. The only child of the Sun and the Moon, Napi wondered how to tell his Parents what he'd done. Talk about high expectations. Napi's stomach gurgled with indigestion as he lay curled on his side holding his belly. Legend has it that he knocked up high red buttes with his hips, knees, and shoulders as he struggled to get comfortable, hollowing out the course of the Apikuni River as he tossed and turned on the rocky ground.

Head in the snowcapped mountains, feet forty miles away on the brown plains of dried bunchgrass, the river is Napi's green blood, running down his curved backbone and along his bent legs, a verdant artery slashing through the otherwise dried brown rattlesnake country. The water loops north at Napi's shoulders around Pyramid Butte, a thin tower of rusty-red rock, then jade-ribbons south and east down his spine. Twenty miles and two feeder streams later the river is a hundred yards of trout wide when it hooks west at the seat of Napi's pants. Six miles after that the water bounces east at the knees when it collides with the massive cliff wall of Square Butte and the Head-Smashed-In Pishkun, a buffalo jump that North Americans have been using to get meat since before the pyramids were built in Egypt. And on the gravel road where the river crooks west at the waist there's a saloon in the old style, the Mountain Palace, and since I was thirsty it was a good thing I still had nine dollars.

It was the first hot day after a week of rain. I parked in the shade of a spreading cottonwood tree at the edge of a rutted lot half the size of a football field. I was studying the green cheese in the cooler thinking I'd borrow ice at the next motel that didn't lock its doors when a black hearse with oversized tires towing a cedar-strip driftboat skidded to a stop fifty feet away in the loose gravel. Doors creaked open on a tall Blackfoot Indian with long black braids, another Indian with a hairless brown gut and no shirt, a slender white woman in a short-sleeved blouse, and a pudgy white boy in a blue Cubs cap.

The woman stood on her tiptoes and kissed the tall Indian on the cheek.

"Kingfish," she said, "I don't know how to thank you. That you could teach Lester to . . . that he could catch all those trout . . . . I just . . ."

The woman was trying not to cry. They both looked at the boy. Lester had been born with bad neurons, something like Down's syndrome. The

7

adjustable band on the blue ball cap was opened all the way but it was still too small for his big round head. And even that smooth white basketball of a head was too small for Lester's thick-lipped red banana of a grin.

"The plane . . . ," said the woman, still not finishing any sentences, "We'll be late if . . ."

The three of them walked to a blue Ford compact with an AVIS sticker parked by the split-rail fence in front of the bar. The woman climbed in the driver's seat; the Kingfish seat-belted the boy in beside her, then put his brown palm on Lester's pink bulging forehead.

"Let's go over this one more time," said the Kingfish. "Back in Chicago, when you tell people you went fishing, and they ask you how you did, what do you tell them?"

Lester lost his smile, nodded solemnly, then held up ten pudgy fingers. "Twenny," he said. "We got twenny."

"And how big were they?" asked the Kingfish.

Lester was still solemn as he held his hands up about a foot apart.

The Kingfish scratched his head and looked sad. "How big?" he asked again.

And now the grin was back. Lester laughed and laughed as he thrust his hands so far apart he hit his mother in the shoulder. The Kingfish stepped back from the car.

"See you next year," he said, waving good-bye with both hands.

The blue Ford pulled out onto the frontage road, the woman biting her lip and staring straight ahead, so oblivious she nearly rammed a rusty pickup with green fenders and a yellow tailgate. The Blackfoot maiden hunched behind the wheel of the pickup truck gave Lester's mom the finger then accelerated directly toward the potbellied Indian without the shirt who had all this time been slouching against a wheel well on the shady side of the hearse. The man's eyes darted left then right before settling on the woman behind the wheel as the truck fishtailed to a stop directly in front of him.

"Easy there, Katy," the man said, edging along sideways with his back to the hearse and both hands up. "Whatever you heard, it ain't true."

Katy opened the door and climbed down. She had twenty-inch biceps, a sixty-inch waist, almond eyes, and a cast-iron frying pan in her right hand.

"You lying sack of shit," she said. "Maybe you forgot you got three kids."

Lying-Sack-of-Shit faked left and went right. For such a big woman Katy was surprisingly light on her feet. The sickening thunk of metal on skull told the story. Katy nudged the unconscious man with her toe just to make sure.

"That'll teach you not to come home nights," she said, then looked over at the Kingfish who had been watching the drama unfold from behind the safety of the driftboat. "And you," she said. "You can get your ass over here and help me load him up."

"Sure I will," the Kingfish called over, "soon as you throw down that skillet."

Together they lifted Lying-Sack-of-Shit into the back of the pickup truck; a yellow dog with ribs showing through licked the unconscious man's face as the truck disappeared down the road. The Kingfish looked straight up at the sky, his long, shiny black braids hanging down his back nearly to his waist.

"Tell Katy," he said to a cumulus cloud shaped like a turtle, "that she forgot her skillet."

He flipped the frying pan into the hearse then headed for the bar. I followed him in. The Mountain Palace was cool and dark. I stopped at the back to let my eyes adjust after the bright sun. Across the room the Kingfish was on a stool, a shot and a beer on the mahogany bar in front of him, talking with a spindly bartender in a white shirt and black vest.

"So Kingfish," said the bartender. "How'd it go last night?"

The Kingfish lit one cigarette with another and grinned.

The bartender threw down his towel and slicked back his thin brown hair.

"You and that damn sweat lodge," he said.

The Kingfish blew a smoke ring then drank off half his beer in two thirsty gulps. "Did you see what happened out in the parking lot?" he asked.

The bartender fingered the pearl buttons in his vest as he nodded. "The showdown was coming," he said, "You could see that."

"Yeah," said the Kingfish, "but it would have been nice if it came next week. I have more clients coming in tonight and now I'm a guide short."

It was a unique opportunity to expand my investment portfolio. Stocks, bonds, and real estate were out of the question. They were all reliable long-term speculations, but I needed to make money fast. A quick killing based on insider trading in the volatile commodities market was my only hope, so I immediately invested everything I had in beer.

"A pitcher," I said, sitting down at the stool next to the Kingfish.

He stared impassively down his long brown tomahawk of a nose.

"I heard you say you needed a fishing guy—" was as far as I got.

The Kingfish leapt to his feet. "You're a fishing guide?" he said.

I wasn't, but to prove I had what it takes to become one, I lied. "Sure," I said, "I'm a fishing guide. And I'm looking for work."

The Kingfish raised his muscled arms like somebody had scored a field goal. "I pay a hundred a day," he said, "and you can start tonight."

We shook on the deal, Indian style, his vast hand limp as wilted lettuce.

"Dinner's at seven," he continued. "You eat with the clients. And you gotta be polite, real polite. Tell them how many fish they're going to catch. If you need a place to stay, pitch a tent down by the creek. There's a shower in the garage. Tomorrow morning, you load the rafts and make the lunches. Then we'll go."

That was the sum total of the job description. I felt guilty over misrepresenting the amount of guiding experience I had, which was actually none. On the other hand, how bad could it be? From what I'd heard so far it didn't sound much harder than remembering to chew with your mouth closed.

It was too good to be true and then it got better. That evening I discovered an entirely new category of alcohol: fine red wine. We were in a big upstairs room with rain-spotted picture windows that looked out over the green river at Trout World, the Kingfish's two-story fishing lodge. The clients had arrived: the Yale class of 1929, the surviving members of the baseball team that won the Ivy League championship in extra innings their senior year.

They'd been catching trout together every year since they graduated. That had been such a long time ago you could put all their best parts together, they bragged, and still not field one decent body. The fine red wine was compliments of Cappy, a San Francisco restaurateur who had been accumulating rare vintages since before World War II and was bald as a bowling pin.

"To Loopy," he said in a frail voice, "and that great infield in the sky."

Liver-spotted hands clenching long-stemmed glasses rose all about the room, toasting the second baseman who wouldn't be joining them for the first time in nearly fifty years.

"To Loopy," echoed an equally frail chorus of voices.

Drinking red wine is like eating spaghetti with a spoon; if you don't know how, mimic someone who does. I stood in the corner by the antique jukebox, swishing wine in my deep glass, sniffing it, trying unsuccessfully to sip slowly because fine red wine tasted better than any liquid I had so far tried on the planet.

Around me the room was done up in kind of an art Indian deco, six-sided feather-and-willow dream catchers alongside glossy Picasso reprints framed with antlers. The jukebox was a mahogany Wurlitzer loaded with scratchy old-time country seventy-eights. It was hard not to tap your foot to the banjo music. I tried to be casual as Cappy walked up with a green bottle.

"You have to try this," he said. "It was Loopy's favorite."

The ceremony, the pomp, the fact that it was free—it was a heady experience for a guy living in his van, especially considering that the wine

I knew best was a fortified variety advertised as Mad Dog 20/20, which when mixed with 7 UP made a sweet drink the sorority girls called Going-All-the-Way. That story comes with another story, a story I decided not to tell.

I figured it was like chewing with your mouth closed.

"Drink the best bottles first," said Cappy, raising his glass.

It was the same toast he'd been using. I knew the proper rejoinder as we clinked glasses. "And don't buy any green bananas," I said.

The wine was so purple it was almost black, sloshing in sheer viscous sheets around the inside of the glass above Cappy's trembling hand.

"You got that right," he said.

The jukebox clanked, the record changed, the Kingfish walked over.

"Did you hear that high part?" he said. "Who is that fiddle player anyway?"

Trout World had originally been built as a boardinghouse when the first railroad came up the Apikuni River valley after the Civil War. The jukebox looked to have been around for a lot of those years, producing music from the vibrations in a needle on a tonearm that bounced along the tightly packed grooves in a disc of black vinyl spinning around at seventy-eight revolutions per second. The carved wooden tonearm was counterweighted with Scotch-taped pennies, and the Kingfish tapped cigarette ash onto the plank floor as he read the label on the spinning record.

"Mike Williams," he said. "I wonder how many other great musicians we've never heard of?"

Cappy's jaw dropped so fast all three of his jowls jiggled.

"You know who else could read a spinning seventy-eight?" he said. "Babe Ruth."

Babe Ruth? "You knew Babe Ruth?" I said.

"I hunted woodcock with him," said Cappy "Once a year in upstate New York."

No wonder the Babe could hit a curveball. The faded print on the label of the spinning record was an absolute blur. When I looked up the Kingfish's gray eyes were already waiting.

"Tomorrow let's try and find some salmonflies," he said. "How about if we float from Harry Morgan's Bridge down to County Line Campground? You think we'll find the bugs?"

Sweat trickled down my arms despite the evening chill.

I'd never even heard of Harry Morgan's Bridge. But I couldn't bring myself to admit it—not in front of everybody. Not when the room had grown so silent at the mere mention of salmonflies that the only sound was the whispering wind through the open window. I was the guide; I was supposed to know what I was doing. Confidence is critical to the catching of fish. And, I assumed, to getting paid. So that is why I said decisively: "Harry Morgan's to County Line. It sounds good."

It did, too.

I'd spent the three previous days camping at County Line. The huge orange salmonflies were out every day at about noon. I knew what flies were working. I knew the fish were holding in seams off the heavy current. If I wasn't familiar with the Harry Morgan's Bridge access point, I couldn't see that it mattered. I wasn't driving.

"That stretch of river below Harry's," I said, "has been great for big browns."

I said Harry like I knew him personally, then pulled a fly from my sheepskin hatband. "This has been what's working," I added authoritatively.

Cappy reached for the high-floating fly, an Orange Stimulator. The flat white wing of elk hair flared along the number two hook nearly spanned his palm.

"A fly that's easy to see," he said. "I like that. Have some more wine."

The Shortstop hobbled over wearing shorts and carrying an empty glass. Sheer varicose support hose covered withered shanks that legend had it once stole seven bases in a single game.

"A salmonfly hatch," he said dreamily "Do you think we'll hit it?"

As best I could tell, Cappy's smile was genuine.

"If we don't," he said, "we can always blame the guides."

The next morning I was up at dawn to make a good impression but the boss wasn't around. I ate four aspirin and took a shower; still no sign of the Kingfish. Bonnie, the Mormon cook, stood over the stove in the kitchen, her big sapphire hair spreading up and out like a giant blue mushroom.

"Where's the Kingfish?" I asked. "Does he always sleep this late?"

"Usually," she replied. "But today he was up early. He left you a note."

The note was scrawled on a brown grocery bag with a wide-tipped black marking pen, the letters barely legible, the message blunt and to the point: "Went to the airport to pick up the rest of the team. Take Mister Dead and meet me at Harry Morgan's Bridge at ten. Bring lunch for eight."

I squeezed my temples with my palms, willing the aspirin to kick in, trying to think.

Mister Dead was the hearse, I knew that much. I saw all too well from our conversation how the Kingfish could leap to the conclusion that I knew both Harry Morgan and his bridge. But there was no way I could have predicted the Kingfish would up and vanish in the night. He should have said something. He shouldn't have just left. But right now both blame and hindsight were nothing but water under the bridge.

Wherever the bridge was.

"This Harry Morgan," I asked Bonnie "Do you know him?"

"Harry Who?" she replied over the snap of sizzling bacon.

I was lost and I hadn't even gone anywhere yet. I hadn't even brushed my teeth. Bonnie didn't know anything; she'd just moved up from Salt Lake. And something else I'd prevaricated was that in my short time in Montana I'd never actually been above County Line Campground, the reason being a steep and rugged canyon that limited access.

In my van I had a dog-eared paperback copy of *The Floater's Guide to Montana*. The map of the Apikuni showed a river access point ten miles upstream of County Line called River Junction. I had to go somewhere. It seemed promising. I didn't have many choices—it was the only marked route into the canyon. Ten miles was a good day's float. Harry Morgan's Bridge had to be somewhere in the vicinity.

The book also described the road into River Junction as treacherous, especially if it had been raining. And there had been torrential thunderstorms every afternoon for the last week.

Sometimes I know I'm making a mistake but do it anyway.

The fresh set of tire tracks in the mire of the River Junction road was reason enough. Hoping it was the Kingfish, I followed, chattering nervously, pointing out ravens and quaking aspen, pine beetles and red-shafted flickers. Behind me the 1929 Yale softball team bounced on homemade plywood seats upholstered with antelope skin. Behind them a trailer stacked high with three fully inflated rafts and aluminum rowing frames jackknifed through the trees.

It was like a dream—a bad one—as I yanked back and forth on the steering wheel through an endless succession of 180-degree switchbacks. The rain had transmuted the road into the purest form of genuine Montana gumbo. And gumbo, a water-saturated bentonite clay, is not a material to be trifled with. Imagine the geologic equivalent of snot. It's awful stuff, the absence of friction, and the hearse didn't have power steering.

Sweat dripped off my nose and into my lap when the tire tracks I'd been following disappeared to the right straight up what looked like a creek bottom. The main road stretched ahead through a green tunnel of trees, virgin untracked gumbo. The Kingfish hadn't come this way but it was too narrow to turn around. A hundred yards later the road dropped like a roller coaster of sharp, slimy turns. I kept Mister Dead on the road, but the whipsawing trailer clanged trees twice that I heard. At my shoulder huge Cappy was riding shotgun and too big around the middle for his seat belt. He was bouncing all over the place. On the springs beside him, it was like sharing a trampoline.

"Are we lost?" asked the Shortstop from the backseat as I slammed on the brakes.

It's a good question and gets right to the core of existence. Heisenberg's Uncertainty Principle says that you can't know exactly where a particle on the scale of an electron is, only where it was, because the tiny particle ricochets randomly off the energy it takes to locate it. By the time you locate the particle it's already bounced off to somewhere else. At any given moment all you can ever know is where that particle was.

The significance in the Church of the Reduced Humanist is that by the time you realize what's happened it's already happened. Anybody can bounce anywhere, and since at the most fundamental level we can't ever be completely found, we can't ever be completely lost, either.

"No," I said. "I know exactly where we are."

We were back in river bottom. The trees had opened up into a meadow, and a pair of wood ducks floated in the pond where the road should have been. It was quiet in the backseat; too quiet.

Now Cappy, the captain and catcher of the team, took charge. "Are you sure we're not lost?" he asked in a stern voice.

All I had was the strength of my convictions, which at that moment could have stood to do a few push-ups. I couldn't be much of a fishing guide if I couldn't even find the river. And just so the morning would be perfect it started to rain.

"You're going to love this float," I said. "It's remote."

The recent storms had flooded the alpine meadow through which the raised road ran. But parts of the berm were above the water, and the rest didn't look that deep. And we were out of the hillside gumbo, back in the washed rock and gravel of an ancient river terrace. The tires would grab, even underwater. I couldn't turn around now, not when I was so close.

"Hold on," I said, "we're almost there."

I revved the engine, turned on the windshield wipers, and jammed the accelerator to the floor. Pond water sprayed up in a V-shaped roostertail. It was deeper than I'd hoped. At one point the trailer was actually floating, but it could have been worse because the water wasn't much more than calf-deep when we finally stalled twenty yards from the far shore.

"Well," said Cappy. "What next?"

It was another good question and I wished Science had a better answer.

"I'm going to put on my waders," I said, "and then dry out the spark plugs."

We finally pulled into the River Junction Campground at eleven o'clock. The Kingfish was nowhere to be seen. Wherever we were supposed to be, we were an hour late.

The sun was back out as I scurried around the hearse opening doors. Considering everything, the team was in pretty good spirits now that they thought there was a chance they actually might live through the day. I'd just helped the pipe-cleaner-thin Left Fielder out of his seat and onto the ground when he started jabbing at the blue sky with his cane.

"Look," he said. "Look! They're here. They're here!"

It isn't fly fishing without the flies. Overhead the flapping translucent wings of a dozen salmonflies sparkled like thrown handfuls of broken glass in the sunlight. Salmonflies are big and bulky, the size of a woman's ring finger, and lumbering in flight. It's a big easy meal for a quick-turning bird, a gob of glittering light disappeared in the yellow-and-orange swoop of a western tanager.

"D-d-damn," said Cappy, already stringing his rod together. "D-did you see that?"

You're always low on the flies that are working best because you've already used them. I searched my dwindling stash of high-floating Stimulators and gave Cappy the best one I had left. Cappy hobbled down to the river with the rest of the team except the Left Fielder, who tripped me with his cane to make sure we'd have a chance to talk.

"Are you sure we're not lost?" he said.

I looked up from the ground, searching for the right words. In that instant the Left Fielder's rheumy eyes widened behind his bifocals as he looked over my head.

"I don't believe it," he said. "You did know what you were doing."

I rolled over in the mud, looked at the river, and found a paradigm example of the Uncertainty Principle. We don't know precisely where anything is, but we do know where it's more likely to be. It's a question of energy, of probability. Some routes are more likely to be traveled through the fabric of space and time. Electrons are more likely to be in certain orbits, and certain fishermen are more likely to be on certain rivers.

The Kingfish was pulling into shore rowing a raft full of people. The Yale class of 1929 was reunited. The first and second basemen in matching brown neoprene waders waved sticklike arms from the front seat. The Kingfish had also brought two more guides, both Indians who studiously ignored me. Without a word they set to untying the rafts on the trailer behind Mister Dead. The Kingfish took me aside.

"Harry Morgan's Bridge," he said, scratching a rough map in the sand with his foot and pointing with his toe. "You put in a mile up the North Fork and float down to the main river. That way you don't have to drive the canyon."

His eyes were shiny and too bright. I started to look away but then stared him right back. I didn't need this damn job. I was about to tell the Kingfish what I thought of his leaving in the middle of the night when Cappy whooped from down by the river.

"First cast," he yelled. "You can't do any better than that."

Who was I kidding? I'd spent my last nine dollars on beer. I really needed this job.

"At least I had the right river," I said. "That's something anyway."

Cappy whooped again. The rest of the team stood around insulting his ancestry as the trout on the end of his line jumped twice in quick succession.

"And that fly that Cappy's using," I said, "I tied it."

Then Cappy smacked his forehead as the line went slack.

"He got away," he yelled to the team. "The knot broke."

The Kingfish kicked at the map in the sand and I knew what he was thinking.

"I didn't tie that bad knot," I said. "Cappy tied his own knot."

"Always tie the knot," said the Kingfish. "Always tie the knot. That way you know it'll be done right. Remember, Cappy hasn't tied a knot in a year."

"Hey," yelled Cappy. "Do you have any more of those flies?"

"Well?" said the Kingfish.

I took off my hat. The meager collection of well-chewed flies in the fleece band was self-explanatory.

"You sure you're not an Indian?" said the Kingfish. "Because you sure act like one."

Then he reached in his pocket for a plastic box and dropped a dozen gaudy orange flies into my palm, flies that by the end of the day had all been chomped to shreds. Salmonflies on the water are both large and help-less. It's the easiest meal of the whole year, and when the bugs are thick even the hugest brown trout slip from their private sanctuaries deep within the undercut banks to join in the feeding frenzy. The bright flies bobbed along in the cliff-wall chop as we floated, disappearing in one splashy trout take after another.

That's not to say catching fish was easy.

I was guiding the First Baseman and the Shortstop. The Shortstop was legally blind, and the First Baseman had lost most of the feeling in the left side of his body after a stroke. The Shortstop couldn't see the strike, and the First Baseman couldn't react to it. Helping people help themselves; it's the essence of guiding. I found that if I yelled "FISH-FISH-FISH!" in the Shortstop's ear when a trout ate his fly, and spun the boat to tighten the line to help the First Baseman set the hook, then all those missed strikes started turning into jumping fish.

Both rods were doubled over with tugging fish when a peal of thunder rumbled across the hills. I beached the raft on a gravel bar alongside the other boats. There's no good place to wait out a thunderstorm on a river but we did our best, as far as possible from the nearest trees, huddled in the lee of a shallow hole in a limestone cliff while the full fury of a twenty-five-thousand-foot-high cumulonimbus cloud broke around us.

We were so close to the center of the storm that sound and light arrived simultaneously in jagged bolts of electric blue thunder. There aren't many jobs where you get to be a hero, and I was replete with vicarious fish-catching pleasure. Those old guys in my boat had appreciated the day so much. Then, without any warning at all, Cappy darted out into the pelting rain.

He left like a sprinter from the blocks, if the sprinter is wearing waders over a Humpty-Dumpty costume. Cappy had always been stout, the team catcher, with a center of gravity so low he must've been an immovable object when defending home plate. A lifetime of good food and drink had extended that center of gravity considerably. Cappy gave it everything he had, but you can only do so much when you're eighty-one and round as a grapefruit.

Cappy said later he had to run. He said it was like a command coming from everywhere at once, he could do nothing else but obey, and it probably saved his life. Cappy thanked his Guardian Angel but I think he ran for secular causes. He was compelled to enter his first race in fifty years because he was the geriatric version of the bionic man, his premonition simply a positive charge building up on all the metal he packed around inside him.

Cappy was held together with pins and plates, a legacy of his hard-fought athletic career. He had steel knees, steel hips, two hearing aids, a pacemaker, an oxygen tank for emergencies, and a battery pack in a shoulder harness that delivered electrical pulses to stimulate the muscles in his back. With all that to go wrong, you wouldn't think it would be the back that would finally catch up to him.

Cappy ran downstream directly away from the upstream trees as if he really had been warned, so fast he kicked up squirts of gravel with every step. A dozen strides later he was still accelerating when the top of the tallest cottonwood tree vaporized in a resounding crack of lightning that wasn't nearly as loud as Cappy's high-pitched scream. The backpack spit a stream of yellow sparks and blew soft puffs of white smoke; Cappy pitched forward facefirst into the gray, sticky river mud.

We all leapt out into the rain. The air stunk of sweet ozone, and the backpack sizzled in as the Kingfish sliced Cappy free of the harness with a bone-handled sheath knife. I helped roll him over on his back. The Kingfish leaned forward to check Cappy's vital signs.

"Does he have a pulse?" I asked. "Is he breathing?"

"Not only that," said the Kingfish, "he's smiling."

Cappy was, too, a beatific smile, like he knew something that nobody else did.

"Quick!" he said "Call my wife."

I was thinking *Last Will and Testament*, but the Shortstop knew better.

"A stiffy," he said, and there was wonder in his voice, "Cappy has a stiffy."

And there it was, the telltale bulge in Cappy's waders.

"Geez," said the third baseman—and there was wonder in his voice, too—anymore just going to the bathroom is about as much fun as I can handle."

"Oops," said Cappy. "Never mind."

The team at this point was of a single emotion. Their long, sad faces and slack jaws all told the same story: Some things are worth dying for. Cappy's friends weren't concerned, they were jealous. Cappy had come within a whisker of frying like a grub on a griddle but every man there would gladly have traded places with him.

And these were wise, learned men.

It's a lesson I've never forgotten.

We fished until cocktail hour then stopped at the Mountain Palace for local color, the taste of sweet grease wafting on the prairie breezes. A cowboy in a sweat-stained Stetson folded his hand at the poker game as we walked inside. I was standing beneath the talons of a stuffed golden eagle, broke and sober, not my favorite combination, when the Left Fielder limped up on his cane and slipped a folded bill into my hand.

"Good job out there today," he said gruffly.

"Thank you very much," I called out as he headed immediately back to the bar.

I turned around to be discreet, opened up the bill, stared, blinked, then stared again.

Ben Franklin stared right back. I was a hundred-aire and I hadn't even gotten paid yet. But already I could see how much I had to learn about fly fishing. Just watching the other guides, there was a lot going on out there. A lifetime didn't seem long enough to learn it all, so I decided to get started right away, with the gaunt man leaning forward on his elbows at the end of the bar.

He had the look of somebody who had spent his entire life outdoors, that weathered look of indeterminate age. He could have been forty or he could have been ninety. Either way he'd forgotten more than I'd ever know about the Apikuni, and the leathery skin on the backs of his hands appeared to be about as tough as the Bunyan Bugs stuck in his fleece hatband.

And that's tough for skin, since Bunyan Bugs are made out of wood. It's an old salmonfly pattern from way before my time. The fly body is carved, usually from pine, then painted orange and crossed with deer-hair legs. I'd never even seen a real one before, only pictures in books, and since monetarily-wise I was now walking in high cotton I bought him a drink.

"Thanks," he said with a quick, sidelong glance as I sat down.

"It's a pleasure," I said, "for a craftsman such as yourself."

This time the glance was even sharper, like he thought I might be selling something.

"I couldn't help noticing those beautiful flies on your hat," I added. "Did you tie them?"

Finally he smiled. It doesn't matter if you're in Fiji or Montana, fishermen love to talk.

"It's more like building than tying, " he said, "with all that wood and glue."

Up close, they were bulkier than you would like. "How do they cast?" I asked.

"Like a horseshoe," he admitted, "but that ain't why I use 'em. I could tell you it's because of the memories, but that ain't it neither. I use 'em 'cause they float low and you can still see 'em."

I settled to get comfortable on my bar stool, then offered my hand and introduced myself.

"The name is Morgan," he replied. "Harry Morgan."

Destiny

UNLESS ACTED UPON BY AN OUTSIDE FORCE, a body at rest or in uniform motion tends to stay at rest or in uniform motion, and in the Church of the Reduced Humanist this is as true of the animate as the inanimate. Consider couch potatoes. It's inertia, Newton's Second Law, and for the next ten years the Apikuni was as far removed from outside forces as you could get and still be in America.

I was, to my bemusement, still guiding. I always thought I'd go back to college and get more degrees but I never had. It was an odd skill for the end of the twentieth century that I'd discovered in myself, the knack of teaching people to catch fish, and I raised my glass to Harry Morgan's picture on the Wall of Fame behind the mahogany bar at the Mountain Palace.

"Thanks, Harry," I said simply.

It isn't easy when your friends go. The Wall of Fame is a black-and-white collection of photographs of all the regulars over the decades who have departed for that great Trout Stream in the Sky. From Harry I'd learned about bugs. His library of entomology was comprehensive, a collection of

25

well-thumbed first editions that he'd bequeathed to me on his passing a month earlier. Squatty, the black-haired bartender with one bushy eyebrow that grew without interruption from earlobe to earlobe, saw my raised glass and came for the ketchup-spattered plate that lay on the counter before me.

"How was dinner?" he asked.

At the Mountain Palace they fry everything, even the water.

"Dinner was great," I lied.

Prior to metamorphosis, many species of mayfly nymphs rise explosively from the streambed with the help of an internally generated bubble of gas. If you've ever eaten at the Mountain Palace you'll know just how those nymphs must feel. It's not the kind of cuisine you follow with a cigar. Depending on your choice of entrée, you could go up like the *Hindenburg*.

It was a Friday night and the place was packed. Every accidental elbow to the stomach was a potential detonation as I shuffled through the shoulder-to-shoulder throng. The narrow corridor accessing the rest rooms was lit by one bare sixty-watt bulb. The rough plank door marked POINTERS was sprung wide open on its one remaining hinge. Four potbellied bikers jostled in the beer-recycling line—and that was just the overflow of black leather and silver chains into the hallway. Both toilets and the sink were already occupied.

I'm not above using the ladies' room in an emergency, but I was too late. A woman with hair black and shiny as raven feathers, a diamond necklace, and a torso-clinging orange sweater beat me to the punch. The diamond dangled on a gold chain, bouncing between breasts pointed like cashmere traffic pylons, then disappeared behind the water-stained door marked SETTERS.

The woman's necklace was worth more than the four bikers' combined annual salary, but that's the nature of a Montana fishing bar: You never know who you'll meet. Then I did what I should have done in the first place and hobbled out the back door to the sage-speckled bluff above the Apikuni River. The Kingfish was already there, head back to the night sky, his baritone voice slightly forlorn as he contemplated the eve of his fifty-second birthday.

"It's hell getting old," he said, "and the bladder's the first thing to go."

My bladder was nearly twenty years younger than his but I was stretched as tight as a carcass in the hot sun. Depending on what gave first, things could get decidedly messy.

"It better be," I grunted.

The planet earth, with the exception of incremental additions from meteorites and volcanoes, has had the same water since the first oceans formed more than three billion years ago. That water is us. Thinking about it like that, a toilet seemed disrespectful. No wonder there's déjà vu. My water splashed into the silver river of the reflected heavens, swirling downhill through the Great Plains to the Deep South and the Gulf of Mexico where pirates once roamed.

"Next stop, New Orleans," I cried as the aft cannons fired.

The Kingfish wrinkled his nose and turned upwind toward the vast northern sky.

"No way," he said. "That won't stop until it gets to the Milky Way."

"Chili dogs," I gasped.

The white stars pierced the clear black sky, as bright as stars ever get, as bright as the porch lights on the next hill over. Like you could get there if you wanted. I thought about Harry. To the extent that we're all destined for the recycling bin under the sink of the celestial kitchen, to the extent that mass and energy are neither created nor destroyed, then it seemed mingling fluids did offer an indisputable sense of immortality. It was a theory I could embrace wholeheartedly because it made such a good case for two of a fishing guide's favorite food groups: beer and coffee.

A place in the afterlife assured, the Kingfish and I walked down the loose gravel shoulder of the blacktopped road that followed the river. We stopped by the sign we'd spent a whole day making, red block letters on white plywood spelled out:

ONE NIGHT ONLY:
The North Fork Nitwits

I played a little but the Kingfish was the head Nitwit, guitar and lead vocals. Music came out of him easier than most people sweat. He was also six-four so when he kicked something it generally stayed kicked; the plywood barely budged under the heel of his cowboy boot.

"The Taj Mahal of signs," he said. "Maybe this will be the one that lasts."

"I hope so," I replied. "I'm tired of making signs."

This was our fourth sign. The first three were casualties to a wind that starts hard at the North Pole, then builds up a head of steam on the straightaways of Alberta. By the time it gets to Montana it can blow a truck off the highway; our first sign, hardboard screwed to a single wooden stake, never stood a chance. It just vanished. The next two incarnations fared slightly better: Although they were destroyed, at least they didn't end up in Wyoming.

But this sign was built to last. We'd abandoned the concept of stakes completely. It was an A-frame sandwich sign, stout plywood squares hinged at the top, spread at the bottom, and weighted down with burlap sandbags at the edge of a parking lot paved with eclectic vehicles.

There were plenty of late-model four-wheel drives gussied up with power everything and out-of-state plates, but there were more disheveled pickups squatting low on bald tires with palomino rust jobs and local plates. And in front of the bar's peeled-log porch railing angled chevrons of low-slung Harley-Davidsons heeled over on chrome kickstands. The gleaming renegade motorcycles were mostly without any license plates at all.

"Well," I said, "the sign is working anyway. I've never seen it this crowded in March."

The Kingfish sighed, his copper skin glowing in the brief flare of orange light as he lit a cigarette with a wooden kitchen match. "It's a sign all right," he said. "A sign of the times."

Then he blew smoke through both nostrils at a folded page of glossy paper he pulled from the pocket of his red flannel shirt. Blue light buzzed from the mercury vapor lamp on the parking lot pole. The folded paper opened origami style into the cover of a fly-fishing magazine, and the Apikuni was featured in big, block letters.

"Did you see this?" said the Kingfish disgustedly.

"No," I said, wishing I had been the one to click the shutter on the cover photograph.

It was called *The Triple Rainbow*, starting with the twin arcs of a full-spectrum double rainbow that curved to low yellow hills on both sides. Those two red-to-purple rainbows framed perfectly the third rainbow: a leaping trout, flash frozen in an arc of mercury spray. The Kingfish tacked the paper to the creosoted light pole with his pocketknife, stepped back, and drew on the photograph with an imaginary bow and arrow.

"We never should have let those wagon trains through in the first place," he said morosely, "and this picture will bring in a lot more people than the wagon trains ever did."

There was a definite upside to more people if it was April and you were a fishing guide who hadn't had work since October.

"Bring 'em on," I said, "MasterCard and Visa will gladly be accepted."

The Kingfish looked down his long tomahawk of a broken nose. "You wait," he said. "You'll eat those words."

If I did, I hoped they went down better than the chili dogs.

The new-moon night was too cold for idle chatter in shirtsleeves. The Kingfish yanked his knife from the pole and we shouldered through the double swinging doors back into the smoky sweat of the bar. The Kingfish headed for his guitar. I leaned against the wall, eyes closed, still fizzing with chemical turbulence.

"Excuse me, but might I have a word with you?"

The diction was perfect, the accent twangy New England. I opened my eyes to the girl in the orange sweater I'd watched disappear into the bathroom.

"My name is Destiny," she said "And I wish to hire you."

Up close she had tangerine fingernails and matching lipstick to go with the sweater. And no way could that diamond on her chest be real, they were far too large. It, not they. It took me a moment to realize my mistake. I was staring, and I looked up from the jewel set between the pylons in her plunging cashmere neckline, totally distracted.

"Hire me?" I said.

Destiny looked amused as she scrutinized the green palm trees on my red cotton shirt. "The bartender suggested I speak with you," she said. "You are a fishing guide?"

I struggled to maintain a calm, professional demeanor but inside I was jitterbugging. Work! I could buy propane!

"I sure am," I replied in an even voice. "And tomorrow will be a good day to catch some fish. It's supposed to get up into the sixties. The blue-winged olives should start hatching about noon."

Then I cleared my throat. I'd never been comfortable with the business end of guiding. Even after all those years the sums involved in merely going fishing seemed slightly ridiculous.

"It's three hundred dollars a day," I said. "But that includes lunch and dinner."

Destiny didn't blink at the price.

"And the following day?" she asked. "Are you available?"

I now have a confession to make. Actually two confessions. First, the going rate didn't ordinarily include dinner. And second, I have no idea whether Destiny actually blinked or not because I was no longer looking her in the eye.

"I'm available," I replied.

Destiny was astounding in her ability to defy gravity, like maybe there were hidden wires, but not that much was hidden. In the presence of beautiful women I'm capable of nearly anything, most of which is stupid. It's as if my brain takes on a life of its own. This time two little high-pitched children's voices regaled me with a knock-knock joke between the ears.

Knock, Knock.

Who's there?

Silly.

Silly Who?

Silicone.

The punch line surprised even me. What a great joke I'd played on myself. I'd just been offered six hundred dollars to take a pretty girl fishing. Now, not only was I staring at her breasts, I was laughing at them. Even by my standards of stupidity this was off the charts.

Destiny cleared her throat I followed the hollow in her pale neck past the sharply defined tube of her larynx to her almond-shaped eyes. There I saw something I'd only read about. Her brown eyes turned gold. It's a recessive gene trait that three hundred years ago in Salem, Massachusetts, was enough to get a woman burned at the stake as a witch, and Destiny smiled yellow like a jungle cat before it feeds.

"Then it's settled," she said. "I assume you take credit cards?"

It was a balmy fifty-two degrees at ten o'clock the next morning as I rowed my fourteen-foot fiberglass driftboat down the placid green river. Darting goldfinches flashed yellow in the olive bank willows. Reclining in the front seat with her feet up on the open bow, Destiny was resplendent in her own plumage, lavender waders with matching lipstick and eyeliner.

I tucked an oar under a knee, tapped Destiny's shoulder, and pointed downstream. "That cliff coming up on the right," I said. "That's Head-Smashed-In, the pishkun you were asking about."

Pishkun is the Blackfoot word for buffalo jump but it translates more like "deep-blood-kettle." Head-Smashed-In was such a reliable place to get meat that back at about the time of the Boston Tea Party ten thousand Crow and Blackfoot warriors fought for its possession. Archaeologists describe it as one of the largest battles in Native American history, and Destiny pushed her dark sunglasses up onto the black bangs on her forehead for a better look.

"What makes that particular cliff so special?" she asked.

The sheer red precipice is a hundred feet high and half a mile long, but it doesn't appear to be that different from a dozen other cliffs along the river. What makes Head-Smashed-In special is the long, natural, steep-sided trough behind the drop-off. I let go of the oars and, with both hands free and the boat drifting sideways down the river, drew the shape of a funnel in air.

"Once the buffalo got in," I said, "they couldn't get out."

Destiny spread her hands flat, her palms smooth as a fresh sheet of white paper. "But why would buffalo run for the cliff in the first place?" she asked.

The way it worked was, a medicine man would dress up in a buffalo skin. In this disguise he would bellow and paw out a challenge to the lead bull in a passing herd of buffalo. The medicine man would then retreat into the mouth of the trough, pulling the lead bull in after him. The herd followed the lead bull. When they'd ventured far enough the trap was sprung as the rest of the tribe rose up from behind strategically placed brush piles that defined the edges of the funneling trough, hazing the buffalo with flapping antelope skins into stampeding off the cliff.

Leaping buffalo didn't always die in the fall, so the Blackfoot helped them along with a stockade built from sharpened, fire-hardened tree trunks jutting up at the bottom of the cliff. A deep-blood-kettle of screaming, gut-impaled buffalo is a far cry from cellophane-wrapped sirloins, but the more gore I described, the greater the detail Destiny demanded.

"Bones and skulls wash out of the ground after a hard rain," I continued. "Some of the Blackfoot say you can still hear the screams of dying animals on a full-moon night."

We rounded a corner. Urbane Destiny switched gears to a more familiar topic. "Who is that man?" she asked, "and why is he staring at me?"

Not many girls can make a pair of waders look good. The lanky man in the pea-green boat was probably the only guide on the river who wasn't staring at Destiny.

"Don't worry," I said. "That's Secret Agent Man, and he's looking at me, not you."

Destiny arched her thin black eyebrows suggestively as she smiled. I could never tell for sure when women were flirting. It was true they sometimes wanted more than just a guide trip, but a girl like Destiny must've been used to men falling at her feet. My best chance was to play it straight. At the very worst we'd have a good time catching trout.

"Not like that," I said. "In ten years I've never seen Secret Agent Man with a boy. Or a girl, for that matter. All he does is fish. He'd shoot a hole in his boat before he'd show you his flies, because then his secrets would be safe even if they were lost at the bottom of the river. He's watching us because he's afraid we might be watching him."

I stepped on the lever that dropped the anchor. Thirty pounds of lead splashed off the stern. We watched as Secret Agent Man rowed madly away down the river.

"Textbook paranoia," said Destiny. "My shrink would have a field day. Are all guides this crazy?"

"Pretty much," I said. "Otherwise they'd be able to hold real jobs."

Destiny leaned so far forward her long hair tickled the backs of my big hands. "And what about you?" she said. "What's your secret?"

The secret to guiding is to put fish on the end of the line as quickly as possible because then and only then will people pay attention to what you have to say. You can't teach if they won't listen. It all boils down to credibility, and when it comes to beginners catching fish on flies there are three cardinal rules.

"I have three secrets," I said. "The first and most important is Rule Number One . . ."

I paused for dramatic effect. Daffodil-flecked whirlpools began to swirl around the black pupils in Destiny's brown eyes as she waited for the most important maxim of all:

"Slack is Evil."

Destiny blinked. When her lavender lids popped open, her irises were all the way yellow.

"Not just bad," she said, "but Evil?"

"Worse than landlords," I replied. "Slack in the line is Evil because you can't cast slack, and you can't set the hook with slack. The best way to control slack is to keep the rod tip low, so low it's nearly touching the water. If you try to cast slack you'll spend all day undoing tangles. And every time you're tangled, that's another fish you didn't catch."

I held up the rig we'd be using, a weighted nymph tied on thin monofilament line about four feet below a dime-sized foam bobber. We were anchored in the shadow of a cliff that human beings had been using to get meat since the last ice age. In terms of putting fish in the boat, weighted nymphs are the most effective technique to come along since nets and sharp spears.

"Rule Number Two," I said: "The best cast is the one you don't make. Just leave the fly in the water. That's where the fish are."

Destiny took the rod and studied the fly. The green nymph was ribbed with gold wire, less than half an inch long, and fuzzy because it was tied with the stiff guard hairs from inside a rabbit's ear.

"The best cast is the one you don't make," I repeated, "because that nymph imitates the bugs that live at the bottom of the river—the bugs that make up eighty percent of what trout eat. The trout are down at the bottom looking for the bugs. You have to get the fly down to the fish. Depending on current speed, it takes the fly five or ten seconds to sink to the proper depth, so if you cast every five or ten seconds the fly will never get to where it needs to be. You see it all the time: fishermen flailing away constantly all day long and complaining in the bar they never catch any fish, like maybe they thought fish lived up in the air because that's where their flies were."

Destiny bounced the tapered nymph up and down, trying it out for heft. "The best cast is the one you don't make," she said. "Like a Zen thing."

"Exactly," I said. "And Rule Number Three: You can't set the hook too quickly. Did you ever watch fish feeding in an aquarium, how they flick their food in and out quick as a hummingbird's tongue, testing before they swallow? Trout are the same way. By the time the bobber moves, the trout is already spitting out the fly. That's why we're using a fuzzy nymph. It sticks in the trout's teeth a little bit longer, and it's easier to detect the strikes."

The silver hoops in Destiny's earlobes jiggled as a trout jumped next to the boat.

"Okay," she said. "Three rules. That's easy enough. I have it."

"Okay," I said, even though I knew she didn't.

Destiny, on only her second cast, attempted to pick a loose coil of slack off the water by waving the rod back and forth. *Slack is Evil:* That quickly, the entire leader was lashed in a knot of unholy matrimony, and curled nylon has a memory. Once monofilament pigtails, it wants to pigtail again. The best thing to do is cut out bad tangles and start over with fresh line.

The silent repair time offers an opportunity to teach, but the caliber of people who can afford guided fishing trips aren't used to taking instruction. The captains of industry and finance you're likely to meet didn't get where they are by being told what to do, especially when they've just made a mess of things. I prefer an indirect approach to the art of teaching, subscribing to the Parable School of guiding, beginning with the gospel of Saint Stephen.

"Don't worry about it," I told Destiny as I reached for a knife to slice the knot out of her line. "It happens to everybody. This tangle is nothing, not compared to what happened to Saint Stephen his first day of fishing."

In all honesty Stephen wasn't so much a Saint as a Sinner, a three-hundred-pound black man who liked his rum.

"How much fishing have you done before?" I'd asked Stephen when he first climbed into my boat.

"None," he replied. "Shee-it, I never even seed real cows before today. Everything I knows about nature I learns on the Dee-scovery Channel."

The ghetto English was all an act; Stephen could also enunciate like the king of England. He was a successful stockbroker with a degree from Oxford, but Stephen was smart enough to act dumb, and he was good at it. What he wasn't good at was managing slack.

A little slack in the line on the water is good. It helps promote a drag-free drift, but too much slack and you can't set the hook. Stephen was compensating for the slack in his line by rearing back with every ounce of his six-foot, six-inch body every time he had a bite. The boat was rocking so much I was getting seasick. Finally I pulled over, beaching the boat on a shallow mudflat on the inside edge of an eddy formed by a large rock.

"Try it here," I said. "Just flip it upstream and let the flies sink. The bobber should run right down that current seam below the rock. And remember, keep that line tight."

"Yassuh," he said. "I knows. You teaches me good. Dat slack is sho 'nuf eee-ville."

Don't let the self-deprecation fool you. At this point, sitting there in the front of the boat, Stephen had metabolized into a highly focused bundle of fishing energy. He'd had dozens of bites, a couple of fish on, but had yet to land a trout. And it was making him crazy. Or maybe it was the rum. Either way, what Stephen wanted more than anything else in the world was to catch a fish. It's an atavistic urge I've watched overwhelm hundreds of people over the years; this time when the bobber plunged down, Stephen was ready.

At three hundred pounds, he was more than ready. Stephen set the hook so hard he fell over backward and snapped the plastic seat right off its swivel. The only part of Stephen still in the boat was two size-fifteen feet in leather lace-up shoes. The rest of him lay in the shallow water, half buried in the soft mud.

The fish was still on; in plunging over backward, Stephen had pulled the trout close enough to the boat that I was able to net it. I held up the trout, sixteen inches long, his first fish ever. Stephen smiled with his floppy ears still in the water. And now when he spoke, it was in the clipped British English of Winston Churchill.

"You know, old chap," he said, "it isn't easy being a large black man in America."

I'd told that story enough to get it right. Destiny snorted as I imitated Stephen's Oxford accent then grabbed with both hands for her rerigged rod.

"I get it already," she said. "Slack is sho 'nuf eee-ville."

Slack is Evil, the Prime Directive; she'd take it to her grave. Once you master slack, the next hurdle to catching trout on weighted nymphs is detecting strikes by sometimes infinitesimal movements of the bobber. It's easier with a guide. You'll be able to detect strikes right off by the way he screams.

"FISH, FISH, FISH," I yelled, but Destiny never moved.

"Too late," I said.

"What?" she said. "What!"

"That was a fish," I said. "That little twitch of the bobber, that was a fish."

I'd shipped the anchor. We were floating down the river, still in the shadow of Head-Smashed-In. Destiny was casting plenty well enough to catch fish. Her flies were in the perfect position, twenty-five feet out and slightly ahead of the boat. The bobber danced slowly down the swirling current seam. It hadn't gone another twenty feet when it dimpled again.

"FISH, FISH, FISH," I yelled.

Destiny stamped her foot. "It barely moved," she protested. "That wasn't a fish."

"Too late," I said.

Sometimes the bobber doesn't move at all; it just slows down. And sometimes it doesn't even do that much. The leader is never absolutely straight between the bobber and the flies. By the time the bobber moves, the fish is already spitting out the fly.

"Rule number three," I said, "you can't set the hook too qui—FISH-FISH-FISH!"

The bobber plunged down in a classic take. It had already popped back up to the surface by the time Destiny reared back on the rod. Everybody pulls too hard at first, and Destiny turned to watch as I unwrapped the fly line from my neck.

"Now that was a fish," she said.

"They were all fish," I said. "You have to believe."

As I repaired the second tangle I told Destiny the Parable of Alex, a twelve-year-old boy who was the best I've ever seen at setting the hook. Alex was barely five feet tall, but he went to the head of the class for two reasons. First, he had the hand–eye coordination of a middleweight boxer. He was quick enough to dodge a striking snake. But his rapierlike reflexes mattered less than the fact that Alex was still young enough to believe in Santa Claus. When that bobber twitched there wasn't any doubt in his mind. It wasn't a rock or a stick or a weed at the end of his line; it was a fish. Adults think it's a fish, kids know it's a fish.

"And the moral here," I finished, "is that if you have to think about setting the hook, it's already too late. That fish just got away."

Destiny took the rod, her slender fingers trembling with adrenaline.

"Thank you very much, Mister Aesop," she said.

Lavender legs locked in the knee brace, Destiny stood in the front of the boat. She was bent forward at the waist, her pointed chin jutting forward in concentration, and this time when the bobber went down the rod stayed bent. A gleaming trout jumped as silver as her sterling earrings. Line sizzled from the reel as Destiny held on with both hands, her arms extended straight down toward the water.

"Keep the rod tip high," I said, "If you lower . . ."

Wild trout are surprisingly strong. I've seen them yank rods right out of people's hands.

"Shit," said Destiny. "Shit, shit, shit."

The bend in the rod acts like a shock absorber. With the rod pointed straight at the fish, there's no flex in the system. In the face of that unyielding resistance, the first thing to give is the hook in the corner of the trout's mouth. It's a disheartening feeling when the taut line goes slack as the fly rips free.

"Don't worry about it," I said. "You'll get the next one."

"Shit," said Destiny. "Shit, shit, *shit!*"

The good old days on the Apikuni really were. The aquatic grass flats across from Head-Smashed-In were so thick with fish that it was common to get a hundred or more strikes in a day. There's an excitement in catching fish that goes back to a time when it was the difference between eating and not eating. A surprising number of women over the years have described that prehensile pleasure in sexual terms. Tired fish should always be released in slow currents, and I pulled the boat to shore. Five minutes of deep-throat squealing later Destiny's face glowed like angel skin as she gently cradled her first trout in six inches of clear water.

"The trout's heart," she whispered, "I can feel it pounding in the tips of my fingers."

By releasing that fish Destiny was giving life. There is a God-like sense to it, especially at first, the resurrection of a connection to a natural order long buried in the casket of overscheduled city life. Destiny knelt over her trout, leaning so far forward that her black hair dragged in the weak current. The purple crescents of her long fingernails were cupped lightly behind the flaring red gills. The blue carotid artery pulsed in her pale extended neck.

"Whose heart is beating faster?" I asked. "Your heart or the trout's?"

Destiny looked up. At the movement the trout flicked its tail and eased away.

"My heart," she said.

She stood up and bounced on her toes like a ballerina, if ballerinas wore purple rubber suits and grabbed their guides with both hands by the collars of their Hawaiian shirts.

"Let's get another one!" she said. "Let's get another one!"

People lose themselves in good fishing and the trout that day, as Destiny so poetically put it, "were stacked like the hoagies in the window of Fred's Broadway Deli." When people are catching fish they relax for what might be the first time in months or even decades, then they forget. What job? What phone bill? What house that needs painting? What nagging spouse? What pregnant teenage daughter? None of that stuff matters.

Fishing well requires an utter concentration that somehow slows the hands on the cosmic clock. Einstein showed that time is relative to the fabric of space. Depending on factors like acceleration, time slows down and speeds up like a car, and when time stops there's only the moment. Poised for the moment with a fly rod in the front of the boat, Destiny had become perfectly intent on catching trout: Just to let them go.

She was utterly absorbed: On accomplishing absolutely nothing.

Catch-and-release fishing must be what Samuel Beckett envisioned with the Theater of the Absurd. Only more so. It's one thing to wait for Godot, it's another thing entirely to actively pursue him. And in this absurd theater, a unique drama premieres daily. No matter how much you know, there's always something new to learn. No matter how much you've seen, you haven't seen it all, and later that afternoon Destiny rotated her head, rubbing at the top of her knobbed spine like she'd pinched a nerve in her neck.

"How are you doing?" I asked. "Are you getting tired yet?"

"My arms are exhausted," she said. "Even my hair is exhausted. These fish are strong."

Then the floating orange bobber darted crazily sideways in a hard take by a wild trout.

"But not that tired," she said.

Destiny's curved body stiffened as she lifted the rod to set the hook. Biologists say trout aren't capable of cognitive reasoning, but I'm not so sure. If you catch and release a fish enough times it seems plausible that it could learn from its mistakes and come up with better escape routes. An evasive maneuver I see more trout using all the time comes straight from the pages of Moby Dick: Hooked, they speed directly back at the boat.

It's a good trick because it puts slack in the line, and Slack is Evil. Now the fish is in control of what happens next. Most trout employing this tactic swim under the boat and keep going, which breaks at least the tippet and sometimes the rod, but Destiny's fish tried an airborne attack. It was a prodigious leap of Olympian proportions.

The trout had plenty of height to carry the boat, and would have had the distance if Destiny's face hadn't gotten in the way. The two-pound muscle of solid trout slapped her a punishing blow, hard enough to send her sunglasses clattering to the bottom of the boat. One of her eyes was brown and the other yellow. With crossed irises she rubbed the red welt rising on her cheek in the forked shape of a trout's tail.

Her mouth opened, her lips moved, nothing but bubbles came out. It's not often you see a lawyer speechless. The trout was doing back flips at Destiny's feet, but when I reached for the fish my curled fingers stopped dead inches short.

"A tarantula!" I said. "Get back! Get back!"

A huge, black spider was waving its long furry legs alongside the flopping trout. I didn't know how a tarantula got in my boat and I didn't care. The important thing was that it wasn't getting out. I once lost a chunk of my leg the size of an apple to a spider bite in Costa Rica. The muscle grew back but I still mash spiders as a matter of phobia. I was hard at work stomping the spider into arachnid hereafter when Destiny squeezed my arm.

"That's no tarantula," she said. "That's my eyelash."

I closed one eye. The curled mascara of a giant false eyelash snapped into focus.

"Sorry," I said.

Destiny's tittering belly laugh ended abruptly as she spread ten thin fingers on her suddenly rumbling stomach. And when she held out her hands the once white palms were red with blisters from catching so many fish.

"I'm hungry?" she said. "It must be time for lunch?"

She sounded puzzled, as if food was a foreign concept, hunger an alien experience.

"Not lunch," I said. "Dinner."

"Dinner!"

Good days fishing vanish as if they never happened, as if the hours won't be counted against the sum of your life. It's that relative-time thing again, the diametric opposite of a boring job. The sun was already a golden smear in the wispy pink clouds above the western mountains. Destiny had been so focused on her bobber she'd never taken the time to look around. Now she turned a full circle in the boat, a bright lavender orchid in the drab Montana sagebrush as she threw both arms in the air.

"What a day," she said. "What a glorious day."

A good day guiding, when you've done everything right, is uniquely gratifying. In the eyes of the client you're like a hero in a century when crooked bookkeepers have the run of the land. It is a crime against nature not to straddle the forces of the universe when they align, and Destiny was renting a cottage in the foothills just down from Beaver Head Rock. The Beaver Head cottages come fancy, with everything from hot tubs to stereos, and a shooting star lit the night sky as I turned off the engine in my truck in the graveled driveway.

"Come in for a minute," said Destiny. "I have a little something for you."

Gratuities are all that stand between most fishing guides and death by slow starvation.

"Thanks," I said, "I really appreciate it."

Regular tips keep the show on the road. They pay for gas, flies, lunch, the bar bill, all the everyday expenses. Side tips are different. They define the lifestyle. Side tips are the difference between living and merely existing. Now I made Bombay martinis from the ingredients on the kitchen counter while Destiny put some old jazz on the tape deck.

"Sit," she said, leading me by a cool hand over to the leather couch.

Over the years I'd received side tips of everything from twenty-five-year-old Scotch to Cuban cigars to Mexican fishing vacations, but this was the first time ever for lingerie. Ella Fitzgerald sang and Destiny danced, sweet-scented-nothings piling up in my lap one wiggle at a time. It was a slow two-martini tease. Destiny was down to a lacy black thong and gray wool socks when the tape ended midsong in an abrupt hiss of static. My heart stopped along with Destiny, her thumbs already hooked in the thin elastic waistband. But we really do live in the Golden Age. Thank God for autoreverse.

Married men live longer, and guys like me are the reason why. The bed was a four-poster, peeled-log, grape-arbor kind of an affair and that first night we broke it, twice. I'd always had either four girlfriends or none and for a long time that had been enough. But now, even though I knew it was a mistake, because it really isn't a choice, I did it anyway.

With Destiny, for the first time, I fell in love.

It was a mistake because she was a high-powered defense attorney in Seattle, and I was a Montana fishing guide. The cultural differences were extreme, and long-distance relationships are tough to begin with. Absence might make the heart grow fonder, but dinner for one gets old in a hurry. And phone sex only goes so far. It's a wonder nobody was electrocuted. Then one humid evening the phone rang. Without preamble Destiny said: "We have to talk."

This was a lie. We didn't have to talk; it had already been decided. I just wasn't willing to admit it. What we had—it didn't seem possible it couldn't ever be there again, no matter how many other people there were in the world. We couldn't just give up. I was certain we could work things out face to face. Without calling to let her know I was coming, I started driving. Fourteen hours later the smooth interstate highway had left the lava flats of eastern Washington to climb the Coast Range and dump me in the bustle of downtown Seattle.

Destiny had moved closer to the Space Needle since I'd seen her last; what I had was an address. The Sunday-morning sidewalks around the Pike Place Market were crammed with pierced bodies and Day-Glo hair colors. The area was unusually bohemian for Destiny's decidedly upscale tastes, but all I could think about was a coffee shop on the corner. They roasted their own beans, and after a hard day's night I desperately needed a jolt of caffeine.

Drool rose at the back of my tongue over the rich coffee aroma as I pushed through the plate-glass door. Service was slow because the place was packed. I got a triple espresso to stay. The only available seat was at a window table for two. A slender man with a green Mohawk and silver rings in his nose, eyebrows, and ears slouched back in his wicker chair. He was staring out the window, but sat up straight when I pointed wearily at the empty chair across from him.

"Is there anybody sitting here?" I asked.

Green Mohawk smiled, the rings in his nose jingling together like wind chimes.

"There is now," he said. "Be my guest."

The steaming coffee was too hot to drink. The heavy ceramic mug clinked as I set it on the glass table. When I leaned forward to pull up my chair, startled blue eyes looked back from my reflection in the polished glass. It wasn't so long ago on the banks of the Puget Sound that salmon dried in the sun while men compared details on totem poles; the conversation now was the two women at the next table over who were comparing notes on the seven most erogenous zones of the female body.

This was one seminar I didn't want to miss. I leaned farther forward, grabbing both sides of the table with white-knuckled hands. A burly woman with a shaved head was doing all the talking, a skinny redhead with lips painted to match her black leather vest nodding in agreement. The response centers weren't where you might think. Well, that one was. Green Mohawk had good reason to look startled—at that point I'd practically crawled across the table into his lap.

He smiled and said something. I had no idea what, so I smiled back and said: "I'm a fishing guide," as if that explained everything.

The bald woman slapped the table; the redhead chewed her split ends. Green Mohawk took a dainty sip of coffee with his finely manicured right hand. I watched in slow motion through the glass table as his left hand slid up my tanned leg and disappeared under my grass-stained shorts. It suddenly made sense that half the women in the room sported mustaches.

Until that moment I'd had no idea gay coffee shops even existed.

What Green Mohawk found up my shorts was misleading, entirely misleading. I leapt up and caught the edge of the low table with the tops of my thighs. It tilted, and my steaming espresso slid into Green

Mohawk's lap. He threw up his right arm in a reflex reaction. The coffee from the cup in his hand was launched over his shoulder in a spreading black blob.

The hot coffee splatted on the back of the bald woman's sleeveless white T-shirt. She turned, the stiff hair on her upper lip bristling as she screamed her outrage. A smart captain knows when it's time to abandon a sinking ship. Too late, I realized I had no business being in Seattle. I was making good time down the sidewalk toward Montana when my flapping feet were stopped dead in their rubber river sandals.

I'd nearly run down two women, Destiny and an Asian woman I didn't know, at a crosswalk. Arm in arm, they stood with their cheeks pressed so close together that their hair fell in one ebony shower. Women are essentially incomprehensible to men; I knew it then. But I didn't care, I missed her so much already. Destiny took a step backward, then crossed her arms on her chest with her hands clenched on opposite shoulders. Her lips curled up and down at the same time. It didn't seem possible that a smile could be so sad yet so sweet.

"I'm sorry," she said.

If I follow my heart and things go wrong I don't mind so much. But if I follow my head and things go wrong, I wonder if I should have followed my heart. So I pretty much always follow my heart. The head, naturally, is jealous, and likes to say *I told you so*. This time the head got even with the heart by flashing a picture of one possible future.

It might have been thirty or even forty years later. I was walking into a café with one shoe on and one shoe off. There were egg stains on my shirt, and my hair hadn't been combed in weeks. I was mumbling incoherently. The other customers and even the waitress looked away in an embarrassment they didn't quite understand as I sat down alone at the counter.

What a vision. As if things weren't bad enough. Nobody should have to deal with a head like that. No wonder I was crying.

Head, said my heart, *lighten up*.

Because once you've known love, nothing else will do. And ladies really do love outlaws, for about two weeks to a year. It's a fact of fishing guide history. In my heart I knew already that being broken was just something the head was going to have to learn to accept, in my head I knew already that the heart was going to be tough on all of us.

Heidi

ADULT MIDGES SKITTERED FRANTICALLY on and above the river, but trout rose only to the midge pupae mired in the sticky tension of the surface film. These pupae, as they sprout wings and struggle free of the nymphal shuck, have long been regarded as helpless, but recent studies by the Bureau of Underwater Growth (or B.U.G.) have shown that not only are they vulnerable, they're confused. Fortunately for their parents, there is no cause for alarm.

Confusion is normal in teenagers, and midge pupae have it worse than most. Their entire adolescence is crammed into a scant minute or two. It's human puberty in hyperdrive. Imagine hair, breasts, and genitals swelling like time-lapse flowers. Acne, *ph-t-t-t,* come and gone. All those bad hair days in the same follicle of time. The weight of a thousand awkward moments dumbbelled together; all those nights in the back of Jimmy O'Malley's Ford distilled to one giant grope then, suddenly, back there between that third pair of legs, full grown and begging for penetration: There it is. Whatever it is.

"It's no wonder those poor bugs are confused," said Heidi.

At least that's the way she saw it. Lately, to catch more trout, Heidi had been trying to think like a bug, and now she tied a flea-sized black-and-red midge pupa to her 6X tippet.

"I think like a girl," she said to the fish that had so far refused seven different flies. "It only gets me in trouble."

She'd put the trout down with a rushed cast. Now Heidi was waiting for the fish to rise again, certain she was on the right track with the new fly. Midge pupae were fresh vital food. There was more energy per mouthful. Trout ate pupae for the same reason elk in the spring followed the snow line feasting on the first shoots of green grass: nutrition. These bugs were going to metamorphose, mate, and die all before she had her next beer. With all those vital juices flowing, it would be astonishing if trout ate anything else.

"It's like having hot mustard on your bug," said Heidi.

If asked, Heidi would deny talking to herself, but over the years she'd spent enough time alone that it had become as natural as blinking. She was dressed all in black, even her waders, and the thick braid cascading the length of her spine was a vivid blond streak in the gathering darkness. Except for her lips Heidi was motionless as the bark on a tree in thigh deep water, her fly rod flat to the river behind her, waiting for the trout to show itself one more time.

"Maybe I'm getting flat feet," she muttered. "These boots used to fit just fine."

Her wading boots pinched and her feet were throbbing lumps of pain. Heidi wondered if her toes were purple yet, or just blue, and the last she'd heard Jimmy O'Malley was still in jail.

A while later she said: "I'm too young to get flat feet."

And a while after that she said: "Okay, so I lied."

She'd been hoping the wind would die at dusk, but if anything it was stronger. Heidi stared without blinking at the dark green water twenty feet away where she'd seen the nose of a good fish, but not in the last five minutes.

Six minutes.

Seven.

Eight, and Heidi was back to thinking like a bug, considering the barrier of surface tension. It's a formidable obstacle for a hatching insect. She'd read it was like a person digging up through three feet of dirt, but Heidi saw it more as a thick layer of ice overhead. And below the ice there would be hungry fish, gaping tooth-filled maws everywhere she looked.

Heidi saw herself submerged in shark-infested waters, trying to break through the ice. It was taking too long. She had a crowbar, but couldn't get a good swing, because she was wrapped in a straitjacket. And it hurt. God, it hurt. Like an explosion with nowhere to go. Legs, wings, antennae, and all manner of bursting organs were mashed against the constraining straitjacket. And despite her most frantic wriggling, she couldn't quite work free.

And then in the cold blue water, drifting to the surface, a hungry shark.

"It's about time," gasped Heidi.

She couldn't even feel her feet anymore. The trout was rising again, dimpling in the film, not moving even an iota to either side. Midges hatch tens of thousands at a time. With so many bugs on the water it's not about how many casts you make, it's about making each cast count. Heidi paused, getting the rhythm of the rise. She cast on the four-count, her drift was perfect, and the trout took a natural half an inch away from her fly.

Her second cast received the same refusal. So did the third, fourth, and fifth.

"Well if it isn't the pupae," said Heidi, "what the hell is that fish eating?"

The trout had been rising with the tiniest of rings, barely denting the surface, but now the hooked jaw poked all the way out of the water as a wispy cluster of mating midges rolled down the river. Heidi shuddered. It's not often the secrets of the universe are revealed. Revelation, by definition, is unexpected, and this time it came with an exquisite full-body rush. Raised Catholic, Heidi wondered if Moses felt anywhere near this ecstatic on the Mount.

"It's the taste," she said. "Of course. It's the *taste!*"

Heidi reached in her frayed fishing vest for the palm-sized aquarium net she always kept handy. A walnut-sized orgy of feathery midges tumbled by. She caught it with a quick scoop of the net, then popped the clump of bugs in her mouth, chewing with a quizzical expression.

"Hm-m-m," she said, licking crunchy chitin off her square front teeth "No wonder."

Heidi bit the pupa off the end of her line and tied on a Griffith's Gnat. This bushy-hackled dry fly looks nothing at all like an individual midge, but everything like a cluster of uninhibited midges engaging in passionate group sex. There can be dozens of panting, sweating midges participating in these wispy orgies, tumbling lightly about the river in a tangle of airy appendages, caught up in a moment of glorious intensity that must be the coq au vin of the bug world. No wonder trout went out of their way to eat certain flies.

This thinking like a bug was really paying off.

"Scratch-and-Sniff Flies," shouted Heidi. "I'll be rich."

Heidi shouted because she'd grown up poor; the prospect of rich excited her. She also shouted because the fish was larger than she thought, and things were happening fast. The trout had gulped the Griffith's Gnat in a splashy take on the first cast. At the touch of the hook the fish had bolted directly back at Heidi. She stood on her tiptoes with the rod held up to the first stars now popping in the night sky, furiously stripping in slack.

More quickly than she could pull it in the line snaked back out, bellying in a long, taut curve, hissing as it sliced a trail of foaming bubbles through the dark green water. Heidi chased the trout downstream to the next pool, following until the river was as close to the top of her waders as she dared go on a cold night in April. Twenty feet of bright yellow backing showed at the end of the bent rod when the line sagged limply. With all the resistance of the line on the water, the tiny fly had torn free of the trout's jaw. Heidi's mouth opened, then closed, then opened again as she began to sing softly in a clear alto voice:

> I lost the fish and I feel so glad;
> It fought like Attila the Hun.
> It was the best fish I ever had;
> I fought the fish and the, fish won;
> I fought the fish and the, fish won.

Half humming, half making up her own words to the melody of the rock 'n' roll classic, "I Fought the Law," Heidi cranked the line and leader onto the spool of her reel. The corners of her blue lips turned up toward the jade earrings that matched her eyes as she clipped off the Griffith's Gnat and stuck it in her hat. Heidi grabbed her three-piece rod by both ends, and tugged it apart—and her smile drooped in dismay as the center section of the rod plopped into the water.

"Being blond," she said. "It's not for everybody."

The middle of a five-hundred-dollar rod was sinking out of sight. Heidi pinched her nose shut but kept her eyes open as she dropped through the silver mirror of surface tension, seeing but not feeling her fingers close around the thin graphite cylinder in the dark green water. The water was so cold her jaw ached. Back at the surface a few remaining midges washed loose as Heidi shot a ribbon of water through the thin gap between her front teeth.

If she'd been cold before, now she was freezing, and it was a mile back to her truck. Jogging helped; halfway back Heidi was warm enough to walk. A good thing, too, she thought, wheezing. The last time she could remember running a whole mile was a lifetime ago in track practice. When the roaring in her ears disappeared Heidi noticed the wind had finally eased. A pheasant crowed in an uncut irrigation ditch, a squadron of geese honked against the rising moon, a distant coyote howled in the purple sage, and Heidi joined the chorus.

"Catching fish with my," she sang, "wet buns . . ."

The well of lyrics had long since run dry when she arrived back at the potholed two-lane highway. A green rubber-tired tractor rolled past with the headlights on. Heidi stared at the dented camper that reared above her Ford three-quarter-ton pickup. Her nose dripped, she wiped with the cuff of her black wool sleeve and said to the broken tailgate: "If this is what happens when you think like a bug, maybe it's time to start thinking like a girl again."

The wood-paneled camper walls had been home for seven months now. The evening swim in the freezing water had given Heidi a splitting ice cream headache; she ate four dry aspirins, then stripped by the dim blue light of the naked twelve-volt bulbs over the tiny table. She was big without being fat, the Montana state record she'd set throwing the discus for Butte High still hadn't been broken. In the cracked mirror her bronze tan went all the way to the bikini line and was starting to fade. Two weeks earlier she'd been in Mexico, on assignment, and the fuzzy beach towel Heidi used to rub her muscles dry still smelled of the sea.

Heidi, a professional photographer, had been around the world twice. And she was thinking that twice was enough. It was good to be back in Montana.

"For a smart girl," she said to the mirror, "you sure have done some dumb things."

Especially coming from Butte, she should have known better. The copper mines were shut down, the richest hill on earth was now the biggest pit on earth, a green-stained hole so big it had eaten half the town. It was like if life came with a set of instructions, she wouldn't bother to read them; like it didn't count unless she figured it out the hard way. What bothered Heidi most was that after ten years of scrabbling, all she had to show for her travels was the pickup truck that rocked on its heavy-duty springs as she stepped to the tiny closet for dry clothes without feeling the least bit like camping.

Not on a Friday night.

The bar back up the road had been crowded even earlier that afternoon when she'd driven past; now the only parking spot left was on the gravel road shoulder. Heidi backed into the narrow space, yawning with the heater cranked too high. She was yawning again, thinking she'd just crawl into her bunk if the aspirins didn't kick in soon, when a dull thud was immediately followed by a sharp, splintering crack. Heidi jammed on the brakes with both feet and smacked the steering wheel with the heel of her left hand.

"Not again," she groaned, wondering what it would cost this time.

Despite the largest mirrors money could buy, a blind spot that Heidi had come to think of as her blond spot remained directly behind the camper. In the past seven months she'd backed into a gas pump, a car, a cow, two trees, and a palapa in Oaxaca. This time it was a sign. In the mud behind her truck Heidi pieced together jagged chunks of plywood like a giant jigsaw puzzle until she could read the red letters.

"The North Fork Nitwits?" she said.

Heidi wiped her muddy hands on the dried yellow bunchgrass beside the split-rail fence and stood up. The parking lot was lit by one flickering vapor light nailed to a stubby creosoted telephone pole. Her breath caught in her throat. It wasn't the first time she'd seen the black hearse now centered like a bull's-eye in the blue glow of the overhead light.

Yesterday morning she'd been photographing nesting horned larks in the spring-fed prairie above Beaver Head Rock, totally concealed in a willow-and-burlap blind in a dense brier patch at the edge of the rocky bluff above the river. Hunched over the camera on her tripod, Heidi could hear an engine coming half a mile away. The motor knocked as it died fifty yards of thorny rose thicket away. Doors creaked open, then slammed shut; a tall brown Indian with long black braids and four white men in baseball caps sauntered into Heidi's view along the edge of Beaver Head Rock. The five men gazed down on the river where four fishermen were already fanned out on the gravel bar, two with fish bending their rods.

"Shit," said a man in a Mets cap, "they're in our spot."

"I told you we needed to leave earlier," said a gaunt man in a green parka.

"I told you we needed to leave earlier," mimicked a man who held his head like it hurt.

Long Black Braids rubbed his hands together as if he were making fire. "I think it's time the Indians staged an uprising," he said.

Green Parka wrung his hands. "What are you going to do?" he asked.

Mets Cap smiled. "You sure are a sneaky bastard," he said appreciatively.

"Remember that," said Long Black Braids, "when you're writing a check for the tip. Now you guys go get ready to move fast. Put on all your fishing stuff."

The men disappeared. Car doors creaked; then it was quiet. Heidi was zeroed in on a lark as it shredded a piece of orange baling twine to use as lining for its nest. The motor drive on her camera whirred as Green Parka's reed-thin voice said: "What are you looking for?"

Long Black Braids replied in his radio announcer's baritone. "Someday," he said, "I gotta clean out under this seat. I know that tape from the last powwow is here somewhere."

A car stereo suddenly boomed, ceremonial drums and guttural chants storming like avenging ghost riders over Beaver Head Rock. The echo of three quick high-powered rifle shots startled Heidi enough that she bumped her head on the bent sticks at the top of the blind. The fishermen on the gravel bar looked nervously over their shoulders as they fished. Moments later Long Black Braids danced into sight at the edge of the bluff. He brandished a half-gallon bottle of whiskey with one hand, a lever-action deer rifle with the other, all the while stomping up a miniature cyclone of dust as he skipped a tight circle to the beat of the pounding drums.

The music got faster and faster, building to a feverish crescendo. Long Black Braids stopped as suddenly as the drums. He now stood facing the lake with his legs spread and arms up, the whiskey and the rifle silhouetted against the blue morning sky. Just to be certain he had the undivided attention of the four cowering fishermen below, he squeezed off another round.

"Hey," he called, "you white guys won't mind if me and about twenty of my buddies come down and do a little shoot-and-release fishing, will you?"

The drums started up again. Long Black Braids danced slowly back out of sight.

"Get ready," he said. "They'll come up that path there. We'll go down over here."

As if it were choreographed, the four fishermen on the river hurriedly gathered their gear and left by the quickest trail out, their heads popping up and down at the edge of the bluff like worried gophers. Meanwhile Long Black Braids and his crew ran a back-door play through a narrow cut between the granite outcrops that formed the head and shoulders of Beaver Head Rock. The displaced fishermen wandered around scratching their heads for a while, wondering where all the Indians went. After much discussion they finally decided that since the coast appeared to be clear they should go fishing again, but when they walked back to the bluff they found that someone had taken over their sweet spot on the gravel bar.

"Hey," said a man in rose-colored glasses, "isn't that the guy with the rifle down there?"

He pointed to the lake where Long Black Braids was walking between fishermen. Every time he stood beside one of them he'd say something, and the guy would catch a fish.

"He looks like a guide," added Rose-Colored Glasses.

They stood there quietly. They still hadn't quite figured it out yet.

"He is a guide!" said Rose-Colored Glasses.

They talked big for a while about going back down to the lake, but they weren't fooling Heidi. Those four were in way over their heads. In a boardroom they might have had a chance with Long Black Braids, but maybe not even then. Heidi had packed up when the rich low-angled light that made good photographs was gone for the morning. Long Black Braids and his crew were still fishing. She'd walked right past their vehicle, a black hearse modified at the corners with plate steel and oversized knobby tires.

The hearse in the blue parking lot glare was the same, complete with deer-antler gun racks in the back windows, only now it was hitched to a trailer loaded with a high-sided, wooden driftboat. A boat is personal. It reveals personality as much as any of those secrets you ever hid in the bottom of your underwear drawer. This boat had four-toed, painted yellow clown feet centered on the floor in front of the seats that said: STAND HERE.

Heidi was so stunned she had to lean back against the light pole.

"Brilliant," she said out loud. "What a great idea."

She'd guided one summer during college; the money was good, but she didn't have the patience for it. Fish-counters were bad but boat-rockers were worse, standing on the chines, digging in the edge of the boat, the full weight of a born-again couch potato behind every body cast. The boat would rock so bad you'd need Dramamine, just to keep down your lunch. Heidi checked the parking lot for prying eyes then flipped open the lid to the scuffed plastic cooler.

Crushed beer cans, soggy corn chips in half-melted ice, a jar of green mayonnaise.

H-m-m-m, she thought, *no girlfriend*.

The double plank doors to the bar were thrown wide open, propped back against the log wall with stainless-steel beer kegs. The smoke inside was dense enough to box and ship. Heidi forced her way through the crowd to the edge of the worn mahogany counter. The bartender was a thin man in a leather vest with the sad eyes of a clown.

"What'll it be?" he called out.

"Just a Coke," replied Heidi.

Two things could happen when you grew up in Butte: Either you drank too much, or you didn't drink at all. Heidi went back and forth. Still chilled to the bone, her straight-backed reflection shivered in the mirror behind the liquor bottles as the bartender scooped cubes into a pretty-clean glass.

"No ice," she yelled.

The bartender nodded without looking up, dumped the ice, filled the glass.

"Four bits," he said, slapping the drink down on the scarred counter.

Heidi slid a five across the bar, then pointed at the musicians clumped on the stage.

"The Nitwits?" she said.

The bartender nodded. "In the flesh."

The band comprised seven men and two women. Instruments ranged from banjos and mandolins to clarinets and kazoos; there was even an upright bass. Long Black Braids stood front and center, chopping out bar chords on the arched spruce top of the dreadnought acoustic guitar strapped across his chest.

"I need to talk with one of them," said Heidi. "I'm afraid I have some bad news."

The bartender looked both ways then leaned in close out across the bar. "What?" he said. "Is it your daughter that's pregnant?"

Heidi blinked. She didn't think she looked old enough to have a pregnant daughter. "It's nothing like that," she said. "It's just that I ran over their sign."

The bartender relaxed, grinning as he made change from a sheaf of loose bills. "They'll be glad to hear that," he said. "They love making signs." He was still chuckling as he left to fill drink orders.

The Nitwits finished a hillbilly version of Bob Dylan's "You Ain't Goin' Nowhere" on mostly the same beat—at least everybody reached for their beers at the same time. The banjo player was a month overdue for a haircut as he leaned down close to Long Black Braid's guitar. "Give me a G," he said, "These new strings are still stretching."

Long Black Braids strummed a chord. A woman in a yellow sweater and a fishing vest stuffed full of harmonicas wrinkled her pointed nose as the banjoist twisted pearl tuning pegs. When all the notes were just right, Long Black Braids looked back over his shoulder at the rest of the band. "I wrote a song," he said, "For that fishing album we keep talking about doing. You want to try it?"

"That depends," said the woman in the yellow sweater. "What's it called?"

Long Black Braids smiled and said: "Our Bodies, Our Flies."

"That's what I was afraid of," replied the woman as she reached for a harmonica.

"Any tricks?" said half the band altogether.

Long Black Braids shook his head. "You'll hear it," he said. "Straight country blues."

"Are there any other kind?" said the man with gray hair playing the bass.

"In C," said Long Black Braids.

He tapped out the rhythm with his cowboy boot, walked up a bass line to the root chord, then threw back his head to the log ceiling and sang:

> Our bodies, our flies; We're not like other guys,
> Except that when we're using them, Everybody lies.
> We twist 'em and we tie 'em, We dip 'em in cement,
> We fondle them all over, In basements and in tents.
> We might be pathological, Most certainly we're bent,
> 'cause when we feed them to a fish, We think it's excellent.

> Our bodies, our flies; We're not like other guys,
> For the silly things we do, I have no alibis.
> We lock them up in boxes, We wave them in the breeze,
> And sometimes we even, Throw them up in the trees.
> It could be contagious, Like mad-cow disease,
> But it's better than using, A yellow ball of cheese.

> Our bodies, our flies; We're not like other guys,
> Except we like to argue, About the relative size.
> There's Hendricksons and Sulphurs, And Pale Morning Duns,
> But my favorite is the Humpy, That's Golden like the sun.
> Our bodies, our flies; We're not like other guys,
> Except that the point, Is to try and get a rise.
> Except that the point, Is to try and get a rise.

The last note still ringing, Long Black Braids was already stomping his heavy cowboy boot, shouting: "One, two, three, four."

The Nitwits funked right into a horn-driven version of "Satisfaction" by the Rolling Stones. This was especially impressive since none of the Nitwits actually owned horns. They settled for a harmonica, a clarinet, and a scared-looking man with the hair of Albert Einstein tooting away on an oversized kazoo. All around the bar women young and old looked at each other, giggling nervously as Long Black Braids swallowed the mike with his rumbling diesel voice, calling for volunteers to help with the backup vocals.

"The Nitwits are looking for some Nit-wettes," he said. "Anybody feel like singing?"

Heidi couldn't remember a time when she didn't feel like singing. She'd read that classical music stimulated infants to learn by relaxing their brains into a receptive alpha state, and wondered how it changed things that her dad had squeezed lead accordion in a six-piece polka band. Either way, the music was in her soul. Her mother worked graveyard shifts at the hospital, and three nights a week starting as a seven-pound, seven-ounce infant Heidi practiced with the band, lulled to sleep in the bassinet on the scratched Formica kitchen counter, her little pink toes twitching with the downbeat.

Heidi hung her plaid wool coat on the back of a chair, shook out her hair, and climbed onto the stage in a red T-shirt that said CANCUN. The cheap cotton was tight across her chest because it'd shrunk in the first wash. Without wondering why Heidi grabbed up a pair of wrinkled brown maracas hanging by leather thongs from the aluminum microphone stand. She didn't play them so much as they played her, sharing the microphone with Long Black Braids, his high brown cheekbone pressed to her soft white temple. He did the slow "I can't get no"; she did the quick "No, No, Nos"; they both did the slow "Sat-tis-fac-tions." They sang the last verse together, the whole band except a guitar player in the back ending together in an abrupt "NO-NO-NO" of barwide pandemonium.

Heidi's arms dropped like chain-sawed trees at the final note. Long Black Braids took a step back, studying her. Up close his eyes were the color of milk chocolate.

"Hey," he said, "you sing good. The band's taking a break now, but after that, come back up, let's do some more songs."

Heidi pulled her T-shirt back down over her navel. Her hands had been so far over her head as she shook the maracas that CANCUN had ridden up nearly to her shoulders.

"What's with these maracas?" she said, her voice jittery. "I thought my arms were going to fall off. It was like I couldn't stop. I just kept going faster and faster."

"Rattles," said Long Black Braids, "not maracas. My grandmother made them."

He reached for the rattles; Heidi, oddly reluctant to let go, held them up for a better look. They were pretty simple really: a hard, wrinkled sphere fixed with glue and rawhide to the end of a carved wooden stick.

"What is that?" asked Heidi. "Some kind of dried squash?"

Long Black Braids reached for a duct-taped guitar case. "Buffalo scrotum," he said. "The leather lasts forever."

Heidi ran a tongue over dry lips. It was as if those rattles somehow anticipated the beat. "But what's inside?" she said. "What makes that sound, like shattering ice?"

A bottle was making the rounds as the musicians put away their instruments. Long Black Braids took a double-bubble swig.

"Goose beaks," he said, with a silly whiskey grin. "Or is it geese beaks?"

Her headache was nothing but worse. Without drinking Heidi passed the bottle. She didn't know what she'd expected to hear, but *geese beaks* wasn't it.

"Geese beaks?" she said. "And that's all?"

"There's more," said Long Black Braids. "But Grandmother never said. She was a very powerful medicine woman."

Then he fingered a calfskin pouch hanging at his neck.

"In the old traditions," he said, "that rattle was a way of honoring a spirit helper."

His brown eyes lost their focus as he stared through the bar to the horizon; like maybe he saw campfires and tepees instead of bikers smoking cigarettes.

"A hundred and more years ago," he said, "the buffalo were about gone. Grandmother was a young girl who hadn't eaten in many days. In those days the animals still visited the people to help them in their dreams, to give them advice. Grandmother was sleeping on her back in the hot sun, perhaps thinking it was a good day to starve, when Honking Goose flapped his wings and landed on her growling stomach.

"'Honking Goose,' she said, 'what are you doing here?'

"'Look up,' said Honking Goose.

"And when Grandmother looked up the sky was dark with flying geese.

"'I'm here,' said Honking Goose, 'because I eat the white man's grain.'

"And with that, he flew off."

Long Black Braids regained the focus in his eyes but Heidi thought she might be lost. "I'm not sure I understand," she said.

"A hundred years ago there were fifty thousand geese," he replied. "Now because of all the wheat fields there's five hundred thousand. If you can't beat 'em, join 'em; that was Goose's message. Grandmother was the last of the great medicine women, and the first to rent out rooms to make ends meet. She homesteaded a chunk of river bottom up by Pyramid Butte. That's where my fishing lodge is, in the . . ."

Nostrils flared beneath the hooked obelisk of Long Black Braid's monumental nose.

"Hey," he said, "What were you doing yesterday morning in them bushes up by Beaver Head Rock?"

Heidi tapped the rattles together as a cold spot iced the curve of her spine. There was no way he could have seen her in that dense thicket of briers, not in her painstakingly constructed blind, not when she was invisible even to the horned larks.

"How did you know I was there?" she asked.

"Not many people on the reservation use cucumber soap," he replied.

"You smelled me?" said Heidi uncertainly.

"You were upwind."

"And fifty yards away!"

"You never answered my question. What was you doing in them bushes?"

Heidi felt like she'd been swimming against the current and it was time to let go.

"I was in the bushes taking pictures of birds," she said, "for my port-folio."

Long Black Braids sniffed the stage like he smelled a storm on the horizon.

"What did you say your name was?" he said.

"I never did say, but it's Heidi. Heidi Jaspersen."

Long Black Braids jabbed the air between them with a crooked brown finger. *"The Triple Rainbow,"* he said. "That was you!"

Heidi smiled with even white teeth. It was gratifying when people recognized her. And *The Triple Rainbow*—a photograph of a rainbow trout chasing an emerging caddisfly into the air, the leaping fish perfectly framed by a full double rainbow in the sky—she'd always considered a masterpiece. And a lot of work; she'd spent seventeen days standing covered with caddisflies during the evening thunderstorms before the vision in her head finally came together in the polarizing filter on her fifty-millimeter lens.

"I feel so famous," she said as she lightheartedly flipped her long blond hair.

Long Black Braid's expression remained an inscrutable droop-eyed frown. "You are famous," he said. "That's why you shouldn't name rivers in the stories you write. Especially the name of this river. It just can't handle the pressure."

Heidi lost her smile. So that was it. She was so-o-o tired of being blamed for crowded rivers. It wasn't her fault there were more people than there was world. She pushed the rattles back into Long Black Braid's hands.

"Here," she said, "why don't you shove one of these up your ass."

Long Black Braids blinked. "And you seemed like such a nice girl," he said.

Growing up copper-mining poor could make living in a tepee look pretty good. Heidi remembered the barefooted winter of the '59 strike. She steamed at the thought of the coupons they'd get from Union Hall, pasteboard stubs good for tins of hoof- and hair-laden meat so rancid that even her dog Ralph wouldn't eat it.

"Don't you be telling me to turn down a paycheck," she fumed. "My father's grandfather cashed his first paycheck at Marcus Daly's Copper King Saloon and the money was gone before he ever got out the door. My family's been under the company's thumb ever since. So don't you be telling me how to make a living."

Heidi's hand with a mind of its own had darted out and grabbed back a rattle. She used it like a period, rapping Long Black Braids on the sternum at the end of every sentence.

"And another thing," she went on. "How the hell do *you* get off criticizing *me?* You're an outfitter. I saw what happened at Beaver Head Rock yesterday morning. You catch fish, people come back. You've done it for years, you're as much to blame for the crowded river as anybody."

Long Black Braids held up his hands with his palms out, the sign for peace, but Heidi was still on the warpath as she rapped away with the rattle at the end of every word.

"And another thing," she said. "I broke your damn sign."

The Nitwits hadn't gone anywhere. They'd been standing around the back of the big stage during the break watching Long Black Braids and Heidi with rapt attention, like it had been a long winter and they'd just gotten cable. The man in the Hawaiian shirt who had been playing the fiddle was suddenly having trouble breathing.

"*Broke?*" he said, "What do you mean *broke?*"

"I'll pay for it," said Heidi.

The fiddle player groaned. "Not another one," he said.

"And next to the light pole," said Heidi pensively, "there was a cedar-strip driftboat."

She fingered her blond hair like an excuse. Long Black Braids squeezed her by the shoulders. He'd built that boat himself from old-growth timber. It was irreplaceable, a labor of love, hundreds of hours of gluing, sanding, finishing love.

"My boat," he screamed. "My boat! What did you do?"

Heidi shook her head sadly. There was terrible anguish in her voice, like no matter how hard she tried, she just couldn't bring herself to relay the awful news.

"Well," she said morosely, "somehow I managed to miss the boat entirely."

It took a split second to register. Then the Nitwits lived up to their name. Long Black Braids collapsed in mock relief to the plank stage. Sitting with his knees apart, he fumbled in his shirt for a packet of tobacco. Leaning back on one arm, with his free hand he twisted a gummed rolling paper into a tailor-made; Heidi wrinkled her nose as he lit up.

"Maybe the news hasn't spread this far north," she said, "but cigarettes will kill you."

Long Black Braids blew a smoke ring that elongated in the shape of a trout. "It isn't when you die," he said serenely. "It's how you die."

Heidi's skull throbbed with every beat of her heart as she hung the rattles on a nail in the log wall. She hadn't realized just how bone-weary she was after the long day, and her green eyes squeezed shut as she knuckle-rubbed both temples.

"If your head hurts," said Long Black Braids, "take off your shoes."

Heidi opened her eyes and looked down at her black sneakers. "My shoes?"

"And your socks."

"My socks?"

"Your foot is an energy map of your whole body," he said. "Your head's right there between your second and third toes. It's Chinese medicine. I learned from Grandmother. Let's go find a couple of chairs."

If it was a line to get her to take off her clothes, Heidi thought it was a good one as they walked to a plank corner table. Heidi sat in a high-backed wooden chair, unlacing her shoes as she studied the tall Indian with the chocolate eyes as he pulled a chair in front of hers. He looked Chinese the way a rabbit looked like a buffalo.

"Your grandmother," said Heidi. "She couldn't have been Chinese."

"No," agreed Long Black Braids, "But she did run a boardinghouse. Chinese labor built the railroads. Grandmother learned from a Manchurian coolie who sold herbs and lived upstairs when the tracks came up the river valley."

Long Black Braids whistled as Heidi's bare foot settled in his lap.

"Totem toenails," he said. "Very impressive."

Passing hours mattered less to Heidi than the changing seasons. The designs she painted on her toenails kept track of time as she saw it. The ends of her feet were now decorated with midge pupae in the throes of metamorphosis, glowing red, green, and white jewels of expanding sequined glitter.

"Totem toenails," said Heidi. "They're a lot harder to lose than a wrist-watch."

She groaned as Long Black Braids pulled on both little toes at once. The skin on the backs of his hands was smooth. Heidi wondered how old he was. He could have been thirty or he could have been sixty, and she'd always had a certain fascination for older men.

"So," she asked, "do you always storm fishing holes you want with live ammunition?"

Long Black Braids smiled with a full set of slightly crooked teeth. "Sometimes I light the prairie on fire."

Heidi's mouth opened then closed. Hot tingling pinpoints of relief burned in the wake of his hard roving thumbs. For the first time since she swam in the river Heidi began to feel warm again, but when he kneaded the soft crease on the outside of the heel below her bony ankle she shivered uncontrollably.

"You're cold?" said Long Black Braids, like he was surprised. "After we sing some more songs, you know what would help? Have you ever been in a real Indian sweat lodge?"

Whoever Dies with the Most Stories Wins

NEWTON THOUGHT IF YOU CHASED after a beam of light, you could catch it. Einstein says you can't. According to Einstein, no matter how fast you're going, the speed of light stays the same. The paradox is that everything else changes: everything. Objects gain mass as they pick up speed. They also get shorter. And the faster you go, the slower time passes.

People view the universe differently depending on their relative states of motion. It's Einstein's Theory of Special Relativity, and it has practical implications because it means some battles simply can't be won. No two people, even though they see the same thing, can ever make exactly the same observation. Consider the seat-up-or-down issue. Women blame bad aim but men argue that toilets aren't built big enough. It's all relative to the observer. Time and space are constructed in such a way so as to avoid a definitive answer.

Everybody's right, everybody's wrong.

The solution, I decided, was never to live in a place where you couldn't pee off the front porch, so I once spent everything I had on twenty acres of trout stream. *Everything* wasn't much, and there's a reason the Blackfoot wintered on the plains and not in the mountains. Life gets harder and land gets cheaper as the elevation rises. The money in my cookie jar came in exactly one mile high up the tumbling North Fork of the Apikuni. The river here is turquoise-green with glacial silt. Foaming rock-studded riffles pour into deep mirrored pools; the trout are squirming quicksilver, gleaming native cutthroats.

"See-suk-kumea," said the Kingfish, swimming his hand through the air "In Blackfoot it means 'spotted fish.'"

In English the cutthroat takes its name from the twin diagonal orange slashes below the rosy gill plates. The back and tail of the cold, twelve-inch trout in my hand were peppered with black spots and too plump to circle with thumb and forefinger as I smashed its head on a chunk of gray limestone. The bright eyes filmed over as the Kingfish held a reed-stemmed medicine pipe up to the plains hazy with blue dust that stretched away far below to the east. He turned to the north and south, saluting the pine and fir forest, and last he turned to the west, holding the pipe by its carved red soapstone bowl up to the shark-toothed mountains, a skyline dominated by massive, snowcapped Napi Peak.

"See-suk-kumea," I repeated. "See-suk-kumea."

I grew up on packaged bologna and canned tuna. It's easy to forget your place in the food chain when death comes disguised with Saran Wrap in a stainless-steel grocery cooler. Eating what you kill is the ultimate reminder to respect life, the difference between ownership and stewardship, a serious reminder not to take things too seriously because you might be next.

"Carpe diem," I said as I put down the fish and reached for the pipe.

The Kingfish's steep and oft-broken nose winds around like a giant slalom course; his darting eyes come from so many directions, it's as if everybody is skiing at once.

"Seize the carp," he agreed, "but wash your hands first."

Melted glaciers are cold even in summer. I dried the goose bumps on the seat of my faded jeans. The medicine pipe was more than a hundred years old, festooned with eagle feathers, yellowed beaver teeth, and broken badger claws that dangled from worn rawhide thongs. I smoked while the Kingfish sliced the trout from tail to gills through the soft strip of white underbelly.

"What was he eating?" I asked between puffs.

The silver knife tip slit the distended length of the long rubbery stomach, olive-green bugs oozing into the sun. The segmented bugs in the stomach near the mouth were so fresh you could still count six legs, two inches down the gullet it was lumpy abdomen soup, two inches more and the insects had been reduced to homogeneous green mush.

"Grannom nymphs," he said. "Look at all the silk."

The Kingfish scooped from the fresh end of the stomach. Dozens of tiny white threads rustled in the breeze as he held the lump of dead bugs on the knife up to the sun. Grannom caddis live in fast water and, like spiders, spin sticky silk. The nymphs use the silklike ropes to rappel about the rocks. It was easy to imagine snapping silk tethers as frantically rappelling nymphs disappeared into dark trout mouths.

"I tried imitating that silk thread last year," I said. "I painted a couple of inches of tippet white above the fly last May when I was fishing Bernie the Billionaire in the riffle below Head-Smashed-In."

The Kingfish was amused I would resort to such chicanery. "Did it work?" he asked.

Credibility is a guide's best friend. That and good flies.

"Sure it worked," I said. "Bernie thought he had the smartest guide on the river."

I yanked a handful of wild purple onions at the edge of the gravel beach to be fried in butter with the trout. The Kingfish held up a scarred thumb to measure the sun above the trees.

"I better get going," he said. "I'm meeting Heidi in Cow Coulee. We're shopping for new beds for the guest cabins."

He said *shopping* with the enthusiasm most people reserve for fever blisters.

"At least stay for lunch," I said.

A grin ran a couple laps around his thick red-brown lips then collapsed in a heap.

"I'm not sure," he said, "but I think I said I'd be there an hour ago."

"That'll make her happy," I said.

"That's why I came up here first," he replied. "Now I can blame you for being late."

"And don't think I don't appreciate it," I said.

At the edge of my rutted driveway I held up the fish, waving good-bye as the Kingfish drove away in a cloud of dusty yellow pine pollen. The engine noise faded away to the popping tune of a missing cylinder, then the thick woods were quiet. Where I live it's as wild as you can get and still have electricity. Along with eight months of snow, a thousand feet of riverfront, and a spectacular mile-high view of the Continental Divide, I had also just purchased my very own wildlife refuge.

Bull moose wallowed in the beaver-pond willows, red foxes in the alpine meadow, ruffed grouse pecked in the whortleberry beneath the lodgepole pine forest. A mountain lion circled one new-moon night, hunting deer, resting outside my bedroom window, and twitching his tail while I slept; the next morning his tracks etched the newfallen snow. There were all manner of creatures on my land, but of all the various animals, only one was ideally suited to its habitat. Unfortunately, it wasn't me.

Until I could get a house built I was living in a trailer that came with the property. The trailer was an awful shade of ugly, the yellow of diseased toenails, rusted metal panels peeling away at the sides, like Shirley Temple on Rogaine, above a rickety wood foundation. The only kind of women I could bring home were the kind who raised wolves and didn't shave their body hair. The trailer wasn't a double-wide but a double-long, so dark and narrow it was like living in a two-dimensional universe. The days had never seemed so gloomy or my moods so bleak. What I thought was depression turned out to be sewer gas from a blocked vent pipe.

It was no place fit for a human to live, but for the bushy-tailed wood rats, the trailer wasn't just a place to get out of the rain. The semi-enclosed crawl space was more of a luxury aboveground suite. There was radiant ceiling heat from the woodstove. There was bale after bale of snuggly warm fiberglass insulation, the ultimate in nesting material, to rip out of the walls. There was wood to chew, wires to tug, food to raid from the kitchen cabinets. There was even hot running water, but only until the leak in the shower fixed itself.

The good news spread quickly among the gregarious wood rats. A stop at my trailer became de rigueur for upwardly mobile rats-in-the-know. Rodents never had it so good. They partied nonstop, like every day was Super Bowl Sunday, and rats came from miles around to join in the celebration. Then the looting began. Wood rats are also known as pack rats, and when they get together they're a bunch of petty thieves. They'll steal anything so long as it's shiny or edible, which for a rat is pretty much everything, and when they lifted the chrome scissors from my fly-tying bench they'd gone too far.

The Rats Wars would begin. This time, for sure. This time, I really meant it.

All along I'd been exceedingly reluctant to trap the rats. I didn't know why until I was standing on the splintered plank floor at the local feed store, surrounded by traps designed to capture creatures from mink to marten. Rat traps came in two varieties: spring traps that killed and live traps that didn't. The chain on a spring trap rattled as I pulled it from the pegboard display rack. Bob, the proprietor, clomped over in steel-toed logging boots.

"That's a fine trap you got yourself there," he said. "It works just the same as it did a hundred years ago. Ain't nobody been able to improve on the design since."

"Good," I replied, "Because . . ."

The memories when they came flooding back were so intense I wondered how I could possibly have forgotten. This wouldn't be the first trapping I'd ever done; I'd made quite a career of it when I was ten years old or so. I'd started with squirrels, luring them with cheese popcorn under a cardboard box propped up with a forked stick. The squirrels ate the popcorn but avoided the stick. I threaded the popcorn on a string and tied the string to the stick.

The box fell but the squirrels knocked the flimsy cardboard aside. I tried a wooden milk crate; the squirrels gnawed through. I was stymied. Then one night while reading by flashlight under the covers about lion hunting in Africa, I had a brainstorm. I'd dig a pit like the pygmies, but squirrels were obviously sneaky, so just to be on the safe side the pit would need a lid, a lid that eventually took the shape of an antique kitchen table with carved wooden legs.

"Look at that old thing," I said. "Nobody will miss it. And besides, we'll bring it back."

Little Johnny, who was my age and lived down the street, eyed me doubtfully.

"Squirrel stew," I said, smacking my lips. "Think of it."

The table was in Johnny's garage, so he had a lot more to lose on this one than I did, but he finally succumbed to the romance of trapping. We took the table, without asking, because the concept of deniability is as important to children as it is to politicians. *You never said we couldn't* is a much better defense than *We forgot*.

The table was solid oak and weighed as much as the two of us put together, but finally we had it down the hill, into the woods, and under the stout limb on a spreading hickory tree.

"How's this?" puffed Johnny, leaning on the table as he looked up at the tree.

The limb was a good fifteen feet high. We'd have plenty of rope. The lid could really fall.

"Perfect," I said, and we went to work on the pit.

We'd borrowed real shovels, man-sized shovels with dull points that barely scraped at the rocky ground even when one of us held the handle and the other jumped on top of the blade with both feet. It was a lot harder than watching cartoons no matter how high we jumped, but we kept at it, and after a time had fashioned if not a pit, at least a trough around a stout section of all-important root.

"How's that look?" I gasped. "Big enough for a squirrel?"

Johnny stepped back to eye the pit critically, his skinny chest heaving.

"Maybe even two," he said, and we went to work on the lid.

With the table upside down on the pit, we tied in a rope where the three claw-footed legs came together in the middle, then threw the rope over the limb of the tree. With rocks in our pockets for ballast, we hoisted the heavy table into the air, then tied the rope off to the root we had exposed in the pit. The table was now suspended above the pit. By rubbing bait on the rope, we hoped to entice a squirrel to enter the pit and nibble away. When the squirrel chewed through the rope, the lid would fall—trapping the squirrel in the pit. To help things along, we thought we'd better fray the rope.

"I'll tell you what," I said. "Since it's your table you get to bait the trap."

"No," said Johnny, "I insist. It's your idea, you get to bait the trap."

Baiting the trap meant being under the table, so we decided maybe we didn't need to fray the rope after all. We mixed crumbled cheese popcorn with enough bacon grease to make it sticky, then played rock, paper, scissors to see who got the honor of baiting the trap. My paper covered his rock. Johnny spooned bait onto the knotted rope at the bottom of the pit. He also spooned bait on his shoes because he was watching the table slowly spinning above his head.

Then came the hard part: We went home to wait. A night never was so interminable. Johnny slept at my house. The next morning the sun was barely above the horizon as we raced down the hill to the woods to check our trap. The rope was limp, the lid was down.

"It worked!" we shouted together. "It worked!"

Johnny's big, round eyes nearly covered his whole face. He looked as surprised as I felt.

"Okay," I said, "you take the net, and when you're ready I'll lift the edge of the table."

Johnny was surprised but not that surprised.

"I have a better idea," he said. "I'll hold the table and you net the squirrel."

We had a fishing net along to serve as a temporary holding cell for the squirrel, and the issue here was hand-to-claw combat. There would be a moment after the table came up and before the net came down that the squirrel would be free. Johnny's scissors cut my paper. I put my thin side of ribs to the ground, my heart thumping up puffs of dust with every pounding beat.

My cheek to the dry ground at the edge of the table, clenching the net with both hands, I was thinking squirrels climbed trees, so their claws must be pretty sharp. And just how fast were squirrels anyway? What if they were really, really fast, and charged like teeth with feet? What if squirrels were so fast they couldn't stop and skidded down your arm and into your shirt? And into your pants? And did they bite? Did squirrels bite!

I wanted to run but my knees shook so bad my legs wouldn't work. I was thinking I should have worn a belt when light flooded in from the edges as Johnny tilted the table up and away. One good look and I immediately rolled away onto all fours.

"What is it?" Johnny demanded. "What is it?"

Too much table, not enough pit.

"It's Wa-a-a-a . . ." I groaned, then vomited all over the table.

78

Waffles was the plump, pampered poodle who belonged to old Mrs. Haberman up the street. Now the dog was spread like red, furry butter across the shallow depression in the rocky soil. The heavy table had cracked even the dog's skull. The slimy sheen of corrugated brains wasn't nearly what I expected.

And we never told. Never-ever.

Not even when a heartbroken Mrs. Haberman asked up and down the street after her poor, lost dog. Not even when she stood sobbing on the front steps, her shoulders shaking, telling us over and over how Waffles would sit up and beg with tiny waving paws for the bits of bacon she'd hold between her fingers. People really do look like their dogs. The vivid memory rolled back in color like going to the movies; when the show was over, I found myself standing flat-footed at the feed store.

Bob was nervously fingering the mother-of-pearl buttons on his starched red shirt.

"Are you all right?" he said. "You haven't said a word in three minutes. You just been standing there all slack-jawed. I was getting ready to call the doctor."

It must be like epilepsy the way my brain spirals down inside itself. Or maybe it's just practice for Alzheimer's.

"It's nothing," I said. "I was remembering why I don't like bacon."

Bob grinned uncertainly and fled for the sanctuary of his cash register. I hung the trap that killed back on the rack. The wood rats would be spared their miserable rat lives. I walked out with a live trap touted as the best money could buy: the "Havahart."

The Havahart is a wire cage with doors designed to close behind the rat when it enters and wiggles a food-covered lever. For bait, I settled on nachos and Vienna sausage. After all it was Super Bowl Sunday. The trap went at one of the main crossroads of Rat civilization: in the bathroom alongside the hole they'd gnawed in the baby-blue fiberglass bathtub skirting.

I stood up, ignoring the first gray hairs in the black beard that needed to be trimmed. Some days the blank stare in the cracked mirror above the iron-stained plastic sink is enough to convince me of the Hindu concept of past lives. Like I'm paying for something and don't have the cash. And whatever I did, they don't take credit cards.

Out and back, left and right, up and down: the three dimensions we see as space. Time is the fourth. Then physicists discovered that if they added a fifth, it helped explain both electricity and magnetism. Additional dimensions helped describe the observed universe so well that cutting-edge physicists didn't quit until they had ten dimensions altogether. These scientists now envision a universe comprising time, with tiny, contorted six-dimensional balls curled up at each and every point in regular three-dimensional space.

These six-dimensional balls that fill the fabric of space exhibit a host of singular properties, including the fact that particles can only get so small before they start to get larger in a reciprocal dimension. A reciprocal is one over itself: things that were ten are now one over ten. Grapefruit are now one over grapefruit, and things that were getting smaller are now one over getting smaller, which is the same as getting bigger.

At the instant dimensions switch, it is possible that the fabric of space actually tears. No wonder bizarre events occur. In an atom the size of the universe, the switch happens at about the size of your average tree. It's unimaginably small, but it's still there. The important point is that nothing, not mass or energy, just disappears. And right there, when space tears, when things can't get any smaller because they have to start getting bigger, that could be reincarnation.

The cosmological implications of naughty and nice in a ten-dimensional universe remain paradoxical. Naughty now might be nice later, but the reciprocal of nice is naughty, which leaves the devout Reduced Humanist right back where he started. Naughty. It could be that the universe is set up to make us pay for our mistakes, and it's going to go on for a long, long time.

If that is the reality, then all you can do is tell yourself it really isn't that bad.

Lots of people live with rats.

A stinging hot shower steamed up the mirror; peppermint soap masked the sulfur in the hard iron well water. And if my hair was going gray, my stomach was still flat as I drove the fifteen miles of county road to the Hilly Chili Café for the Monday-morning meeting of the Joke-of-the-Week Club.

There are times out there guiding when you desperately need a joke. Mondays at the Hilly Chili—depending on who shows up—you can double your repertoire. It's also a time to take care of the business end of guiding, and there's the possibility you'll eat for free, since the best joke by popular acclaim is good for a free breakfast.

The Hilly Chili had been around for a couple of years now, ever since Chef Jeff, a world-traveling Trout Bum with a flair for the taste buds, had moved a used commercial kitchen into an old hand-hewn log cabin on the bend in the road just down from the Mountain Palace. A bright sign on the front door said NO CREDIT CARDS in big sunburst letters. Jeff waved from the back as I walked in, his face and hands white with flour. Heidi and the Kingfish were waiting at the corner booth by the potted rubber tree in front of the big window.

"Hey," I said as I slid into the booth across from them.

"Hey," they replied in perfect thirds.

Some people are connected at the hip, some at the heart, but Heidi and the Kingfish were connected at the ear. Music is an antidote to growing up poor whether you're a copper miner's daughter or a Blackfoot Indian. From their first note together they sang harmonies like they were sharing the same circuit breaker. The two of them, leaning back against the cushioned bench seat—imagine Sitting Bull with his arm around Ingrid Bergman, if Sitting Bull wore cool aviator shades and burly Ingrid played a little hockey on the side.

"I was hoping you'd be here this morning," I said. "I wrote out a bill for those guide days I did last week."

But when I opened the worn leather wallet that doubles as a mobile filing cabinet a sheaf of loose papers fell on the table. The Kingfish glanced at the litter and started chuckling.

"What's that?" he said. "An organ donor card? I hope you aren't planning on donating your liver. That would be like Ray Charles donating his eyes. What's the use?"

The Kingfish hadn't had a drink in two years; it was the only way Heidi would marry him. But sanctimonious was a headdress that didn't fit this Indian.

"I think I liked you better before," I said. "Just pay me so I can pay everybody else."

The Kingfish pulled out a checkbook and started writing with a red pen.

"Don't cash it until tomorrow," he said. "I have to deposit some checks this afternoon."

Heidi opened her backpack, pulled out another check, and signed it on the back.

"If you're going to the bank," she said, "put this in for me. It's from *Vogue* for that last set of photographs I sold."

The Kingfish folded it in half and was pushing it into the right front pocket of his faded fishing shorts when Heidi grabbed his arm.

"Not in the same pocket with your car keys," she said. "You know how you lose things."

The Kingfish said "Yes, dear," but when Heidi let go he shoved it into the pocket anyway. Heidi pinched her lips and drummed fingernails painted with yellow stoneflies on the table. The Kingfish never even noticed as he pushed his sunglasses down his nose and peered at me over the wire rims.

"How's your war with those rats?" he said. "Have you graduated to live ammunition?"

"Too messy," I said. "So I put out a live trap next to the bathtub."

The Kingfish pushed his sunglasses back up and looked out the window.

"If you get anything," he said, "let me know. Eddie's doing better, but I know he'd like live rats a lot more than dead hamburger."

Eddie was a bald eagle with a broken wing the Kingfish had found full of buckshot down by the river. Heidi was still mad at the Kingfish so she took it out with sarcasm on me.

"Next to the bathtub?" she said. "No wonder women are lined up at your door."

The cushion sagged as bulky Captain Bismarck slid into the booth beside me. He owed his name to the old-style, high-sided boat he rowed. It was by far the largest driftboat on the river, a boat so big you could mount twelve-inch guns in the bow and shell England.

"Women?" he said eagerly. "Lined up at whose door?"

"My door," I said. "It's just that they're going the wrong way."

"That'll change," said Captain Bismarck. "Wait until the action figures come out."

"Action figures?" said Heidi gleefully.

Captain Bismarck nodded, crumbs falling from his gray, bushy beard.

"Like GI Joe," he said, "only it's a fishing guide."

Writing fishing stories is like selling defective guns to mercenaries: a good way to die broke. But I'd just had a book published. This was the price of that fame.

"Comes with a billionaire," said the Kingfish. "Other clients are optional."

"And there's lots of accessories," said Heidi. "But most of them are missing."

"And when you pull a string in his back," said Captain Bismarck, "he starts to whine."

Wherever I go I leave a trail of stuff. That crack about missing parts really hit home, but with the Joke-of-the-Week Club, if you don't shoot back they'll fill you full of holes.

"And then there's the Captain Bismarck Action Figure," I said. "It comes with a wrecked truck, a boat full of empty beer cans, and a dead deer."

"Oh you poor thing," said Heidi. "Not again."

Heidi was one of those tactile people who touched when she talked. Her hands and body had as much to say as her mouth, and when Heidi said she didn't have a thing to wear she meant it. She was dressed for a hot summer day, in bare muscled skin and a green spaghetti-strap tank top that went with her eyes; Captain Bismarck grinned like a loon as she absently curled a tuft of the grizzled hair on his forearm around her finger.

"My radiator," he said, "it's like a deer magnet. That's four since January."

The front door squeaked open. Heidi slid over toward the Kingfish to make room.

"I warmed it up for you," she said.

"Hey, everybody," said the Duke, hanging his hat on a dowel behind the rubber tree.

The Duke is a balding ex-football-player who once drove a race car through a hot dog stand, then found his life's work sitting on the toilet. The epiphany came his junior year in college. He was sifting through the teetering stack of literature that had accumulated alongside the porcelain oasis over the years, and under a hundred well-thumbed *Playboys* and one *Good Housekeeping*, right next to an Allman Brothers album with a big peach on the cover, that's where the Duke found a dog-eared copy of *Trout Fishing in America*.

It's a thin paperback by Richard Brautigan. The cover is two hippies standing in front of a statue of Benjamin Franklin; on the inside a trout stream ends up in pieces on the shelf to be sold off just like any other kind of plumbing supplies. The Duke started to read. By the time he reached for the paper and pulled up his pants it was too late. He left that night for the Rocky Mountains, gone fishing. He was ruined for life, but not as ruined as some. Thirty years later, as he plopped down in the brown faux-leather booth next to Heidi, the Duke was the state conservation director for Trout Unlimited, and our resident expert on all matters bureaucratic.

"So what's the latest with the motorboat law?" I asked. "Any news?"

The proliferation of Jet-Skis and Jet-Boats had been hyperbolic. A coalition of grassroots organizations had approached Fish and Game about banning motors or at least enforcing a horsepower limit on the Apikuni. The Joke-of-the-Week Club had even mobilized to testify in Helena before committee during the last legislative session.

The Duke turned over his coffee cup. "There isn't any news," he said. "And don't expect any soon. It's the Wilderness Bill all over again, whether there should be places where motors aren't allowed, and we've been trying to get that passed since nineteen seventy-three."

Heidi squeezed the Duke's shoulder hard enough to leave welts.

"But it's not just the Wilderness Bill all over again," she said indignantly. "It's not just aesthetics, there's a safety issue. Especially weekends. All those kids in inner tubes are floating bull's-eyes. It's just a question of time until somebody gets chopped up by a propeller."

Heidi was preaching to the choir. The Duke reached across her for the white thermos.

"You wouldn't believe the lobbying that's going on," he said. "You'd think we were trying to take away riding lawn mowers the way people are reacting. The snowmobilers, the four-wheelers, the boat dealers, the gasoline retailers—they raised a bunch of money and hired Reagan's old Sagebrush Rebellion crew out of Denver to argue Catch-22. They're contending that since nobody's been killed, the rivers must be safe. And since the rivers are safe, nobody will be killed. And that means there isn't a problem in the first place."

"But that's insane," said Captain Bismarck. "Isn't there anything we can do?"

"Write your congressman," said the Kingfish so seriously everybody burst out laughing.

Children on the reservation grow up drinking Bloody Custers: grain alcohol strained through Wonder Bread then flavored with cherry Kool-Aid. The Blackfoot were once deeded the land that is now the eastern half of Glacier National Park. The Kingfish knew all about government promises until the rivers flow no more forever.

"So," said the Duke. "Has anybody floated the canyon lately?"

"Yesterday," said Captain Bismarck. "We got about fifty."

"Fifty?" said the Duke. "That's a lot of fish."

"Not fish," said Captain Bismarck, "tangles. I was ducking all day long."

"That's why real guides don't wear hats," said the Kingfish. "They wear helmets."

Style points count; the Kingfish didn't miss a beat in entering a potential Joke-of-the-Week in the competition for a free breakfast.

"Football helmets," he continued. "Like the three Texas Aggies who couldn't play in the big game because of failing grades. The coach begged the dean of students to do something, anything. The dean of students agreed to administer a test for extra credit, and the next morning the three football players were seated at their desks.

"'This is a musical examination,' said the dean of students. 'I'm going to play a song for five minutes, and at the end of that five minutes I'm going to ask you a question about what you've heard. Answer it right, and you get to play in the big game. But get it wrong, and we'll be forced to revoke your scholarships. Are you ready to begin?

"'Yup,' 'Yowsa,' and 'Howzzat again?' said the three football players.

"The dean of students took that as affirmation and turned on the music. The three Texas Aggies hunched forward, listening intently as the children's song 'Old McDonald' played over and over again. After five minutes the dean switched off the tape and said: 'Now listen carefully. Here is your question: What did Old McDonald have?'

"Then the dean left the room so he wouldn't have to watch, and the first football player turned to the second football player.

"'Geez,' he said, 'This sure is a hard test.'

"The second football player rolled his eyes. 'A farm,' he said, 'Old McDonald had a farm. Now if I could just remember how to spell *farm* we could play in the big game.'

"The third football player smiled because he was the smart one. He knew something the other two didn't. 'You idiots,' he said, 'It's right there in the song.

"'You spell farm,' said the third football player, 'E-I-E-I-O.'"

Fingers went up all around the scorer's table. It was a solid entry, sevens and eights all around except for the Duke who gave it eight fingers and a thumb, a perfect nine.

"That's because I know that third football player," he said. "The smart one. Now he's the head of Fish and Game."

Our waitress, sixteen-year-old Sarah Dusty-Bull, had been leaning on one wide hip against our table, patiently awaiting the punch line, and now she rolled her painted eyes.

"I'll take your order," she said, "if you'll just please stop telling those jokes."

In Sarah, pop culture squarely collided with the reservation. Her braids were bright electric blue, her eyelids matched, and her mother was doing three months for kiting checks. Sarah was fending for herself in a fringed doe-skin skirt, a fresh thermos of coffee in one hand, a pad and blunt pencil in the other.

"Bacon and eggs," said Captain Bismarck. "Better make that a double."

The huevos rancheros, the huckleberry pancakes, the jalapeño and goat cheese omelet—it's all good at the Hilly Chili. Sarah jotted down meals then swished away in yellow stockings that rubbed together between her thighs. She turned sideways to let Randy Bird pass by. Randy smiled white like a toothpaste commercial in creased salmon shorts, shirt, and cap.

"Do you know how you make a million dollars in the tourist business?" he asked.

It's an old joke. It works for farming and ranching, too.

"Start out with two million," said Captain Bismarck as he slid over to make room.

Russet-headed Randy had just moved in from the West Coast. You'd never know it to look at his curly hair, but he was the bare minimum legal Indian: one-sixty-fourth Yakima blood. It was enough to qualify him for a low-interest government loan to start the newest business on the Apikuni, scenic inflatable kayak trips through the Class II and III rapids in the upper canyon below River Junction. There's money to be made in sportswear, and Randy's blue-and-red company logo of a shark-toothed kayak chewing on a curling white wave was embroidered on every piece of clothing that showed, and probably the ones that didn't. He dropped a manila folder overflowing with white and yellow papers onto the green tablecloth.

"Here's all that paperwork on Freddie," he said. "You got your stuff?"

"That as-s-s-hole," hissed Heidi.

She glared at Randy's papers as if she might ignite them with malevolence alone, then opened her purse and pulled out some more papers. The Kingfish remained impassive as Heidi pinned her papers atop the manila folder with a glass jar of white sugar.

"You do know," he said, "that this won't do any good."

Now Heidi just looked tired. "I know," she said. "But we have to do something."

It all began when Frederick "Just call me Freddie" Mullins III appeared on the Apikuni. Freddie was in advertising and used enough glistening gel to keep his hair down in all but the fiercest of winds. Up and down the river he traveled, soliciting customers, including Trout World, where he stopped by with a proposition guaranteed to firmly position the Apikuni at the top of the map of worldwide fishing destinations.

"It's not what I can do for you," said Freddie, "it's what you can do for yourself."

Freddie was promoting the idea that complementary businesses would spin customers off to each other. He worked the Apikuni like a country preacher trying to convert as many local businesses as possible to sign onto his bandwagon.

"More is more," he said over and over. "More is more. Somebody goes for a horseback ride, that hot spring on the way home is going to look pretty darn good. Somebody rides by the river, they're going to go fishing. Everybody wins. More is more."

It was hard to argue because that was the way it worked. What Freddie proposed was to produce two videotapes of each business, then display the tapes at sportsmen's shows in major metropolitan areas. The first tape would contain five minutes of action highlights of each company and run as part of any endless loop on four big-screen televisions. Anyone expressing an interest in any particular segment would then receive a private screening of the second tape, thirty minutes of hard sell showing each business in detail.

"And that's the best part," said Freddie. "Think of it. More is more. You get to write and star in your own movie."

The Kingfish had been writing songs since he was old enough to pick up a guitar. The chance to make his own music video was a hook he couldn't ignore.

"The soundtrack!" he said, "We could make our own soundtrack."

"Exactly," said Freddie, jabbing excitedly with a fist full of fat fingers. "More is more. That's exactly what I mean by more is more."

Heidi put her head on the Kingfish's arm. They did have those new guest cabins to fill.

"It might work," she admitted. "But what's all this going to cost?"

Freddie folded his manicured hands into a tent and flashed a thousand-dollar smile.

But that wasn't a bad price at all. Not when it included eight three-day shows in eight different cities. Chicago. Anaheim. New York. Seattle.

Minneapolis. All the big shows were covered; the promotional material would be seen by hundreds of thousands of potential customers. The price was especially alluring considering that the cost to set up your own booth at any one of those shows, including travel, would run many times that thousand dollars. It seemed like a great deal, a steal, which is exactly what it was. Freddie, in three weeks of shooting scenes up and down the river, never bothered to put film in his camera.

He wasn't Freddie, he was Fast Freddie, and that's where the police came in. Or should have come in. The crime came under the jurisdiction of the Tribal Police. Black Drum, the detective in charge of the case, said his time was too valuable to waste on crimes as petty as misdemeanor theft.

That was a lie. Black Drum had plenty of time to eat doughnuts and set speed traps on a discount-for-cash basis; the real reason he avoided action was politics. And a long-standing feud. Black Drum hated tourism in general and the Kingfish in particular, but the list of duped businesses was infuriatingly long. If everybody banded together, the total amount of money stolen would render the crime a felony. The crime would be more difficult for Black Drum to dismiss out of hand; young, optimistic Randy Bird had volunteered to organize the paperwork.

"There's no doubt it's grand theft," he said. "Don't worry, we'll get our money back."

Captain Bismarck ran his downstairs as a guest house; he had a thousand in the pot, too, along with a piece of crisp bacon sticking out the corner of his mouth.

"What happens next?" he mumbled.

"I called the detective yesterday," said Randy, "and once I explained the arrangements he volunteered to drive up this morning and pick up the paperwork."

Heidi looked stricken, like she'd swallowed a frog. The Kingfish eased the knife from the sheath at this belt and began to clean his fingernails.

There's all kinds of trouble. Randy was just too new to the area to know any better.

"You're kidding!" I said. "You told Black Drum to come here?"

Randy Bird looked at a watch with his company shark logo on the leather band.

"He should be here any minute," he said. "Since he's twenty minutes late."

The front door squeaked open. The corner blocked my view, but it had to be Black Drum. He was six-five and showed the doughnuts; the creaking floorboards gave him away. He stood at the end of the table in a mustard-green uniform that needed pressing, thumb hooked in his shiny black belt so that his fingers draped over the handle of his gun as he leered down the front of Heidi's shirt.

"The white men may have got our land," he said, "but at least we got their women."

Then he turned to the Kingfish.

"Ain't that right, brother? Share and share alike?"

Black Drum's bald brown hand was halfway to Heidi's shoulder. The Kingfish half rose from his seat, still holding his knife. Black Drum pretended he'd been reaching for the papers on the table all along. He backhanded aside the jar of sugar, still smiling at the Kingfish as he said: "I heard you lost a little money. You can't believe how bad that made me feel."

It didn't happen so fast you couldn't see it happen but it happened faster than you had time to do anything about it. The Kingfish threw the knife with a quick flip of his wrist. The slender burnished blade stuck up quivering where it pierced the papers through the green tablecloth.

"The complaint has been withdrawn," said the Kingfish.

Black Drum's acne-scarred cheeks merged with his thin eyebrows and he shook like his uniform was stuffed with Jell-O. The fit was over as quickly as it began; Black Drum looked up, now cradling his bursting, round belly with both hands.

"Well then," he said, smiling with sharp, yellow teeth, "I guess the case is solved."

And then he winked at Randy Bird. "In record time, too," he said. "Kind of makes you proud to be part of law enforcement, now, don't it?"

Randy started to protest but I reached behind Captain Bismarck and rapped Randy on the back of his thick skull with my knuckles. When he looked over I drew a finger across my throat to cut him short. It wasn't ordinary trouble between Black Drum and the Kingfish. When it comes to revenge, the Hatfields and the McCoys have nothing on the Plains Indians. The trouble between Black Drum and the Kingfish went back four generations, back to a time when the men and women along the Apikuni lived in tepees, ate buffalo, and shot at each other with arrows.

The Kingfish

THE KINGFISH WAS TEN YEARS OLD and waist-deep in Badger Creek. His shiny black braids hung nearly to the surging water, ribs showed through his thin brown chest, and he was so absolutely motionless he might have been dead.

"That water's kinda cold," said Black Drum, "enit?"

Black Drum had him by two years and twenty pounds but the Kingfish didn't even bother to look up. He was crouched in the swirling eddy behind a jagged rock splitting the rushing current, and he just wished Black Drum would go away.

"You froze in there?" asked Black Drum. "That why you don't ever move?"

The Kingfish searched for a suitable insult but settled for the truth. "No," he said. "I don't move because it scares the fish."

Black Drum stared with his mouth hanging open, like he didn't know you could talk without moving your lips. "Well," he said, "I'm asking because we're getting up a game."

Trout flashed in silver streaks at his knees as the Kingfish swiveled around. "A game?" he said. "What game?"

They both talked with their hands, the Kingfish fondling a make-believe basketball, Black Drum raising his heavy arm as if he were throwing a tomahawk.

"Battle of the Big Hole," said Black Drum. "And we need someone to be Chief Joseph."

The Kingfish was on dry land in two giant bounds. The kids never asked him to play, and he stood panting, knock-kneed, and dripping wet in cutoff blue jeans and high-topped Keds.

"You ever get anything like that?" said Black Drum. "With just your hands I mean?"

The Kingfish reached out and carefully parted a thorny tangle of rose hips. Two whitefish and a fat cutthroat trout lay side by side on a bed of wet moss in the shade. "The trout are faster," he said. "It's easier with a spear."

He reached a little deeper into the thicket for his spear: a hickory-shafted arrow with a razor-sharp, four-pronged broadhead point.

"It was stuck in a tree," said the Kingfish. "Somebody missed."

Black Drum rubbed the pad of his forefinger along the point, then licked at the blood that suddenly spurted from a thin red line. "Well," he said, "we might want the fish, but you can leave the spear."

The boys left the creek on a dusty trail that circled Pyramid Butte, scrambled across the sunbaked scree where the rattlesnakes first showed in the spring, then dropped down into the cool, shaded cottonwood bottom where Badger Creek joined the Apikuni. There was a new song on the radio, about a hound dog, by a guitar player named Elvis. The Kingfish was whistling the melody when his left cheekbone exploded in a ball of mud. He wiped his eye clear, then looked toward the trees just in time to catch another mud bomb in the chest.

The Kingfish turned to Black Drum, bewildered.

Black Drum smiled, and punched the Kingfish right in the nose.

"Hey, Breed," said Black Drum. "We're playing a new game. It's called ambush."

Four boys materialized from behind the corrugated-silver bark of the wide cottonwood trunks, each armed with waxed-paper sandwich bags stuffed with clay made sticky with their own urine. The Kingfish stood in shocked immobility just long enough for Black Drum to kick out his legs. Once the Kingfish was on the ground the boys came in with hard feet, kissing his kidneys cowboy style with the pointed toes of their leather boots. The Kingfish was curled up on the ground, bruised forearms protecting his face, wheezing for breath; he thought they were done but Black Drum turned to say good-bye with one last cowboy-kiss to the guts.

"And by the way," said Black Drum, picking up the fish, "thanks for dinner."

The Kingfish remained in the fetal position, fighting the urge to suck his thumb as the taunting boys left. He was ashamed, not quite sure why, and wondering exactly what to tell Grandmother. He dawdled in the canyon up Badger Creek, fishing, waiting, until finally the sun fell pink-red as he watched from the cottonwood grove where the creek joined the river.

A three-wheeled wagon had been there in the trees so long that a cottonwood grew up through the middle of the wooden bed. The Kingfish sat in the wagon, the way he did nearly every evening, leaning against the rough cottonwood bark, watching as bright Coyote's Eyeball appeared overhead. The summer star had once belonged to Coyote the Trickster, but Coyote had tried to impress a couple of girls by juggling his eyes and threw one of them so high it stuck in the sky and became a star. The Kingfish wondered what it was about girls that would make you play with your eyeballs as he finally arrived home at the old farmhouse below the cliff.

At a blade-scarred wooden plank on the back porch the Kingfish used a dull hatchet to scrape the scales from three whitefish. He rubbed the firm, oily flesh with salt and brown sugar, then put the fish on the rack next to the venison haunch inside the rusted white refrigerator that had been converted into a smoker. The electric hot plate in the bottom glowed dull orange and was running low on wood. The Kingfish added wet chips to the smoldering pile of apple sticks and went through the screen door.

His grandmother, Sleeps-in-Blood Woman, sat in a metal folding chair hunched facedown over the yellow Formica kitchen table. Her thin gray hair was stark in the light of a bare bulb hanging from a frayed wire, and Sleeps-in-Blood Woman was poking intently with a toothpick at the tiny spindle in the float-valve of a Holley four-barrel carburetor.

"How was fishing?" she asked without looking up. "Are we eating fat ones tonight?"

The Kingfish dumped two trout in the sink, then slumped down into a high-backed wooden chair.

"Grandmother," he said in a low voice, "what's a 'Breed'?"

His grandmother looked up sharply from the toothpick, sighing when she saw the black eye and bloody nose. "Who did this?" she demanded. "It was those dog-eaters, wasn't it?"

The Kingfish had spent all but a few days of his life within a full day's walk of home. His face remained impassive as Grandmother explained. He'd never even really talked to a white man before; the idea that he *was* one was going to take some getting used to. Sleeps-in-Blood had fallen silent, lightly drumming her fingers on the table. Then she went to the shelf where dozens of dried local plants were stored in an assortment of shiny screw-topped jars.

"I have just the thing," she said. "It will help you dream."

The Kingfish wasn't so sure he wanted to dream. But he was hungry. His mouth watered as Grandmother whipped up a mushroom and bitter root omelet. She sprinkled in various green leaves and brown powders; the Kingfish ate a whole three-goose-egg omelet by himself and was already nodding off as he laid down his fork. He was certain he remembered climbing the stairs to fall asleep in his own bed, but he woke up back in the cottonwood grove down where the creek joined the river.

The sun was up, and the old wagon was looking a lot better with all four wheels and a billowing canvas top as it crossed the shallow riffle in the river behind two snorting oxen. A tall man slouched low on the splintered plank seat, his tattered gray uniform stiff with dried sweat, and he yanked back on the reins as he pulled onto the grassy riverbank alongside the Kingfish.

"Put her there," he said, offering his hand. "The name's Jebediah, Jebediah Armstrong."

Jebediah shook hands with a single hard squeeze, then stomped the floor below him.

"You like my new wagon?" he said. "I won her back up the valley, aces over tens."

The Kingfish ran his hand over the floppy, arched white Conestoga cover. "Nice," he said. "Does it keep you dry in the rain?"

"Sure does," said Jebediah proudly, then picked up his tapered bullwhip and snapped it six inches over the oxen's curved horns. The animals lunged in unison against the massive dropped hickory yoke.

The Kingfish skipped alongside as the wagon began to move. "Do you have to go already?" he said. "I was hoping you could stay a while."

"I can't," explained Jebediah, cracking the whip so hard he bounced in his seat. "There's new gold diggings south down the Prickly Pear Trail in Last Chance Gulch, and the way it works is first come first ser—"

There was another crack; a sharp, splintering crack. You could have stuffed a cannonball in Jebediah's wide-open mouth. He may have been surprised—a wheel had just fallen off an axle—but the Kingfish wasn't. As mammoth as the man was, and as much as he bounced around, a regular wagon was just plain overmatched.

"Well," said Jebediah philosophically, "at least there's some shade."

He leapt down, scratching his forehead by rubbing his stubby-brimmed gray cap up and down as he surveyed the damage. The east wind was bone-dry on the prairie trail, and it was another hundred miles to the gold fields. Splitting a wheel hub in a stand of cool cottonwood at a river crossing wasn't the worst thing that could have happened, and Jebediah turned a slow circle like he was trying it on for size.

"I'm thinkin'," he said, "that this is as good a place as any to sell some whiskey."

Jebediah turned to the Kingfish, eyebrows raised as if he'd just asked a question.

"Probably," replied the Kingfish. "People around here sure drink a lot of it."

"All right then," said Jebediah, and from the assortment of rough wooden boxes stacked in the bed of the wagon he pulled out a boarding-house with a downstairs saloon.

"Wow!" said the Kingfish, who didn't know anybody who was good at making money.

Jebediah was now dressed in fine new clothes, nodding his head in satisfaction. "Better step back," he said. "It looks like this location is going to work out just fine."

The smell of manure wafted in on the hot dry plains. They stepped backward to avoid the train of ox-drawn wagons now plodding down the trail. In the years just after Jefferson Davis surrendered at Appomattox, the low Prickly Pear Pass over the South Fork of the Apikuni served as the main route between the steamboats and the gold fields. Trading posts brought settlers and Indians together in an uneasy and oft-broken truce. A quarter mile upstream scalps flew from the crossed lodgepoles of dozens of tightly stretched buffalo-skin tepees.

Meat-seared wood smoke hung in the summer air as they approached the Indian camp, Jebediah striding so fast past the scattered cook fires and barking dogs that even with his long legs, the Kingfish was half running to keep up. At the last tepee before the clay bluff a willowy brown girl was on her knees scraping yellow fat from a hide with a flat knife. She stood and smiled as Jebediah presented her with a bolt of red calico and box of black licorice.

"Morning-Star Woman," said Jebediah.

The girl kicked up her heels in beaded moccasins with a child's delight as Jebediah swept her off her tiny feet with a smothering hug. It didn't take a medicine man to see what was coming, and the Kingfish took a sudden interest in the horizon. He turned to see a muscular young brave with eagle feathers in his hair playing with a long knife. The brave could have been Black Drum's twin brother, only older, and he was sneering at Jebediah and Morning-Star Woman, his blocky lips curled in disgust.

"She's mine," cried the brave as he leapt forward holding up the bone-handled knife.

But a talking crow flew in the brave's face, spreading its wings so the man couldn't see.

"No, Spotted-Drum," hissed the crow, "not yet. Wait your time."

The Kingfish turned to warn Jebediah, and saw from Morning-Star's big round belly that he had missed more than just a kiss. A mule-drawn wagon full of boiler plate was passing by; the two men on the open board seat both wore the tattered blue remnants of the uniform of the Union army.

The narrow-eyed man behind the reins poked the grizzle-cheeked man on the seat beside him with his elbow and pointed at Jebediah. "Get a load of the squaw-man," he said. "He's gonna have himself a breed."

The other man sprayed a dark stream of tobacco juice at Morning-Star Woman's feet. "I wonder which part will be red," he said. "The top half or the bottom half."

Jebediah looked at the Kingfish and shook his head slowly. "If you let them start," he said, "they'll never stop."

Jebediah vaulted into the wagon with a piece of cordwood held like a sap in his huge paw of a hand. The wagon driver grabbed for a pistol behind the seat, but he was way too late. With one swipe of the wood Jebediah knocked both men unconscious, then trussed them with their own rawhide whips to the undercarriage of the wagon, and held up an earthen pot of salve and a shaving brush.

"Bear grease, black pepper, and peppermint oil," he said. "You want a mule to run, just paint some of this on its ass."

The wagon bounced and crashed behind the braying mules out of sight into the sagebrush prairie.

The Kingfish looked around for Morning-Star Woman. "I don't think she should be alone," he said.

"Piegan women have always borne their babies alone," replied Jebediah.

"But there was this guy Spotted-Drum," said the Kingfish.

When Jebediah heard the news they tried to hurry, but in the way of nightmares the faster they ran the slower they went. Their feet slipped and slipped on ground sticky as honey until it was too late. Only the bone knife handle protruded from Morning-Star's chest, the steel blade deep between her ribs, and in the pool of warm blood a tiny baby girl with the umbilical cord still attached was napping in her mother's arms.

The Kingfish was awake in the dark, Sleeps-in-Blood Woman's face inches above his.

"Cute little thing, wasn't I?" she said, smiling in the moonlight.

And even though he was back in the soft blankets of his own bed the Kingfish shuddered.

"Grandmother," he said, "it was so real. Was I really there?"

"Maybe," she replied. "Who knows?"

Then Sleeps-in-Blood Woman handed the Kingfish an ice-cold Pepsi.

"You come from two worlds," she said. "You can be as smart as a white man and as dumb as an Indian. Or you can be dumb as a white man and smart as an Indian. Think about it."

The Kingfish held the Pepsi against his temple as he thought about it until his head hurt. "Does that mean I'm twice as smart?" he said. "Or twice as dumb?"

"Exactly," she said. "The important thing is to be a warrior. Now get your moccasins. Blue-streak-follows is waiting."

In the old days a horse wasn't worth owning unless it had been stolen, and Sleeps-in-Blood Woman felt the same way about cars. She'd gone all the way to Spokane for Blue-streak-follows, the pick of the herd, a customized '52 Chevy street-rod with oversized pistons in a short-block Hemi. There wasn't a vehicle on the reservation that could touch it, and they roared down the highway with the top down under a canopy of blazing stars.

"Where are we going?" asked the Kingfish.

"It's time we drummed up a little trouble," cackled Sleeps-in-Blood Woman.

Sleeps-in-Blood Woman held up an empty box of Ex-Lax, the jumbo economy size.

"While you were dreaming," she continued, "I was helping Black Drum's mother fix her special stew. It smelled like dog to me."

And this time when Sleeps-in-Blood Woman smiled, the Kingfish smiled back.

Grandmother cut the engine at the top of Porcupine Hill, and they coasted down the long grade to the HUD house where the various aunts, uncles, and cousins of the extended Drum clan lived. Grandmother spun the wheel; they ghosted through the yard and stopped behind the burned hulk of a wrecked truck with bald axles jacked onto rust-streaked cinder blocks.

"There's a logging chain in the trunk," whispered Grandmother. "I'll need your help."

Grandmother was civic-minded: Breakdowns were common enough on the reservation that she'd welded a steel hook to the chassis of her car so she could tow her neighbors home. They linked the chain to the hook then, scrambling through the blackness, looped the far end of the chain around the outhouse planted in the weeds at the edge of the yard.

The outhouse was a ramshackle affair, cardboard and black plastic on a thin wood frame around a bench seat, held together with just enough nails to keep it from blowing away in the chinook winds. Sleeps-in-Blood Woman scanned the heavens, and cleaned her ear with her little finger as she saw Coyote's Eyeball had settled nearly to the western horizon.

"It won't be long now," she said.

They had barely time to settle back in their seats before light blazed on in an upstairs window, and the first groaning Drums stumbled down the well-worn path to the outhouse. They had a two-holer but it wasn't nearly enough. Running Drums poured from the house, trembling as involuntary waves of peristaltic surf pounded the beach of their intestines.

Sleeps-in-Blood Woman cackled again. "Talk about shit-for-brains," she said.

Worn pants and ragged skirts scattered in the dirt yard as the line backed up. Black Drum was on the seat of honor alongside his sister Norma when Sleeps-in-Blood spun the key in the ignition. A well-tuned 440-cubic-inch engine rumbled to life, and even the stars stopped to listen to the bone-chilling war whoop of grandmother and grandson as Sleeps-in-Blood Woman popped the clutch.

Blue-streak-follows was built for the racetrack with power to spare. The rickety outhouse sprang from its railroad-tie foundation. Norma was a big girl, and her spreading cheeks held her stuck in the hole of her seat by suction. She popped free at the first screaming turn, mashing sagebrush like a human rolling pin until she scraped to an abrupt halt against an abandoned washing machine. Black Drum wasn't nearly so fortunate.

"Dog-paddle, you dog-eater," screamed the Kingfish.

Black Drum had been holding himself above his adult-sized hole with both hands. The splintering outhouse slid like it had been buttered out from beneath his skinny shanks. Black Drum plummeted straight down, now he was up to his chin in the fetid morass of festering turds below. Sleeps-in-Blood counted coup with victory laps around the yard while the Kingfish sang and bounced in his seat as seminaked Drums dived headlong from the narrow beam of headlights.

Seventeen years later not much had changed.

The Kingfish was still bouncing in his seat, still singing, still driving too fast, thinking maybe he'd finally found a vehicle he could live with. The middle of the twentieth century had pretty much passed Montana by. It was the kind of a place where you could still hide from time, and the crumbling pavement in the two-lane highway along the river was riddled with cracks, holes, and pits. Conventional wisdom dictated that you proceed with caution under these circumstances, but the Kingfish in his new vehicle had arrived at a whole new Theory of Gravity as it related to Pothole Management.

He reasoned that when it came to any particular hole, the less time he spent over it the better. If only he could get down that road fast enough, gravity wouldn't have time to work. The wheels wouldn't drop into the holes because they wouldn't have time; at some critical escape velocity he would shuck the husk of gravity and skim lightly across the potholes like Robert Builds-a-fire, the hurdler who won state and ran like his feet never touched the ground.

The Theory of Relative Gravity and Pothole Management worked just well enough for the Kingfish to stick with it. He needed more speed. The biggest potholes were the problem, cavernous potholes that could be the size of a dead cow out there in the road. There was no skimming those babies, not without wings, not when true escape velocity was seven miles a second. And there was no swerving, either—not careening around a blind corner shaded by cliffs where the road hadn't seen the sun since October and a blind pit yawned open right now.

On direct hits the Kingfish was launched from seat to roof as if he'd been shot from a cannon, which sure made it hard to sing along with the catchy new song on the radio.

". . . in Margaritaville," he'd sing, then "OH NO!" would be followed by a crash, a scream, "AI-YEE-E-E!" and he'd pick up where the radio left off: ". . . Shaker of salt . . ."

Dirt roads stood up to frost heaves much better than low-budget reservation pavement. The Kingfish took the long way home, down through the cottonwood grove by the river. Jebediah's wagon had grown with the tree, and now floated in a web of branches several feet above the ground. Blue-streak-follows was at the next tree over; the sapling rising through the floorboards was already windshield-high.

Men were walking on the moon when Sleeps-in-Blood Woman finally admitted that she'd blown her last head gasket. She hadn't been convinced until she accelerated through the plate-glass window at Kipp's Market twice in the same week. Sleeps-in-Blood Woman had seen enough of a changing world that she didn't think there was much left that could surprise her, but she was surprised waiting for the latest in a long line of the Kingfish's vehicles to sputter into silence in the driveway beside the pond.

"Ai-yeh," she said as she hobbled up leaning on a cane. "Nice hearse."

"Thanks," said the Kingfish, tapping the shiny black door through the open window.

"Did you steal it?" asked Sleeps-in-Blood Woman hopefully.

"Just about," said the Kingfish. "It was a going-out-of-business sale."

He started to explain, but when he opened the door Sleeps-in-Blood Woman gasped. The driver's-side floor was covered with crumpled blue waxed fast-food wrappers. Sleeps-in-Blood Woman rapped her cane on the hood of the hearse hard enough to dent the heavy black metal. "Haven't I taught you anything?" she demanded.

The Kingfish had the wizened old woman by over a hundred pounds but he hung his head like a bad little schoolboy. You are what you eat and animals have spirits, too. As long as he'd been growing up they'd eaten nothing but wild meat: fish, antelope, deer, grouse.

"It's easier," he said meekly, "being on the road and all."

The Kingfish cringed as Grandmother fingered the leather medicine bundle at her neck. Suddenly he was staring through the vacuous eyes of a cow.

"Is that who you are?" she said. "Is that who you want to be?"

Then a pain grew in his side, a lump that sizzled like a fat haunch roasting too close to the coals as Sleeps-in-Blood Woman shook a greasy McWrapper in his face.

"You know what kind of chemicals they put in these things?" she said. "That lump is what took Jebediah. What are you trying to do? Glow in the dark so you won't have to buy candles?"

The lump dissolved, but having seen with cow-dead eyes left the Kingfish a little queasy.

"I know," he said as they walked toward the house, "I know."

Tufts of grass stuck up through the gravel driveway, the porch needed painting, and the front hall by the antler coatrack dripped with the smell of wild, hot meat.

"Elk roast and camas root?" asked the Kingfish hopefully.

Sleeps-in-Blood Woman leaned on her cane and shook her head. "It's only Gilligan," she replied. "The cannibals have him again, but that white boy is so skinny I don't know why the Indians bother."

The television was an old Magnavox equipped with a goose skull tuner and real rabbit ears; for as long as the Kingfish could remember, the flickering black-and-white picture had arrived with scent as well as sound. Reception improved as the weather got worse. During blizzards they'd have to turn down the volume on the perfume commercials—either that or open the windows. Now Gilligan, Ginger, and Mary Ann were squealing on their stakes as brown men in hula skirts piled brush at their feet. Gilligan was thin gruel, but Mary Ann smelled like fresh baked bread and spicy Ginger made the Kingfish squirm in his worn Barcalounger.

"Now that's better," murmured Grandmother approvingly.

The cannibals were after the real meal deal. They were trying to stuff the Skipper into a cast-iron cauldron, levering at him with coconut poles, but he was so fat he wouldn't fit.

"Butter him up, quick!" said Grandmother, who was rooting for the cannibals.

Then the Professor saved the day with a coconut catapult constructed of vines and sticks.

"I'll be darned," said Grandmother in mock seriousness. "The Indians lost again."

"Hard to believe, enit?" said the Kingfish.

Then a commercial for the new movie *Star Wars* aired. The living room smelled like strikes of lightning as men dueled with slashing gray sabers of light, and Grandmother's eyes lit up as she sliced the air with an imaginary sword.

"A lightsaber," she said. "Now that's the way to lay in a cord of firewood."

"Better sell your chain saw while it's still worth something," agreed the Kingfish.

Sleeps-in-Blood Woman kept a traditional sweat lodge but chopped the ceremonial sweet grass with an electric blender. She'd always been a curious mix of the old and the new, but since the 1930s not much was new. The Great Depression lingered, then interstate highways took away the railroad traffic. The boom times were long gone, the boardinghouse empty for years, and now Sleeps-in-Blood Woman slapped the top of the television to turn it off.

"How long will you be staying?" she asked, a little hope in her old-woman's voice.

The Kingfish didn't notice. "Only until morning," he said eagerly. "But

I'll be back in a month. And I should have enough for that new roof we've been needing."

Her rheumy eyes opened like someone had just dropped a horseshoe on her toe. "What is it?" demanded Sleeps-in-Blood Woman. "What are you up to now?"

The Kingfish scratched dollar signs in the air with both forefingers at once. "It's a sure thing," he replied. "I'll triple my money."

Grandmother sighed. When it came to business matters her grandson was too much like Gilligan and not near enough like Jebediah. Something always seemed to go wrong.

"What about that open-air restaurant?" she said. "Have you forgotten about that?"

"That was nothing," said the Kingfish, dismissing Aztec Joe's Open-Air Seafood Bistro with a wave of his hand.

"Nothing?" said Grandmother. "You call burning down a barn nothing?"

The "Bistro" was three folding chairs, "Open-air" was an umbrella over a folding table, and "Seafood" was brook trout that Aztec Joe caught fresh in whatever stream was handy. It was good work because there were lots of girls and he only opened weekends; singing Spanish songs and selling hot fish tacos at local rodeos, art fairs, and music festivals. Disaster struck on a blustery Saturday at the Miles City Bucking Horse Sale.

The fish for the tacos was cubed, dipped in egg batter, rolled in ground chilis and cumin, then fried crispy in peanut oil on a rusty old two-burner Coleman camp stove. The oil had to be boiling hot, and chronically dirty burner jets make Coleman stoves notoriously funky, especially if you sneak into a nearby barn and borrow some gas because you're out. The Kingfish had no way of knowing the man who owned the barn was a crop duster, or that the five-gallon can was filled with aviation fuel. The wind was gusting to thirty-five when the stove exploded in a ball of orange flame and spiraled up the crinkly red crepe paper decorating the umbrella pole.

A burning paper plate blew into the dry grass, the wind fanned the flames, and now the Kiwanis selling steak sandwiches in the next booth over were on fire, too. The Daughters of the American Revolution were abandoning their quilts to the flames when a game warden doubling as a volunteer fireman knocked over the cooler of "Seafood." Things looked bleak, but once the hay caught there was no saving the barn. The Kingfish managed to slip away in the confusion.

"That was different," he said. "Come and see."

Grandmother followed the Kingfish outside, limping along in the twilight.

"Your hearse," she said. "It's dripping."

"Isn't it great?" said the Kingfish proudly. "I drilled drain holes in the floor."

He opened the swinging rear doors to reveal a white bin constructed of white polystyrene foam insulation and duct tape. It was a giant homemade cooler filled with melting ice cubes and one big, dead gutted salmon.

"Wholesale," said the Kingfish. "That's where the real money is."

Sleeps-in-Blood Woman felt unbearably sad as the Kingfish went on like an infomercial.

"Spring chinook," he raved, "The sweetest salmon there is. Wholesale, not retail, that's where I went wrong before. I get the fish fresh from Quillayute with traditional fishing rights on the Columbia, and guarantee overnight delivery to Montana restaurants. I sold out my first load in only one afternoon."

The Kingfish lifted the stiff fish by its long pink tail.

"But I kept a salmon for the smoker," he said. "Wait until you taste it."

Six weeks later the Kingfish was hauling his largest load yet. He brushed at the tiny bubbles of Styrofoam that clung with static electricity to his silk tie and everything else in the car, sweltering under a huge ridge of high pressure blanketing the entire Rocky Mountain West. Record high temperatures were being shattered from Denver to Calgary. You could cook pizza on the dash, that's how hot it was inside the black hearse, and more fish meant less ice.

Compounding matters, the Kingfish had been enrolled for three days now in a course on the nature of competitive economics in a free market-place. The Montana Fish Company had moved into his territory. The company had deep pockets, refrigerated trucks, and relied on air freight to take advantage of the best deals. The Alaskan halibut run was on, and they were beating his salmon prices by two bucks a pound. His regular customers had all the fish they needed.

The sun burned a yellow hole in a cloudless blue sky as he sped down the highway. The Kingfish couldn't buy ice fast enough; whenever he stopped for more than ten minutes at a time cats came sniffing at the backwash of ripe fish. The Kingfish was desperate by the time he arrived at Pierre's Bitterroot Bistro, ready to sell at any price, when he saw the hand-lettered sign beside the front door advertising that night's special.

HALIBUT.

Pierre Lemieux was acclaimed as one of the finest chefs in all Montana. The Kingfish harbored no illusions about the present state of his cargo, but since he had delivered only the best fish he didn't know how strongly Pierre regarded fish that wasn't fresh. And there was no way the Kingfish could have known what a lousy day Pierre was enduring.

It was partly because Pierre had been cooking now for thirty-three years.

His lower back was an agony of scraping vertebrae. Pierre was weary of cooking, so weary that the thought of another cream sauce made him want to sob out loud. His wife was getting hot flashes, and last night Pierre had overheard his seventeen-year-old daughter admit to a friend on the phone that she was pregnant.

When Pierre smelled the salmon, something snapped.

"You call dese feesh fresh!" he exclaimed.

Pierre reached into the pile and grabbed up an orange fifteen-pounder with both hands by the tail. He spun it head-down in a full circle, springing from the knees and grunting at the release as he opened his pudgy fingers. The rigid fish flew a surprising distance before skidding to a stop in the dirt-and-gravel parking lot. Pierre smiled, a huge release of a smile, like he hadn't felt that good in weeks.

And he grabbed up another fish, and another, and another.

Salmon sailed for all four points of the compass. The Kingfish leaned against a tree and lit a cigarette as Pierre emptied the hearse fish by fish. It was hard work on such a torrid day; by the time he was done Pierre was leaning forward, hands on his knees, huffing and puffing.

The Kingfish stubbed out his cigarette and climbed behind the steering wheel.

"Thanks for unloading all them fish," he said. "I think they was starting to go a little bad anyway."

He'd heard it said on the reservation since he was a kid that you could exist anywhere, but you could only live at home. The Kingfish thought now maybe he knew what they meant. He wondered back to the buffalo days, wondering what returning war parties must have felt like; they didn't always come back with stolen horses. Sometimes they didn't even come back at all. Their hair would be flying from the poles of somebody else's tepee.

The Kingfish decided that anyone who traveled long distances alone and communicated with smoke signals could appreciate the advantages of radio, so he turned his on. He sang along with the Stones and Credence until the spiked silhouette of Pyramid Butte popped above the horizon. The weather had changed, too late for the salmon. The first plump drops of cooling rain cratered into the dust as the Kingfish pulled up to the old farmhouse.

"Grandmother?" he called out, pushing the screen door open with his shoulder.

He had so much to say, tears blurred the Kingfish's eyes as he plopped down into a creaky chair. He stared at the kitchen wall: blue paint darkened with wood smoke. There was a note on the table, carefully scribed block letters on a piece of lined loose-leaf notebook paper in blue ink: "Gone to the Sand Hills. If you're hungry there's pemmican in the microwave."

Then the writing changed to a spidery scrawl in blunt lead pencil: "P.S. Two white guys stopped by to rent a room. Can you believe it! They saw your boat and said they'd pay you to take them trout fishing next Monday. I told them you would."

The Sand Hills are north and east on the desolate plains just over the border. It's where the Blackfoot go when they die, up into Canada, a land of salt hummock and dry swale where the buffalo still roam. Shadow warriors pursue all the slaughtered billions of the once vast herds through an eternity of eating meat. It's a hereafter that cries out for comfortable accoutrements; the Piegan, like the ancient Egyptians, hold that you can take it with you.

The way you take it with you is that it's buried with you. A hundred years ago you'd take plenty of moccasins and a new tepee. You'd need a warm buffalo robe—it was cold in Canada—your favorite lodge chair, pipe and tobacco, plenty of arrows, and some jerky, because for a shadow warrior the Sand Hills are a hard two-day ride even on a stalwart warhorse.

You just don't leave for the Sand Hills without your favorite horse. The Kingfish found Sleeps-in-Blood behind the wheel of Blue-streak-follows, half buried in goose feathers, her arm around the television, leaning against the cottonwood that grew up through the middle of the car. Her desiccated head lolled back on the seat, and she smiled up at Jebediah's wagon in the tree up above. She couldn't have been gone long because the engine under the hood was still warm, and as the rain fell harder dancing drops sizzled on the swept-back pipes of the hot chrome manifold.

The Hanging Judge and the Christian Biker

THE LOGGING TRUCK CAREENED in from behind with a squeal of air-powered Jake Brakes, tailgating so close, my rearview mirror showed nothing but exposed radiator. Loggers get paid by the load and hate to wait. I swerved off in the next gravel turnout. A stack of thick-butted fir passed in a diesel hum. I drank coffee and ate blueberry muffin until the dust settled.

So much for rush hour.

My commute was ten miles of winding mountain road down the North Fork to the main stem of the Apikuni at the edge of the open plains. The local stop signs were all perforated with bullet holes but it wasn't road rage that did it, it was people sighting in their hunting rifles. The nearest traffic light was forty miles away. Turn signals were still optional equipment, which was good because I had a dead bulb in my left blinker.

I looped around Pyramid Butte, thumped across the loose planks of the Badger Creek Bridge, and hung a left through the log arch under the hanging sign that said TROUT WORLD. The Kingfish was out front in the white gravel parking lot, kneeling beside the wide-open door of his hearse, half buried in a heap of litter as he excavated the no-man's-land beneath the front seat. The due date for the filing extension was rapidly approaching, so it was no surprise to see him doing his income taxes.

The Kingfish scrutinized each item as he retrieved it. Anything important—the names and numbers scrawled in empty matchbook covers, the mud-stained envelopes, the receipts dipped in coffee—the Kingfish filed in a rusty tacklebox. Everything else—cassette tapes, a tambourine, four-piece fly rods in stubby aluminum cases—he dropped into the mound of debris surrounding him like an upside-down midden, oldest relics on top.

I rolled to a stop right next to him and leaned out the window of my truck.

"Department of Antiquities Department," I called out. "You have a permit for this job?"

The Kingfish tried to smile but couldn't quite get it out. You have to give him credit for trying. Tax time is no joke for anyone; when you use the floor of your truck for a filing cabinet it can be downright discouraging. I know, because I use pretty much the same system. So do a lot of fishing guides. We didn't get where we are today because we're good at business.

"Because," I continued, "there's a lot of history here. You can't just be digging willy-nilly without a permit. You need a plan, in triplicate. It's the law."

The Kingfish produced a green quart glass bottle from the pile at his feet. "What do you think?" he said. "Would this make you look in the other direction?"

Fifteen-year-old Scotch can make you look in a lot of directions all at once.

"Bribes are good," I replied. "Maybe we could even get you some grant money."

You quit one day at a time in an upscale business where the good stuff is always around at the end of the day, and the Kingfish stared wistfully at the bottle as he handed it over.

"Grant money would be good," he said. "We could study the effects of rock 'n' roll on the central nervous system."

I wrapped the Scotch in an old shirt and put it behind the seat. When I turned back the Kingfish held out a hinged plastic case originally designed for designer sunglasses. The case now served as a sarcophagus for a four-legged mummy splayed out flat on its back, a section of charred speaker wire clenched in its grinning sharp-toothed rictus.

The animal was too big for a shrew, too small for a chipmunk; the gray hair was long and curly, like poodle fur. I picked up a used orange Popsicle stick by the clean end and poked at the mummy. The thin body inside the shroud of frizzy fur was hard as a hubcap.

"I'm thinking *field mouse*," said the Kingfish. "How about you?"

The size and color were right but there was still the smile, an enigmatic *Mona Lisa* smile. It wasn't the expression you'd expect from a mouse. And mice have tiny, black, beady eyes; this creature had wide green pupils the size of nickels that even in death remained zeroed in on something startling in the distance.

"If it's a mouse," I said, "he went where no mouse has gone before."

"I had to cut him out and splice the wire," said the Kingfish. "The snout is clamped shut so tight I couldn't even pry him open with a screwdriver."

"That must have been what happened last Friday night," I said.

The Kingfish nodded. We'd been returning from a jam at the Mountain Palace. It was about two in the morning, and the tape deck was cranked to early Led Zeppelin. Robert Plant with his electric guitar and Jimmy Page with his warbling tonsils were dueling for the highest note humanly possible when all the speakers on the left side of Mister Dead shot sparks, and there was an odor that in retrospect was probably singed fur.

"Wherever this little fella went," said the Kingfish, "it looks like it was a quick trip."

The kaleidoscopic green eyes didn't look as if they'd seen a heaven built of cheese. "It may have been quick," I said, "but I'm not so sure about painless."

The Kingfish snapped the case shut and threw the mouse in the debris pile. "I don't think rodents feel pain the way we do," he replied. "They don't have to do taxes."

The wind shifted. Nostrils flared as the Kingfish looked at the back of my truck.

"Way to go," he said. "Eddie is going to be one very happy eagle."

"Meals on Wheels," I said. "Serving nothing but the finest in avian cuisine."

I climbed out of the truck and pulled back the brown burlap covering a chicken-wire cage in the bed of the pickup. Two bushy-tailed wood rats cowered in the flood of daylight.

"Your trailer sure is prime trapping ground," the Kingfish said admiringly.

It was like living in a giant aluminum mousetrap. All I had to do was bait the kitchen counter.

"Yeah," I said. "Thanks."

The rats went in the cage that used to hold rabbits next to the pile of split wood behind the red barn. In the next cage over Eddie, a molting bald eagle with a willow stick splint on his broken wing, watched intently. The Kingfish was nursing Eddie back to health, and in captivity eagles will sometimes starve rather than eat. Still, live rats were food that Eddie couldn't resist.

"So," I asked as we walked back out front, "who do we have today?"

"A judge paid the deposit, some hard-on-crime guy from Minnesota. It's a wedding thing, future in-laws, I get the feeling they don't know each other too well."

The Kingfish and I were doing a two-boat guide trip that was due to begin as soon as the clients arrived. For a guide it's the sixty-four-thousand-dollar question.

"Can they cast?" I asked.

The Kingfish rolled his shoulders noncommittally. "The judge at least," he said. "He's fished all over, from Argentina to Alaska."

It's always easier with people who can cast, and the Kingfish was in a magnanimous mood now that his taxes were done.

"I'll tell you what," he said. "You want the judge, you can take him out."

"Maybe you better keep the judge for yourself," I said, "in case you need legal counsel. I heard Fish and Game is going to be checking boat numbers on the river today."

Fishing guides were taking public heat for the increasingly crowded rivers, so a group of outfitters proposed that guides be required to place special identifying tags on their boats. If that doesn't seem to make sense it's because it doesn't. Drawing attention to yourself won't make people forget you're there.

The Kingfish refused to comply with the new regulation. "What's next?" he said. "They gonna tattoo the numbers on our skulls?"

It isn't easy being a warrior when all the decent battles are fought in boardrooms and courtrooms; I understand that. But at least be smart about picking your wars. There's no way you can beat the bureaucracy in a frontal assault.

"It's a two-hundred-dollar fine," I said. "Just do what I did."

The numbered decals were on my boat, glued up under the gunwales where you could hardly see them anyway. The Kingfish tapped out a cigarette as he stared off to the west, a couple of Eddie's white tail feathers arranged at the top of his long black braids. He was about to say something when Heidi skipped down the split-log front steps waving a white envelope.

"Your boat numbers are here," she said to the Kingfish, "finally. I wrote away three weeks ago. And it's just such a, a, ah, Ah-choo!"

Heidi turned her head to spray a sinus-shattering sneeze toward the barn. "Damn this hay fever," she said.

The Kingfish stared sourly at the envelope she'd just stuck in his hand. Heidi rubbed her red nose on the strap of her shirt and looked at me. Neither of us had siblings, and everybody needs family. Over the years we'd become like brother and sister. Heidi smiled as she squeezed my upper arm.

"Could you help me with lunch?" she asked too sweetly.

I was wary of the smirk in those green eyes, like she already knew. One thing I'd found was that sisters loved to rub it in. If the Joke-of-the-Week Club got wind of what had happened, they'd be merciless. Heidi tugged me toward the house by the triceps. There was nothing for it but to follow along into the yellow kitchen lush with the chocolate tingle of fresh-baked brownies. Flowing curtains framed country windows, table vases sprouted bouquets of fresh wildflowers, and a pair of green coolers with open lids sat on the round table.

"It smells great," I said. "What are we having?"

Heidi blew her nose on a napkin, washed her hands at the sink under the black velvet painting of the dogs playing poker, then said: "Lemon-pepper chicken breasts, pasta salad, sourdough rolls, fresh fruit, dessert."

Lunch on the river is considerably more of a froufrou affair than it once was. We used to just sit on coolers and eat stuff; now you need tables, chairs, and tablecloths. Potato chips and pressed salami on white bread just doesn't cut it anymore. You serve a lousy lunch, word gets out, and pretty soon you don't have clients anymore. Quality control is just part of a guide's job.

I was testing the brownies cooling on the wire rack when Heidi stopped me in midbite with the backs of her smooth hands. "How do you like my nails?" she asked.

She wiggled her fingers as she held up curved fingernails painted with segmented black ants against a silver background. The huge black carpenter ants swarm like termites in early summer when the ground thaws—so many ants that even the trout key on them. She knew. Heidi knew. And if she knew, everybody knew. She was going to say something but when she saw the pain in my face Heidi bit her lower lip.

"How about a hug?" she said quietly.

The hug was as much for her as it was for me. Indians don't touch much, and Heidi couldn't talk without touching, like she was making up for a lost childhood. I rested my cheek on the top of her hot yellow hair, staring through the kitchen window out into the parking lot. Time sneaks up with a gray-haired hammer and hits you from behind. I wondered how it had gotten to the point that I could bring a girl home only if I never wanted to see her again.

"Who told you?" I asked resignedly.

"Bobbie," said Heidi.

"So." Straight from the source.

Bobbie was the new bartender at the Mountain Palace, and lately she'd been hinting with fluttering mascara that she could be talked out of sleeping alone. Bobbie dressed for the tips, and the leather mini skirt alone was enough to keep her truck in gas. Closing time couldn't come soon enough. I thought it was my lucky night until I flipped on the bedroom light back at the trailer.

Huh, is what I thought next.

A dozen ants had just scurried away into the dark line of shadow beneath the pillow.

"Are those bugs?" said Bobbie. "Because if it wasn't bugs it sure looked like bugs."

I picked up the pillow and wanted to be sick. Bobbie turned away and pressed both hands to her stomach above the big silver belt buckle like she felt the same way.

"That's the most revolting thing I've ever seen," she said.

"I can fix this," I replied.

But I couldn't. The dark line of shadow was a seething mass of migrating ants, so many ants in the exact shape of the pillow they'd lifted it off the mattress. Once their cover was blown the writhing, black swarm formed up into columns, and undulating streams of ants flowed for the sides of the bed in three different directions at once.

"I think I'll go now," said Bobbie, turning on a stiletto heel and showing me the red seam on the back of her fishnet stockings.

"No, wait," I said.

Tapered legs and trim ankles disappeared down the double-long hall that smelled of mildew when it rained. I folded the sheets by all four corners into a sack and ran for the door, ants leaking at the seams and racing up my arms like black streams of tar. They were nearly to my face when I managed to knock some loose by falling down the four iron stairs that opened onto the moonlit forest outside. So far the longest relationship I'd managed was with my boat. I was trying to believe I hadn't run out of chances with people when a battered jeep clanked down the driveway between the flanking rows of trimmed birch.

I let go and stepped back. Heidi looked up at the wall clock.

"Right on time," she said. "Half an hour late."

Montana is where four-wheel-drive vehicles go to die. Ancient trucks bound together with baling wire and duct tape are as common as bumps in the road. Still, the jeep in the driveway was the first vehicle I'd seen held together with bumper stickers. Brightly colored swatches of jingoistic dogma were slapped on everywhere, even the windshield.

THIS CAR PROTECTED BY SMITH & WESSON

BIKERS DO IT WITH THEIR RODS

UNBORN BABIES ARE PEOPLE TOO

ABORTION IS MURDER

CHOOSE LIFE

I walked outside carrying a cooler, thinking when the time came for small talk to avoid the topics of politics and religion. The jeep shuddered to an engine-knocking, part-by-part stop. The driver was in his midtwenties with a bristly buzz cut, and a surprisingly gentle voice for someone with shoulders the size of milk jugs.

"Hi," he said, "I'm Chris. Sorry we're late, but I had a flat tire."

He grabbed the padded roll bar and hoisted himself out over the closed door. A thin man in pressed khaki chinos sniffed in the backseat.

"It's lucky we made it at all," he muttered under his breath.

Chris grinned. "Eight-ply steel-belted radials," he said, "What can you do?"

The other man in the backseat was heavier, even pudgy. He had thick black-rimmed glasses, fat cheeks, and both hands buried up to the wrists between his legs.

"I'm stuck," he said in a nasal voice. "I think I hooked my pants on a spring."

The fourth man with silver hair and a deep-water tan had already scrambled from the front passenger's seat and was pumping my hand with an iron grip. "Judge Svensen," he said, "and I've been looking forward to floating the Apikuni for years. I hear nothing but good things about the river. How's the fishing been?"

"Pretty good," I said, "at least in the . . ."

Thin Khaki Man had interrupted and was now pumping my other hand. "Sawyer," he said, "George Sawyer. Now what's that about the fishing? What precisely will we be using today?"

"That depends," I said, "Either a . . ."

Then the man who had been stuck to his seat was squeezing the Kingfish's hand. "Sawyer, Al Sawyer," he said. "Will a twelve-foot leader be acceptable, or should I go with fifteen?"

"It's going to be windy," said the Kingfish. "Fifteen is a little . . ."

Thin Khaki Man was back with a jacket. "Should I bring this?" he asked. "Will it rain?"

The Kingfish sniffed at the wind. "Maybe about three," he said. "But not for long."

Masturbator, I was thinking, *masturbator, alligator, Al. Al.*

I'm lousy with names so I resort to mnemonic links because once you call a client Thin Khaki Man you can kiss your tip good-bye. It wasn't a great link but what I remembered about Al was how he'd been digging away with both hands in an area generally reserved for the groin. The judge was easy. I'd left him Hanging. Thin Khaki Man was dressed for safari. *George of the Jungle. George. Look out for that tree. George.* Say it over and over until you can't forget it. *George. Al. The judge.* And the big guy driving. He was, he was, he was . . .

I'd forgotten his name already. Now I'd have to wait until somebody mentioned it.

And here he was, with flickering blue eyes and fingers the size of bananas. He had iron pumper's arms, thick with muscle and bulging veins, and a tattoo of a biker in a black jacket rode the cords between wrist and elbow. The biker was slouched back on a chopped Harley, leisurely choking a bright red caricature of Satan from behind with a length of chain.

"Nice tattoo," I said as my hand disappeared in his. "I like a picture that tells a story."

He peered close to see if I was sincere, which I was. If he got mad it would be like going through a juicer.

"Thanks," he said. "Craig up in Cow Coulee did it for me. I'll give you his card."

Then the judge came to my mnemonic rescue. "Chris," he said, looking in the back of the jeep, "have you seen my waders?"

Chris. Christian biker. That I could remember.

The disparate group was not your average group of fishing buddies. They were together because of a wedding that was coming up on Saturday, when the Christian Biker would be marrying the Hanging Judge's youngest daughter. Al and George were brothers, George was Chris's father, and since they had fishing in common this day on the river was the judge's idea of a way they could all get to know each other.

"So," said the Hanging Judge eagerly. "Are we ready to go? Because I just can't wait to see this river."

"Yeah," said Al. "How many fish are we gonna get?"

There is a certain clientele known to guides as "fish-counters." Fish-counters get six and they want seven. They get forty and they want forty-one. There's just no pleasing some people, and Al was counting his fish even before he'd left the parking lot. It wasn't a good sign. I took the Kingfish up on his offer to guide the judge, who was fishing with Chris.

Later that morning we were anchored in my fourteen-foot driftboat on the willow bank just up the river from Beaver Head Rock. The oars dragged loosely in the water. The judge was in the front swivel seat, Christian Biker in the back. I was in the middle, and we were all sitting down because that way you can get closer to the fish.

Chris and the judge were each fishing a two-fly setup, a beadhead nymph below a floating dry fly that also served as a strike-indicator. I'd drilled them on the importance of making each cast count as we drifted flies through a shark pod of feeding fish about thirty-five feet away, using a game called Five-cast.

"Nothing puts fish down like slapping cast after cast down on their heads," I said. "So we're going to play Five-cast. It's simple. You each get five casts, then I get one."

They each made five hurried casts; I made one good cast. Their flies waked through the water; mine drifted drag-free. They didn't have a chance of catching a fish. I landed a fat sixteen-inch rainbow.

"There's only one rule in dry-fly fishing," I said. "Make every cast count."

Chris and the judge slowed down for the second round. Out of ten casts they had two strikes; on my one cast I got another fat rainbow. In the third round Chris and the judge each caught fish on their second cast. Five-cast as a teaching tool is worth a thousand words. As soon as you make every cast count, the game is over. It's the fun that's just beginning.

Chris and the Judge took turns plucking the pod of one jumping rainbow after another. So many fluttering brown caddis were hatching that more fish were rising than when we'd started. The forces were in alignment. It was one of those days you occasionally get guiding when everything you touch turns to gold, and I now have a confession to make.

I have a bad habit.

Actually I have several but since my mother might read this I'll only mention one. When I'm guiding and a fish takes the fly I sometimes scream "FISH-FISH-FISH!" at the top of my lungs. The loud yell is a bad habit because it causes startled fishermen to lunge in place if not outright leap from the boat. This results in a panicked jerk on the rod, and either a missed fish or a broken tippet.

I yell only partly from excitement. I also yell because I care. It's vicarious fish-catching pleasure. I want people to catch fish, and you can't catch fish if you can't see your fly. The tiny dry flies that work best on the Apikuni appear to unpracticed eyes as infinitesimal as specks of floating dust; even experienced clients miss most of their strikes. I have to let them know when a fish eats their fly, I just don't have to yell. I know it's a bad habit, it's just that I've been doing it for so long it's hard to do anything else. Breaking habits is an uphill struggle.

So sometimes I yell, they rear back, and we break the tiny dry-fly tippet.

"Smoo-ooth," I then counsel as I tie on new flies. "To set the hook with dry flies, slow down. Don't use your wrist. Lift from the shoulder—up and out to the side. Give the trout time to close its mouth on the fly. You have to hit them smoo-ooth."

But let's face it. Smoo-ooth is easier said than done when your guide shrieks at unexpected moments. Imagine you're the judge. The problem is, you still can't see your fly. You can see the fish, though. The pod is the size of a living room couch, and trout that are three fingers across between the eyes feed so hard you hear the fish slurp. And since you can't see your fly, you make another cast into the broad current line that funnels down to the fish.

"It's perfect," your guide whispers, his lips nearly in your ear. "Get ready."

You take his word for it because you still can't see your fly. Not for sure anyway. It looks just like the thousands of real bugs on the water; that's why it works. It could be here or it could be there, all you know for sure is that your fly is lost in the cornucopia, bobbing along somewhere in the middle of more trout than you've ever seen rise in one place before.

"They're big fish," whispers your guide. "Huge."

It's a riffle not of rocks but of rising trout heads. You'd heard about it, and now you've traveled thousands of miles to see it. The gulp of swallowing fish is louder than the rustle of the willow leaves in the breeze. Your heart pounds, your throat is dry, your hands shake as you think you may finally have picked out your tiny fly.

Smoo-ooth, you are thinking. Smoo-ooth. But you're epileptic with anticipation. You know it's coming, then, scant inches above your twitching shoulder, there it is, the shriek of:

"FISH-FISH-FISH!"

What are you going to do when somebody screams in your ear?

What the adrenaline-honed nerve ending shaped like the Hanging Judge did was what most people do: He reared back on the rod way too hard and a little too late. The big fish had already spit out the dry fly. Wild fish populations, however, fluctuate naturally with water conditions. The river was loaded with four-inch fish following successful spawning during a wet spring, and the dropper nymph was at that instant in the mouth of a baby trout.

Normally any fish—even a little fish—is cause for celebration, but most fish don't fly.

"Incoming," I yelled. "Look out!"

The judge's ferocious hook-set launched the trout like a tiny silver cruise missile programmed with the impact coordinates of the airspace over the boat. The fish whistled past so close I felt the breeze, following the developing loop into a fine backcast that the Judge reflexively punched into a forward cast. Meanwhile, in the back of the boat, my second scream had startled the Christian Biker into a powerful sidearm backcast of his own. It was exactly what Sir Isaac Newton had in mind when the apple fell on his head: The Hanging Judge and the Christian Biker had become mirror images of equal but opposite casting action and reaction.

Both rods were fully loaded; four flies, a fish, and a combined ninety feet of line and leader were accelerating smoothly toward a common destiny with my openmouthed face. The two rods smashed together like dueling graphite swords. The casting loops collapsed. Coils of line and leader fell like macramé about my head and shoulders—but so far it was just another day, another tangle. It was the return flight of the flying fish that made this moment special.

The fish, which had earned enough frequent-flier miles for a free ticket to Puerto Rico, came in hard on a beeline. The dry fly above the fish hooked the other rod in passing, and the fish swung into orbit around the crossed rods. The taut leader grew shorter and shorter as the fish spun faster and faster in a classic display of centripetal force. It wasn't until the rods were lashed together and cinched tight that the fish finally bumped to a quivering stop against the rod. The tiny trout was so close I could smell him; so close I went cross-eyed trying to focus.

I'd undone plenty of tangles before, but this was the first time I'd ever been in one.

"All right," I said, blinking. "Way to go, judge. You got one."

"I did?" he said.

In the commotion the judge had never even seen the tiny fish he had hooked.

"Right here," I said, lifting line from my shoulders, finally removing the fish from the fly and holding him out. The fish still had the vertically barred parr marks of a baby trout and fit neatly in the palm of my hand.

The Christian Biker sat back, admiring the fish. "Frisky little fellow, isn't he?"

The judge tenderly released the tiny fish. "What a lovely little trout," he said.

The Mother of all tangles was going to take a while to unravel, and it was almost time for lunch. I hacked away the worst of the tangle, then rowed down the river so we could hook up with the Kingfish and the rest of the wedding party. It was time for small talk. Politics and religion were out, but it's hard to get contentious about rocks and scenery. As we passed Beaver Head Rock I pointed to the darker layers of fractured octahedrons in the red bluff that were now eroded into a reasonable likeness of a beaver's blunt head.

"Those are old lava flows," I said. "It seems peaceful now, but four hundred million years ago this whole area was covered with huge volcanoes."

The boat rocked back and forth as the Christian Biker shook his massive head. "That's okay," he said, "if you believe in that kind of stuff."

"What?" I said. "You don't believe in volcanoes?"

"I believe in what I see; it's the four hundred million years I have problems with. All this," he said, sweeping his hand at the sky, the river, the cliffs, "was created in seven days a little over six thousand years ago."

I pulled at the oars, biting softly at my tongue.

"You're a Creationist?" I said finally.

The Christian Biker crossed his Satan-covered forearms on his broad chest.

"And you're not?" he said.

The Hanging Judge snorted, but lightly, under his breath. Fathers never quit loving their little girls. I was guessing there were subjects the judge didn't dare broach with his new son-in-law. I was also willing to bet my tip the judge wouldn't mind if I raised the questions for him.

"Chris," I said, "I'll be honest with you. I have a hard time believing that the whole world was created in only seven days. I mean, for starters, what about the fossils?"

The Christian Biker chuckled at the perfectly ridiculous nature of my question.

"What about the fossils?" he said. "They mean nothing. Geologists date rocks by their fossil content, at that same time they date fossils by their location in the geologic column. Talk about one hand shaking the other. You can't have it both ways."

"But surely," I said, "you don't deny the existence of fossils. If they didn't get there over a period of time as the rocks were laid down in sedimentary layers, how did they get there?"

"It was the flood, dude," he said. "Fossils don't record a succession of life-forms. That's not it at all. All fossils represent is a sorting of antediluvian contemporaneous life-forms."

The Christian Biker had the jargon down, no doubt about that.

"The flood?" I said. "You mean Noah's flood? With the Ark and animals two by two?"

"Exactly," said the Christian Biker.

He illustrated every point with thick waving arms as he explained Flood Geology:

"In four-oh-oh-four B.C., after God made the world, the Garden of Eden was the place to be. It never rained, and people like Methuselah lived for hundreds of years without sunscreen because the harmful rays of the sun were filtered out. Then, sometime after Adam's bit of trouble with the apple and the snake, there was a divine judgment on fallen angels. God's wrath was sufficient to tilt the planet earth twenty-three-and-a-half degrees from the perpendicular in the plane of its regular orbit, which is why we have seasons. The sudden shock as the Earth was knocked sideways created tidal waves that swept twice daily around the globe from east to west, simultaneously releasing massive reservoirs of subterranean water."

The Christian Biker clapped his meaty hands as the Earth was knocked from its orbit.

"The resulting disaster," he continued, "killed first the small and helpless animals, like snails and worms, depositing their remains at the bottom of the flood-generated burial strata. More complex animals, like dinosaurs and buffalo, fled to the hilltops. These animals could run but they couldn't hide, and they were eventually buried above the simpler organisms by the raging flood, and that's why fossils range from simple to complex proceeding up through the burial column.

"In geology," said the Christian Biker, "that's known as the Principle of Uniformity."

It was an affront to a member of the Church of the Reduced Humanist, where science explains everything yet determines nothing. A boat isn't a pulpit and guides should never proselytize, but this reasoning was a philosophical slap in the face to everything I held dear.

"In reality," I said, "that's known as the Principle of Absurdity."

A purple-blue vein throbbed in the Christian Biker's blocky temple.

"No offense," I said, "but what about Noah? What about all the animals, marching onto the boat two by two? How could any creatures survive a flood so powerful that it rearranged the face of the earth?"

The Christian Biker reached up and triangulated his arm slabs like a mountain peak.

"Biblical scholars found pieces of Noah's Ark on Mount Ararat. The boat was made of Joshua wood," he explained, "a member of the cork family. It's impossible to sink."

"That's pretty good cork," I said. "I'd like some for tying popping bugs for bass."

It had gone too far. I tried to joke my way back to secular ground but the Christian Biker was having none of it.

"You'll also like what happened next," he said. "One of the first things Noah did was go on a pretty good wine drunk. After the cataclysm the harmful rays of the sun were no longer filtered out, which not only shortened human life spans to three score and ten but also fermented fruit for the very first time. So imagine Noah's surprise when he knocked back his morning grape juice."

Goldfinches twittered in the willows. Were they on the Ark? With giraffes?

"But what about genetic diversity?" I said. "What about evolution, the variation between people? It's just not possible that all the blacks and reds and whites and yellows and all those body types and all those languages evolved in only four thousand years. It's not enough time for all that to happen."

"There's plenty of time," he replied. "It's not evolution, it's de-evolution, quick rather than slow change, a degeneration of family stocks, and the rate of change was greatest directly after the flood when men and animals were suddenly subjected to what was now a completely foreign environment."

This conversation was going nowhere but at least it explained my friends.

"Degeneration of family stocks," I said. "Is that how we got fishing guides?"

I was still trying to joke my way out of it, but the Christian Biker was dead serious as he squeezed my shoulder like he was testing a melon for ripeness.

"Well, then, friend," he said, "if you don't believe in God, what *do* you believe in?"

There may well be Gods, but when it comes to deities I'm more Animist like the Indians than Christian like the Crusades. The power is in the world around us, not in an omnipotent being created in our own image. And if you need to pray, not many people have said it better than Big-lodge-pole, a Blackfoot chief back in the buffalo days.

Big-lodge-pole prayed to the Great Spirit for wisdom for his leaders, so that they might show kindness. He prayed that his enemies would be strong, so there would be no dishonor in defeat. He prayed the young would have love and contentment, the old would have health and long life, and Big-lodge-pole prayed that he would live each day, so that when day was done, his prayer would not have been in vain.

"I believe in Einstein," I said, pushing with the right oar and pulling with the left, spinning the boat counterclockwise, the same direction as earth. "Mass is energy, and energy has waves, so you and me, the river, the trees, and the sky, we all have our own wavelengths. Our own characteristic and unique energies. Sometimes our waves line up with the world around us; sometimes they cancel out. It's our job to make things line up."

I let go of the oars then leaned over the gunwale and used my sweat-stained ball cap to seine spent caddisflies from the surface film. Spent caddis are wispy, desiccated husks completely devoid of vital fluids. I thrust out the dripping hat.

"Everything these bugs had went into one last glorious mating flight," I said. "That's how you live life, by the moment, interacting with as many other wave forms as possible, so, when the time comes, your prayer won't have been in vain."

The Christian Biker poked a sad finger at the dead bugs in my wet hat. "To think that's all there is," he said forlornly. "You must be so very lonely."

Lonely cut like a dagger. I saw ants. All this time the judge had been quietly listening, which if you think about it is what a judge does best. Now he twirled his sunglasses in his hand as he appraised the Christian Biker with steady gray eyes.

"And you truly believe all this?" said the judge. "The earth was created in seven days?"

The Christian Biker smiled back, serene in his belief. "Everything you need to know," said Chris. "It's all right there in Genesis."

131

Steadfast faith isn't a bad feature in a future son-in-law. The judge leaned back and straightened his khaki shirt collar, then pointed at a large black-and-white bird with long tail feathers flapping across the river. "That bird," he said curiously. "What kind is it?"

This, in technical guide parlance, falls under the category of "nature shit." If you don't know the answer it's usually best to just make something up, but this was an easy one. "It's a magpie," I said, pointing at a jumble of sticks in the crotch of a cottonwood tree. "He's heading for that nest."

A note of tenderness sounded in the judge's stentorian trumpet of a voice. "I thought so," he said. "That bird looked just like Heckle and Jeckle."

"Elaine still watches that show," said the Christian Biker.

"It was her favorite cartoon," said the judge. "When she was a little girl we used to watch every Saturday morning. She'd sit there in my lap on the old overstuffed chintz couch."

"She still curls up on the couch," said the Christian Biker. "She says it reminds her of the smell of your aftershave."

It's the Huck Finn syndrome. There may be no better place to talk than an open boat moving at the pace of the river. People will say things they've never said before. Over the years I've heard confessions ranging from illegitimate children to life-threatening brain tumors. The Hanging Judge and the Christian Biker found common ground in the Minnesota Twins; they were analyzing the pennant race as I came around the sharp corner where the Kingfish was already fixing lunch.

The Kingfish had pulled in the placid flat just above the Rock Garden, a foaming chute of fast green water. It's a good lunch spot because the clients can wade fish while the guides set out the food. Thin Khaki Man . . . George . . . was balanced in the quiet water beside the Kingfish's wooden boat, reaching all the way around himself to fuss with his fly vest.

He looked at Chris as my boat scraped up onto shore beside the other boat. "Praise Jesus," he said sarcastically. "Did God show you where all the fish were today?"

George was Chris's father. I guess he figured it gave him the right.

'No," said Chris, "but He might have showed our guide."

"You guys caught all the fish," I said. "All I did was drop the anchor."

The Kingfish looked up from behind a folding table erected and laden with crackers, hickory-smoked whitefish, a couple of kinds of cheese, and a vegetable platter. George's brother Al stuffed a floret of green broccoli into his mouth.

"Really," he said through dripping ranch dressing. "All we caught was little ones."

George turned around and headed for the table, explaining over his shoulder as he went. "We were in the wrong places," he said. "The water wasn't deep enough."

"There just aren't any big fish in this river," said Al. "Isn't that right, George?"

"That's right," agreed George as he surveyed the hors d'oeuvres.

"I told you we should have gone to Alaska," said Al. "How about some cheese?"

"There's big fish in Alaska," agreed George. "Got any Gouda, or just this Brie?"

The Kingfish finished a Coke and crushed the can with one hand. "There's big fish in Montana," he said. "Why don't you give that one a try?"

The sleeves on the Kingfish's blue shirt were rolled up to the elbows. He pointed toward the glassy flat above the Rock Garden. A trout was rising a hundred feet away, dimpling rings on the drop-off of the inside river bend before the water picked up speed.

Al dismissed the fish with a wave of a broccoli spear. "Not worth the trouble," he said. "That's just one more little fish."

Riseforms are deceiving. Small trout can leave big rings, and big trout can leave tiny rings. I couldn't say for sure, not without getting closer, but the Kingfish has binoculars for eyes. If he said it was a big fish then it was a big fish.

"Somebody ought to try for that trout," I said. "How about you, Chris?"

Chris smiled like Solomon and turned to the Kingfish. "It's a little too tough for me," said Chris. "Why don't you use my rod."

"Please do," said George. "Show us this 'big fish'."

George made quotation marks with his fingers as he said "big fish."

People are always asking me if you get assholes out there guiding. The answer is almost never, and about all you can do when it happens is make sure you wipe clean.

The Kingfish walked to his boat, pulled out a rod, bit off the tippet, and rerigged from scratch. The trout was feeding in six inches of water in calm air with only sporadic puffs of southeast wind. The fish would spook at the slightest disturbance. The Kingfish crept on his knees, moving one knee and letting the ripples die, then moving the other knee and letting the ripples die, until he was about thirty-five feet from the rising trout.

He sat back on his heels, cutoff blue jean shorts in the water, waiting with a fifteen-foot 6X tippet. He used a number eighteen Parachute Adams, a fly that lands softly and hangs down like a helpless bug stuck in the surface film. A gust of wind put a tiny chop on the water, and only then did the Kingfish load the rod on his backcast and shoot the fly out low to the green river with a single sidearm cast.

The drift was right down Main Street, the water bulged under the fly, and the fish took a natural insect floating a quarter inch from the artificial. The Parachute Adams rocked in the backwash of the rise. The Kingfish let the fly swing below before stripping in line and switching to the same fly only smaller, a number twenty, a hook about the size of a letter on this page.

Another riffle of wind, another single sidearm cast, and this time the fish tipped down with a tiny bit of diamond-honed steel in its mouth. A full count later, giving the trout time to close its mouth, the Kingfish lifted the rod and set the hook. In the panic of shallow water the fish had nowhere to go but up, but up is good, especially if your credibility is on the line.

"Jesus H. Christ," said Al.

The Christian Biker gave his uncle a hard stare as the brown trout flipped completely over in the air, crashed down in a six-pound belly flop, then bolted for the safety of the deep water in the main river. The Kingfish sprinted across the gravel bar to the edge of the drop, holding his rod with both hands high over his head as he leapt into the river.

"Well," I said, "I guess there's at least one big fish in this river."

The fish was running the rapids so the Kingfish was, too, steering through the scattered rocks with his downstream feet. Rod, arms, and occasionally head were all that stuck out above the foaming water as the fish jumped again.

"I didn't think he was that big," said George.

"Shit," said Al. "That should have been my trout."

The Christian Biker was smiling up at the sky like he personally knew the clouds.

"Thank you," he said.

The judge put his arm around the Christian Biker's massive shoulders.

"No," said the judge. "Thank you."

Bernie the Billionaire

STEVE FROM STEVE'S MOBILE HOMES SMILED with jagged Copenhagen-stained teeth.

"A thousand," he said. "Cash money."

"You have yourself a deal," I said, "as long as it's gone in an hour."

Steve picked through the oversized pockets on his greasy blue coveralls for ten crumpled hundreds, trying to hide a smirk as he hitched the double-long to his giant red tow truck. The trailer was worth five times what he'd paid for it. Steve smiled behind his hand thinking he'd just fleeced a greenhorn. What he didn't know is that I would have given that trailer away.

It's pointless to waste emotion on inanimate objects like cars that don't run and washing machines that flood during the soap cycle, but I had come to hate that oversized aluminum rattrap. Nonetheless it was with mixed emotions that I watched the big yellow box bang down the driveway through low hanging branches of swinging green fir, because as the trailer disappeared so did my last vestiges of indoor plumbing.

I was building a house by myself, which is slow going. I had roof, walls, and windows, but until the toilet was installed I was reduced like a middle-aged caveman to squatting in the woods, the backs of my legs braced against a fallen tree. You can imagine how much I needed a shower, but the bathtub wasn't in yet, either, and until that happy day arrived I was bathing in the river with biodegradable peppermint soap.

On cold mornings I'd lather up across from the carved wooden hamburger topped by a green pickle the size of a spare tire that marked the Hilly Chili Café. That way as soon as I was clean I could dash inside and get warm. Punk-haired Sarah knew my routine. She had a steaming blue mug of coffee ready and waiting as I plopped onto a stool at the white-pine counter.

"I'm watching my cholesterol," I said. "Better give me the sausage and eggs."

"Good thinking," she said, her brass eyebrow ring flashing as she wrote on her pad.

Sarah was a local girl gone urbane, home for the summer working the café tables to make money for college in Seattle where she studied elementary education and majored in Punk Rock. Today her hair was fluorescent green, the matching rhinestone stud in the fold of her tongue a definite distraction. Sarah looked both ways to make sure nobody was listening, then leaned out over the counter on her pointed white elbows. "You know what works?" she whispered. "For those morning bags under your eyes?"

"Being twenty-one," I said. "That's what works."

What I really needed was more sleep, but winter was coming, and when your toilet is a tree branch that alone is plenty of motivation to pound nails and solder pipes late into the night. I viewed the dark pouches under my blue eyes as purple bags of courage. For the first time in my life I wasn't just talking about doing something, I was doing it. I was building a house.

Sarah leaned in so close I could smell the mint in her mouthwash.

"Preparation H," she whispered. "That's what works."

Confucius say, Beware girls who get their fashion tips from MTV.

"No way," I said, edging back on my stool. "You put it on your face?"

"Way," she said. "It's a tissue shrinker, isn't it?"

Sarah anchored her chewing gum on her tongue stud, blew a big pink bubble, popped it with her teeth, then clipped my order to the revolving chrome rack under the grease-splattered heat lamps. I closed my eyes and bent my clean wet hair over the coffee, warming my chafed red cheeks in the hot roasted steam.

In a couple of hours I was picking up Bernie the Billionaire for a day of guided fishing. Every day you guide you need a plan, and with Bernie— my main hedge against destitution—the plan has to be especially good. You don't get to be a billionaire by sitting around not catching fish. Weather is a critical component of every day's plan, and the ranchers at a table behind me had a scratchy transistor radio tuned to the mechanical voice of a National Weather Service forecast updated every hour.

The prediction was clear skies plus wind and more wind, gusts up to forty miles an hour by late afternoon. That's a killer wind, an overpowering blow for all but the best fly casters. It used to be on the windiest days you could tuck into a lee shore where even the fish sought shelter, huge recirculating pods of trout gathered to gorge in the eddies on all the bugs killed and concentrated by the wind. But now there were more fishermen than protected cliff faces. It was combat getting the good spots.

I still needed a plan, but I was too tired to think.

A copy of yesterday's Cow Coulee Gazette lay folded on the counter. I picked through the wrinkled newsprint searching for the classified ads. Jackpot. A set of used kitchen cabinets for six hundred dollars, and somebody was remodeling a bathroom. The old fixtures were selling cheap, and I clipped the column with the scissors on my Swiss Army knife.

Sarah poured more coffee. The ranchers behind me compared notes on the relative amounts of rainfall they'd received in the only storm we'd had for weeks. I knew one of the hoarse voices without even turning around. His name was Sterling, and he'd let you hunt pheasants if you asked.

"It don't figure," he said. "What did you say you got again?"

"Eight-tenths," said a baritone saxophone of a voice I didn't recognize.

"Eight!" said Sterling. "And I only got two."

Sterling was trying to understand why he'd received two-tenths of an inch of rain when everybody else got at least eight-tenths. It didn't figure because his ranch was right in the middle of all the other ranches. He'd been surrounded by rain, but somehow it had passed him by.

"It's an enigma," said the same deep voice from before.

"Shit, Elmer," said Sterling, "you been pretty damn hard to live with ever since you took up with them condensed Reader's Digest books."

"Maybe a bird perched on your rain gauge during the storm," said a squeaky voice.

That was Bob from the grain elevator, where you could find everything from industrial-strength rat poison to fifty-pound gunnysacks of sunflower seeds to feed the chickadees.

"Maybe you got the moisture," continued Bob, "but with that bird sitting up there, the water just never showed in the barrel."

"I don't think so," said Sterling. "The ground was too dry. Somehow that storm went all around me."

"You want rain," said Elmer, "you have to dance for it. Everybody knows that."

"I tried dancing one time," said Sterling. "And I'd never do that again."

"What happened?" asked Elmer.

"I ended up married," said Sterling.

"That poor girl," said Bob and Elmer together.

"The good news," said Sterling, "is the ground's dry enough I can take a second cutting off that lower hay meadow. I'm gonna get on it right after Paul Harvey does the news, and with that dry wind coming in from the East I'll be putting up bales the day after tomorrow."

Breakfast was served. With ketchup on the hash browns and green-chile salsa on the eggs I ate quickly, left a four-dollar tip on a six-dollar meal, then brushed my teeth in the bathroom. I'd come up with a plan—which is always a relief—and I was whistling a fiddle tune as I pushed open the front door with my hip.

The parking lot outside the Hilly Chili is festooned with tourist-luring, red-white-and-blue wind socks. The wind was up already, the nylon tubes rippling with a sound like playing cards in bicycle spokes. I was almost to my truck when Curly Bear, a part-time fishing guide and a full-time Piegan, rose up between two cars. His oily braids were full of twigs and leaves like he'd slept under the transmission, and all he was wearing was a pair of stiff new blue jeans.

"Hey," he said, "how come you're so happy? Don't you know it's against the law to be happy this early in the morning? You're probably going to get arrested."

"I can get a toilet for ten bucks," I said. "Who wouldn't be happy?"

Curly Bear blinked about a dozen times. You could tell he'd had a rough night. His eyes were red radishes at the end of black tunnels. There wasn't enough Preparation H on the entire western seaboard to shrink all that sagging flesh.

"Goddamn wind," he said, still blinking. "Shit. You working today?"

"Yeah," I said. "All week. Bernie's in town."

"You lucky white prick," he replied.

It wasn't so much an insult as an observation. I let it slide. Curly Bear kicked at the dirt with his hairless brown toes. The cloud of scuffed dust immediately blew away and disappeared.

"Goddamn wind," he repeated. "Shit. Where are you floating today?"

"The canyon," I lied. "Try and find a cliff that's out of the wind."

I had a plan and that wasn't it. Curly Bear scratched his belly with both hands and turned his head to look at me with the corners of his eyes. He knew me well enough to know I wouldn't willingly fight the crowds in the canyon. "Yeah," he said suspiciously. "A day like this, that's about all you can do."

I put up a hand to shade the sun; the angle above the horizon said *Get a move on*. I only had about forty-five minutes, and needed to tie up a few flies to make the plan work.

"I'm going to be late," I said. "I better get going."

Curly Bear watched me sideways like he could see me better that way. "Yeah," he said. "I guess I'll see you out there."

There is a fly-tying vise mounted on the dashboard of my truck but I drove a mile down the road before I stopped and used it. Guitars and banjos dueled on the tape deck as I wrapped chartreuse foam, yellow rubber legs, and white elk hair on heavy-wire number ten hooks. Three flies later the digital clock on the dash said it was time to go.

With Bernie punctuality counts, and I've lost every wristwatch I ever owned. I'd already been fired once and couldn't afford for there to be a second time—not with a half-done house. Bernie comes out to fish a week or two a month April through November. It's as close a situation to steady work as you'll ever find in the guide business, and the job benefits are outstanding, beginning with the fact that you get to hang out with a billionaire.

Bernie had always wanted a place he could take his friends and family fishing, so he bought a mile of river frontage in the marsh and hay meadows across from the Head-Smashed-In buffalo jump, then built a house. Actually it wasn't so much a house as a starter castle, all blue granite with a turret and upper parapet porch. A week a month I shared the lifestyle, and believe me, once you've had a taste of the castle it's hard to go back to the trailer.

The first time I had been fired was the September before, during the doctor's trip. If it was a body part, Bernie had a doctor specializing in it. Every autumn all those doctors climbed aboard a private jet and flew to the castle in Montana for a week of fishing. Bernie took care of everything, including a chef who drove up from Cow Coulee. With so many doctors to feed, the chef needed help, which is how the castle came to be equipped with a Serving Wench.

The Serving Wench understood the importance of ornamentation in a fishing camp. Her first night on the job Rose wore an unbleached linen peasant blouse with an open string bodice pulled tight to squeeze up her cleavage. It was steak night. Bernie winked a silver eyebrow as he instructed me to accompany Rose out back and acquaint her with the barbecue.

I walked Rose through the sliding screen door to the stone patio at the back of the castle that overlooked the river. It was a quirk in a fly fisherman, but Bernie loathed bugs; he'd surrounded the castle with a moat of electrical blue bug zappers. The snap, crackle, and pop of frying insects was constant but resistance was futile. Even Bernie's billions were no match for a trillion bugs, and shape-shifting clouds of black midges swarmed the overhead lights.

You can't live in Montana and not believe in global warming. That's why there were so many midges, enough to occasionally block out the white globes of electricity. It had been the warmest September on record; shirtsleeves were comfortable even in the moonlight. I leaned over the grill and Rose leaned under me in an open profile of thin white linen.

The propane grill was vintage Bernie, the best money could buy, with more knobs than the space shuttle. I pushed a big red button. Rose lit a blue-tipped kitchen match on the heel of her polished black leather boot. She tossed the match and we both jumped back at the orange whoosh of exploding propane as the grill flared to life. I tried to think what to say to a girl in a white bodice stretched so taut that her nipples were poking out.

"So," I said, "I'll bet you're a barrel racer."

I was rubbing my hands in a circle like I was looking into a crystal ball.

Rose's high-heeled boot clicked nervously on the granite patio. "How did y'all even know I had a horse?" she said.

The drawl was Texas or Oklahoma, twangy as barbed wire. The match-on-the-boot thing, that was pure rodeo. There were only a couple of events for women, and Rose didn't look like the kind of girl who roped goats.

"And I'll bet your horse's name is Buster," I said, pushing my luck.

The word BUSTER was inscribed in her bronze horsehead-shaped belt buckle, the knobbed knees below her short skirt slightly bowed.

Rose glanced down at her waist, half-smiling as she looked back up. "I ride Buster," she said. "But he ain't no horse.

"He's more of a horse's ass."

It was an open invitation and not for the first time. The vicarious glamour of castle life inspires romance, but if you ante up with a cowgirl you can't be too careful. They play for keeps.

"So who's Buster?" I said.

"My boyfriend," she said, "the bull rider."

It was reason enough to run screaming. Bull riders are not boyfriends to be trifled with. For them, breaking bones is a way of life.

"You know, what I need"—I smiled—"is another gin-and-tonic."

The main room through the double doors off the stone patio was long and high with oak floors and ceilings. Your first time in a castle, it's mandatory to gawk; Rose was looking around enough that she bumped into me from behind as I opened the sliding screen door. Back inside, Sinatra crooned on the castle stereo. A fire blazed in the travertine fireplace, while the open kitchen at the other end of the room smelled of fresh-baked bread. In between an ornately carved slate-topped billiard table got plenty of use. I was lining up an eight-ball bank into the side pocket when the chef grabbed his throat and went white as his puffed hat.

"Oh, Jesus," he said, looking toward the patio. "Oh, Jesus."

The fortress had cracked. The castle was besieged. The sliding screen door was open maybe two inches, and a marauding horde of midges swarmed the thin seam of light. An inky ribbon of insects unrolled into the room in a visible carpet. I leapt up and slammed the door but the damage was done. Bugs were everywhere. I swatted with a dish towel but that only smeared the furniture. I tried spray insecticide from the garage but that bubbled the wall paint. Only minutes later the swarm was out of reach, flocked to the bright light of the high dining room chandelier.

Oh, Jesus, didn't even begin to cover it.

First of all, Bernie was Jewish.

Second of all, it was pathological the way he hated bugs.

Bernie had grown up in the poorest part of the Bronx. Maybe as an infant he was terrorized by a giant cockroach. Or maybe it was the part where the bugs got you in the end that bothered him. He was having so much fun in life he couldn't stand the thought of leaving. It was why he kept all those doctors around—doctors who would be coming downstairs for dinner at any moment, downstairs to a medieval table set with crystal glasses and scalloped china plates below a chandelier nearly hidden in a black tornado of madly circling gnats.

A *vacuum cleaner*, I thought. *And a stepladder*.

The bug-sucking idea had merit, but I was out of time. Bernie strode down the spiral staircase, trailing a string of doctors. Bernie was in his seventies but the first thing you noticed about him was his commanding posture, tall and erect. He wore a fitted black sweatshirt like a tailored suit as he marched over, massaging his right bicep.

"It's a good day when your arm hurts," he said, "from catching fish."

When the boss feels good everybody feels good. It's probably the same no matter whose castle it is. There were smiles all around as Bernie raised his hands and declared: "I'm starved."

"It's ready when you are," said the cook.

It's exactly the right thing to say to a billionaire, and we all sat down. The first course was spinach salad with lemon dressing. So far so good. The bugs were still congregated way up by the chandelier. We might get through dinner, but only if nobody looked up, and in the chair immediately to my left the Patent Doctor had a wandering eye.

It was his first time to Montana, and the Patent Doctor was giving the castle the once-over. He looked like an oversized version of one of the seven dwarfs, with a gray beard that grew in patchy tufts. I didn't know much about him, only that he was a stem-cell specialist who dabbled in cloning and now bought up patents to market through his own company.

The Patent Doctor was leaning back in his chair to better see the ceiling when I tapped his plump shoulder.

"Bernie told me," I said, "to ask you about an interesting new product."

"Ah," said the Patent Doctor. "Investments."

I didn't have any money but sure wished I did as the Patent Doctor leaned forward, his gleaming forehead so close you could smell the Aqua Velva.

"There is this vasodilator," he said.

The Patent Doctor described how vasodilators opened capillaries to stimulate blood flow. The original patent was on a vascular cream that stimulated male erections. But Viagra had significantly cut into the market share of this particular company. The stock could be had for a song, experienced management was in place, and in terms of market share the salient point was that the company had developed and was now testing a vasodilator for women.

"You mean . . .," I said.

Beneath giant eyebrows that sprouted like rows of half-watered corn his brown eyes were laughing. The Patent Doctor was one of the happy dwarfs. "That's right," he replied.

"You're kidding!" I said. "How do you test something like that?"

At first they'd tried it in the usual way, with partners, but relationships introduced a variable that was impossible to quantify. Next, in the name of science, each woman was charged with her own happiness. The laboratory was furnished with a stool, an assortment of toys, a 3-D virtual-reality helmet, and a comprehensive collection of erotic films. For control purposes, sometimes the girls were given real vasodilator and sometimes they were given fake vasodilator, to document the relative pleasure doses. For purposes of comparison the proceedings were videotaped from start to finish.

"Do you get a lot of volunteers?" I asked.

"Oh, they don't volunteer," said the Patent Doctor. "It's piecework."

No matter how long it took or how hard she had to work, each girl was paid one hundred dollars for her efforts. Now, there's a way better job than most jobs. I wondered who did the hiring.

"What kind of women apply?" I asked.

"Mostly nurses," said the Patent Doctor.

That I could believe. It isn't easy being around death and dying on a daily basis. The nurses I knew best tried to cope with the stress by sneaking into the morgue to giggle over particularly well-endowed cadavers. It was easy to imagine them in nothing but a 3-D helmet and sensible white hospital shoes.

"So this vasodilator," I said. "Does it work?"

"It must," said the Patent Doctor. "The nurses call it Scream Cream."

The cure for common frigidity is a hard act to follow, but the Patent Doctor was stopped in midchew. His mouth was open and pieces of spinach stuck to his teeth as he leaned down over his plate.

"Bugs?" he said in a puzzled voice.

Insects had been sifting down out of the air for a while now. It started slow, a bug or two at a time, and I'd been ignoring it, like it might go away. Instead it increased exponentially. Dying insects piled up on the white china plates so fast you could see it happen. Bugs are my bailiwick, and I was supposed to know. The Patent Doctor's eyes were no longer laughing as he squeezed my arm.

"What kind of bugs are these?" he said. "Are they contagious? Should we be worried?"

I didn't say anything. I couldn't. Because I was looking at Bernie and it was now raining dead bugs. So many bugs were dying all at once that they covered the table and its sterling-silver place settings like a gray mat of formed felt.

Bernie leapt to his feet, slashing with his salad fork in one hand and his knife in the other. "How did these bugs get in here?" he demanded, staring at Rose.

"The door . . . ," she stammered. "The grill . . ."

Bernie jabbed at the air between them with the fork. "So," he said, "you left the door open."

Technically Bernie was right. I distinctly remembered Rose following me through the door; she'd bumped me from behind. And I was hoping it might happen again. Nobody needed to get fired here. If anybody had a chance of weathering the storm, it was me after a good day of catching fish, so in a misguided act of employee chivalry I took a deep breath and said: "I did it, Bernie. I left the door open."

Bernie swiveled around. You don't make a billion dollars without having a ruthless streak; I'd just never seen it before. Bernie looked to be about eleven feet tall with fierce gray eyes. It was clear I'd badly misjudged the situation as Bernie forked a wad of bugs from his fluted wineglass and thrust them out over the table.

"Do you know how many wines are rated a hundred-plus?" he said. "Do you? Do you!"

The label on the green bottle said Mouton-Rothschild 1961 and burst like tannic grape shrapnel on the back of the tongue. The fork full of dead bugs dripped in lumpy purple splotches onto the white lace tablecloth.

"Do you have anything to say for yourself?" screamed Bernie. "Do you? Do you!"

My brain was firing blanks and Bernie didn't give me enough time to load a chamber before he dropped the spoonful of bugs back in his glass and said: "I can't think of a single reason to invite you back."

It wasn't what he said so much as how he said it. At the very least I'd just been banished from the castle; it felt more like the ax had fallen. It didn't seem possible that things had gone so wrong so fast. If I'd just been tossed from the gravy train, I was taking my wine with me. I picked up my glass. Since Bernie was standing, I stood up, too.

Now he only looked about eight feet tall.

"I'd like to propose a toast," I said.

At its most fundamental the fabric of the universe is a turbulent froth of quantum foam punctuated by constant explosions as matter and antimatter trade places in the spaces between the stitches. It's anything but smooth sailing, and it's the fabric of the universe. It's chaos, and in the Church of the Reduced Humanist it underlies everything we do. The absurdity is built right in and sometimes you have to embrace it. In the sifting shower of still-falling midges I held my wineglass up toward the chandelier.

"To the bugs," I said. "To the bugs that feed the fish that feed the fishermen that feed the guides. It's only fitting the bugs broke us apart, because it was the bugs that brought us together. To the mayflies and caddisflies and midges, to the bugs that remained loyal until the end."

Bernie's eyes opened from narrow and fierce to horrified and round.

"No," he gasped, an arm up in protest. "No . . ."

I swallowed deeply. The bugs had been marinated perfectly. "Tastes like chicken," I said.

After that Bernie came more and more to regard me as the wayward son he could have had but never wanted. That I had my job back was helped by the fact that if he fired me Bernie would have to break in a whole new fishing guide, choosing from a notoriously feckless local gene pool. It must have been a daunting prospect even to someone as forceful as a billionaire.

The deeper truth was that, wayward son or not, I'd have work as long as we caught fish. When you live by the fish you die by the fish, and yesterday doesn't count. Each and every day you have to prove yourself anew. So each and every day as I drove up to the castle, I inspected my face in the rearview mirror for anything stray or unsightly.

The morning after I'd left Curly Bear standing in the parking lot the purple bags under my eyes were still visible but fainter than they'd been at breakfast. I cleaned salsa from the corner of my mouth with a wet napkin and put my toothbrush in the glove compartment. The yellow aspen trees lining the blacktopped driveway were quaking in the wind. Bernie was out front and raring to go as I pulled up to the attached garage at three minutes after the appointed time of eleven o'clock.

"You're late," he said as I loaded his rods and gear into my truck.

"I was tying some special flies," I said. "You'll be glad I was late."

Bernie leaned forward and unbuckled the flap on his green waterproof fishing bag, checking that the satellite phone was secure in its padded compartment. I loaded his gear into the boat and we climbed into the cab of my pickup.

"I have to make a very important call at twelve-thirty," he said. "We'll need to anchor somewhere out of the wind so I can hear."

"Twelve-thirty is perfect," I replied. "The fish won't be biting until one o'clock."

At the end of the driveway I turned left toward the plains. North to Alaska it's nothing but bunchgrass and wheat—two thousand miles of rolling flats—which gives the wind a chance to build up a head of steam.

Bernie drummed his lean manicured fingers on the dash. "Why did we turn right?" he said. "We need to fish the canyon in this wind."

Bernie hates surprises but I think they're good for you.

"It's a surprise," I said. "You'll see."

Body language is a prime negotiating tool, and Bernie had a pretty good idea of what people were thinking just by what they were doing. I stared straight ahead through the bug-splattered windshield. I could feel those pale gray eyes boring into my ear. It wasn't often you got Bernie's full attention, but I had it now as he pushed back his pressed chino sleeve and glanced at his bright gold watch.

"One o'clock," he said. "Sharp?"

My plan was time-specific. If the fishing didn't happen by one, it wouldn't happen. But if it did, I'd look like the oracle at Delphi. It would be money in the bank to help pay the fine the next time I did something like filling the castle with bugs.

"One o'clock," I said. "Sharp."

It was enough for Bernie. He settled back in his seat as we headed east. The rocks along the lower Apikuni are tipped-up flows of dry ancient lava—snake country. The Prairie Dog Put-in is about as far as you can get from the mountains and still have water cold enough for trout. There aren't as many fish, but there are some whoppers, especially the brown trout.

Twenty-five minutes later I stood in the middle of my driftboat, wrestling with the west wind. I was pushing off the concrete boat ramp at the Prairie Dog Put-in with an oar, but every time I pushed off, the keening gale pushed me back in. The fiberglass boat chines ground against the traction ripples in the concrete as we bounced against the ramp. Each year somewhere in the world clients die in the hands of fishing guides—a fact that Bernie was only too glad to bring to my attention from the front seat as he held on with both hands.

"Remind me," he shouted over the wind. "What part of this is a surprise?"

Bernie was restless enough to call the whole day off. He'd done it before, but I always felt better about the money I was being paid if we at least fished. And if things worked out the way they might, a thousand-dollar tip wasn't out of the question. He'd done it before.

"I didn't say it was going to be a good surprise," I shouted back.

Bernie had something on his mind, something big. It all had to do with the twelve-thirty phone call. I was relieved when the river finally had the boat; there was no turning back now. The sky was hot blue and so dry as I pulled hard at the oars that sweat crystallized on my skin as salt. The wind was downstream, the boat anchored in the Bay of Pigs with ten minutes to spare.

The Bay of Pigs was a big-fish spot, a deep kidney-shaped hole where the high water in flood years had undercut a soft clay bank. Down low and close to the steep bank it was calm enough to blow smoke rings, while fifteen feet overhead at the top of the white clay bluff the wind was chunky with airborne tumbleweed. I leaned forward over the oars. Bernie held out a polished brass lighter that roared like a propane torch.

"Just so you know," said Bernie, "in some circles it's considered gauche to leave the label on your cigar when you smoke it."

Bernie was a thoughtful guy. He'd dealt me the cigar to help me pass the time while he was on the phone. As tobacco it was bigger than most baseball bats.

"The kind of cigars I usually smoke," I mumbled around the giant dark Churchill clenched between my teeth, "you have to leave the label on just to keep them from unraveling."

At twelve twenty-nine Bernie picked up the satellite phone. He thumbed a red speed-dial button, turned the gain down and the squelch up, then held a plastic box that was about the size of a big shoe up to his ear.

"Is the mayor in?" he said. "He's expecting my call."

The cigar was tasty, hand-rolled by a wrinkled old man in Havana. His name was Rogelio, and he stood at the front door of his gray adobe shop in an oil painting that hung over the humidor back at the Castle. The Cuban artist was big and grand like Monet, the pungent tang of fresh-stacked tobacco leaf dripping in the dark wafting brush strokes.

"Good afternoon, Your Honor." said Bernie, "Did you receive my letter?"

There was the distant wind-driven sound of a tractor starting up as Bernie listened into the phone. A couple of sharp-billed diving ducks floated by, looking for minnows.

Bernie said: "The Board of Realtors was delighted to sell out that fund-raising dinner at ten thousand a plate."

He listened, frowned, stared at the water, then shook his gray curly head.

"Three-point-five won't work," he said. "Here's how you sell four: *It will be the death knell to new construction downtown. The unions are going to scream out in favor of jobs.*"

Bernie hardly listened at all before he smiled. "Better yet," he said.

And then he smiled again, the happiest I'd seen him in all of the last year.

I once had a strict no-exceptions rule that prohibited phones in the boat, but it's true: Every man has his price. Every woman, too. It wasn't the first time I'd compromised myself, but it was one of the few times I was glad of it.

It wasn't just about history, it was more like being part of the history. I smoked as the computer age met the stone age. We'd float by a buffalo jump, and between fish Bernie would buy skyscrapers. The son of an immigrant handyman who spoke no English, Bernie had grown up during the Great Depression playing stickball in the worst of the Bronx alleys. He partnered with his brother-in-law to buy his first building using money they'd raised five dollars at a time advertising for investors in the *New York Times*. Nearly fifty years later Bernie had sold his Manhattan real estate holdings for $860 million.

That deal had been consummated exactly one year ago to the day, and as part of the deal Bernie had agreed not to purchase Manhattan commercial real estate for one year. It was hard on him. Bernie missed wheeling-and-dealing so much that his health had deteriorated, but now the moratorium had expired. There was no question Bernie had a big deal cooking; it was just a question of how big. He smiled into the boxy plastic telephone.

"The rumors are true," he said. "The Port Authority has agreed to consider our counteroffer on the World Trade Center. They should have the paperwork any minute now."

And then Bernie smiled like he'd been sainted.

"Thank you, Your Honor," he said. "That would be most helpful."

He punched out, settled the phone into its case, and looked at his watch. He shifted gears faster than anybody I'd ever met. Bernie's brain was always running four programs at once. Now it was time to fish.

"It's ten minutes to one," he said pointedly.

"The World Trade Center?" I said. "Really? Can you get it?"

Bernie once told me you're not bargaining hard enough to get rich until ninety-five out of a hundred negotiations fall through. I could only guess how much he yearned for that building. The World Trade Center would be an exclamation point to a rags-to-riches career, but Bernie did not look sanguine as he flattened his hands and shrugged.

"Everybody wants it," he said. "It just isn't worth what's already been bid."

The problem was that the other moguls craved an exclamation point just as much as Bernie. The price war had been fierce enough that the high bidder was having trouble raising money and was now on the verge of missing the deadline for a hundred-and-some-million-dollar down payment. Bernie was running a back-door play, offering more money down but less money total. I rowed the boat out from the calm shore to give him room to cast. Twenty feet from the lee a swirling gust of wind caught me by surprise and blew my green baseball cap into the river. Bernie looked again at his gold watch.

"Five minutes," he said pointedly.

I dropped anchor and scooped my hat out of the water with my long-handled rubber net. "This is going to be more fun than buying buildings," I replied.

I'd been feeling confident ever since I'd heard the tractor start up, and now I tied the first of the special flies I'd tied earlier that morning to the end of Bernie's line.

He put on his black-rimmed reading glasses, scrutinized the neon green dry fly with its long yellow rubber legs and a flat elk-hair downwing skeptically, then frowned. "What the hell is this thing?" he said.

"It's all part of the plan," I said, and then I explained:

The Bay of Pigs was a big-fish hole that hadn't been fishing well lately. The weather had been so hot and the sun so bright that the trout were buried deep in the weeds. It would take something special to bring them up from the bottom. That morning at breakfast I'd heard the rancher Sterling say he was going to cut his hay field. He'd said he was going to start at twelve-fifteen, right after Paul Harvey finished the news.

Sterling was a fourth-generation rancher and no dummy. He'd surely start mowing on the upwind side so the chaff wouldn't blow in his face, cutting laterally toward the river, working downwind to the point that formed the Bay of Pigs. With all the hot weather we'd been having, that field would be lousy with baby grasshoppers, their bodies bright green and tender because their exoskeletons had yet to harden. For trout it doesn't get much better than that. It's soft-shell crab served up under a chartreuse neon dinner bell.

Baby grasshoppers with immature wings usually crawl close to the safety of the ground, but now it would be hop or get chopped. The grasshoppers would be blown by the wind ahead of those threshing blades, herded in droves across the field until they ran out of cover and were forced into the river. The green flies with the yellow rubber legs were meant to be stripped in six-inch bursts in an impressionistic imitation of a baby grasshopper swimming for its life.

As if on cue a grasshopper jumped into the boat. Bernie looked at his watch. "All right," he said. "I'm impressed."

Trout live in a constantly changing environment; they key into new food sources almost immediately. The grasshoppers were a big hit. Fifteen minutes later the trout were feeding like barracudas, leaving garbage-can-sized wakes as they charged Bernie's fly in rod-ripping takes. He was seventy-two, and until Bernie had bought back enough buildings to recharge his blood he had to rest after every couple of fish. I'd just released a yellow-bellied brown trout that stuck out both sides of my twenty-inch net when Bernie dropped a bombshell.

"You should come work for me in New York," he said. "Make some money."

Bernie leaned back in his seat, smoking a cigar, studying me for my reaction. A lot of what he says is best taken with a grain of salt. With Bernie, sweeping statements are more like negotiations that have just begun. The devil is in the details, but when your toilet is a branch over a hole in the ground it's easy to dream.

"What would I do?" I said.

"Buy low," he replied. "And sell high."

I pictured myself in Armani as I reached for the Magic Box. Bernie's fly had been gnawed down to green thread and half-chewed rubber leg, and the Magic Box was where I kept all my special flies. It was everything that works in a flat plastic rectangle, dozens of tiny compartments crammed full of flies for all occasions, including the two remaining baby grasshoppers.

I set the Magic Box on my knees and opened the flat hinged lid, feeling so good it was too good. Life is bungee jumping with reality for a cord. It's not that the universe is unfeeling; it's just that the fabric can only stretch so far, and then you get pulled back. In that contented moment my energy spike was evidently more than the space–time continuum allowed, because out of the clear blue sky I was abruptly flattened.

The cigar stub shot out of my mouth like I'd been slapped on the back. The boat lurched forward hard enough that the thirty-pound lead anchor dragged. The Magic Box somersaulted off my knees. I followed in slow motion, bouncing hard on my hands and knees as I hit the bottom of the boat. I saw it but couldn't quite grasp the reality. The Magic Box was upside-down in muddy brown bilgewater, a thousand of my best flies slowly seeping out of sight.

"Bloody hell, came a mite too close. Saw you catching those fish."

I lifted my head. Just past the curved fiberglass gunwale I came face to face with dark sunglasses straddling a sweet-potato nose. The man, having smashed into us in a windblown float tube, was now cartwheeling along the side of my boat. Everything was still in slow motion and the spinning was dizzying like bad clams. The red nose dissolved to an overcooked cauliflower ear to sunburned neck wattles and back to another ear beneath a floppy leather hat. A full revolution later puffy lips smeared with white zinc oxide reappeared beneath the knobby nose. The man had rotated all the way down to Bernie's end of the boat.

"Hey, mate," the clown lips said amiably.

"You ran into us," said Bernie in disbelief.

From the beginning, I always said I'd quit guiding when it wasn't fun anymore. It's too easy to grow to hate what you once loved. As crowded as the river had become, I didn't see how the subways could be much worse.

Dear Old Dad

HEIDI RESISTED THE IMPULSE to pound her sweaty forehead on the steering wheel.

I never should have cut so many math classes, she thought.

To take her mind off the traffic Heidi was calculating the odds that she'd been born on the same date as her father. August 1. One day out of a year of days, so one out of 365 seemed right, or maybe one out of 366 since she'd been born in a leap year, or maybe 365½ since he hadn't.

"Whatever the odds," she muttered out loud to the shiny craters in the rock-chipped windshield, "they're a lot better than finding a parking space in this damn town."

It was her fortieth birthday, something she'd just as soon forget, and idle mathematics hadn't helped. Heidi had never seen Cow Coulee so crowded. Where did all these people come from? And what did they do? Work at Wal-Mart? It reminded her of the search for an avalanche-covered body the way she systematically worked an ever-widening grid of streets in search of a place to park.

A neatly scribed list of errands on a yellow legal pad lay beside her on the sheepskin seat cover. When she'd worked her way through the stores and chores it was three hours of interstate highway home to Butte for the traditional joint birthday celebration. Heidi blew air through the gap in her front teeth, hoping her mom would sweeten the cake with carrots instead of the chocolate angst they usually consumed. And finally, in front of the boarded-up saddle shop, an empty parking spot.

Heidi glanced in the rearview mirror. She'd have to beat out the gleaming Honda Civic with Jersey plates coming up hard on the right. She downshifted and popped the clutch, her canary-yellow half-ton pickup truck with the mismatched blue tailgate spurting forward and angling to cut off the Honda. Spinning the wheel with both hands, Heidi pumped the brakes as she drove up and over the curb, swerving left to just miss clipping the parking meter as the front-right tire thumped off the sidewalk and back down to the pavement.

Horns blared and Heidi felt the best she had all morning as she stepped from her truck. The tallest building in Cow Coulee was only four stories high, but in August there was still enough glass and pavement to turn downtown into an inferno of reflected heat. It was only four blocks to the Wells Fargo Bank, but the air-conditioned lobby was sweet relief after the sweltering city streets. Behind the counter the pigtailed teller with the round bursting belly looked too young, like she should be selling lemonade instead of eight and a half months pregnant.

"What exactly happened to this check?" she said. "Are these tread marks?"

"Probably," said Heidi. "My husband dropped it in a mud puddle in the street."

"Men . . . ," said the teller. "You can't . . . They're just . . . I don't . . ."

And then the girl smiled apologetically with bright red lips as her voice trailed off completely. Heidi wondered what it would have been like to have kids; at forty, it didn't look like she was going to find out.

"Your husband?" asked Heidi. "Does he remind you of your father?"

"Not at all," said the teller.

Heidi nodded. "He will," she replied.

The teller frowned as she held the check up to her face. She used her long painted fingernails like a crab used its claws—poking, pinching, and twisting the paper as she examined it.

"And this was written when?" she said. "Three months ago? Is that right? And it's been in a mud puddle all that time?"

Heidi sighed. "It should still be good," she said. "It's legible. Mostly."

"And who's it from?" said the teller. "Vague? Vague what?"

"Not Vague," said Heidi. "*Vogue*; the magazine. I sold them some photographs."

"*Vogue!*" said the teller. "Really? But that's so cool. Down at Doctor Ramsey's, he's my pediatrician, I read *Vogue* all the time. I adore the clothes. In another three weeks I'll be able to get back into some fashions myself."

"Well," said Heidi, "if you know the magazine, you should know this check is good."

The teller cradled her belly that hung like a watermelon inside her loose black dress. "I'm going to have to speak with my supervisor," she said. "Please wait here."

The teller pigeontoed in scarlet pumps toward an older woman who was wearing so much mascara she looked like a raccoon. The woman made two phone calls from behind her metal desk, then wiped her hands on a Kleenex after handling the check. Heidi watched, leaning forward on both elbows as she stared into the barrier of bulletproof glass.

"Happy birthday," she said.

"Happy birthday," her reflection said back.

Heidi rolled her eyes and her eyes rolled back.

"Forty," she said.

Despite twice-daily applications of aloe lotion the back of Heidi's hands flat on the green marble were starting to show wrinkled sun; then the teller was back, her smile wider than ever.

"Good news," she said. "We can deposit your check with a ten-day hold."

"It's good news," said Heidi, "if you have ten days."

Back on the street the heat hit like a fist. Old trucks and rough roads made Montana the land of leaking head gaskets. Heidi coughed at the petro-stink of used motor oil roasting on an asphalt griddle. She leaned against a light pole, studying the yellow legal paper list of all the things she had yet to do before she could escape the blast furnace.

Heidi was humming the *Mission Impossible* theme as she crumpled the list and tossed the yellow wad down the rusted grate of an iron storm drain. She'd decided to take the long way home, through the cool mountains, along the dirt road that followed Telegraph Creek to Priest Pass and the top of the Continental Divide. Before she could dangle her toes in the icy spring creek water the only thing Heidi absolutely had to do was to get her dad a birthday present.

"Maybe I'll get him a game of Monopoly," she said to the light pole.

He could use the "Get Out of Jail Free" cards. Her father, Jack, was eligible for senior citizen discounts, and Heidi couldn't believe he'd just gotten another DUI. She bought a shirt with bold vertical stripes, the latest in fashionable, buttondown prisoner wear, hoping her dad would take the hint. If not, at least he'd have something to wear.

And finally, as a birthday present to herself, Heidi watched Cow Coulee disappear in the rearview mirror. The dusty prairie gave way to gradual green forest. Higher still wildflower meadows blossomed with red Indian paintbrush, nodding yellow bells, and purple sticky geranium. The thin needle on the temperature gauge crawled toward the red zone as the truck lugged up the steep switchbacks below the divide. Heidi cut the engine in the shade of green aspen gone silver with roadside dust, walked around front, and pulled at the lever that unlatched the hood.

The radiator was plugged, the fins completely clogged with a skeletal layer of cooked caddisfly husks. Heidi smiled, remembering the evening dry-fly fishing these last few weeks. Fifty feet away the creek gurgled through the flowers. She couldn't scrape off the bugs until the engine cooled, and Heidi smiled again as she tugged her banjo from behind the seat.

She dipped her feet in the chilly creek, sitting on a streamside boulder sculpted by the eons into a smooth swale-backed hippopotamus, tuning to the low note of the river. Heidi plucked the strings, following the lead of the rollicking current. The repetitive gurgling finger rolls were almost but never quite the same, emptying her mind like meditation. The world was smooth blue granite, cool rock on her bare thighs, hot sun on her shoulders. The creek water was like snow on her feet, the wildflowers in the meadow so beautiful they hurt her eyes, the same as that cold December morning so long ago she'd still had pigtails.

It was the cruelest Christmas ever. The company still decorated the gallows frames above the mine shafts with holiday lights, but there had been a strike in the mines, the worst anyone could remember. Dad finally had to go north to look for work on the railroads. He hadn't been home in weeks, but he was coming for Christmas Eve, except he hadn't arrived.

The night before Christmas came and went, and starting at dawn Christmas Day tiny Heidi kept vigil with her button nose pressed to the sitting room window. Her breath froze in white circles on the icy glass, and when the rusty old Cadillac with the soaring tail fins finally skidded to a stop at about noon she'd darted straight outside for a hug.

"Now, Heidi," Dad had said, pointing to her bare feet, the crimson toenails like drops of fresh blood in the snow. "What would your mother say?"

But Heidi couldn't talk, she could hardly breathe, that's how beautiful the flowers that filled the backseat were. The solid wall of blossoms was a vision, daffodils and tulips and lilies and poinsettias blazing red and yellow and blue against the backdrop of brilliant white snow.

"Don't tell your mother," Dad had said, "but last night I struck a deal down to the flower shop. They was making way for a load of New Year's roses."

And Heidi caught a deep breath, the frigid air first burning then settling into a dull ache at the bottom of her lungs. Color is more intense at twenty below zero. It's so cold it's as though the photons don't check any spectral baggage with the atmosphere, they just carry it right on through, and when that vivid light burst against those bright flowers it was something like perfection.

Heidi had reached through the broken back window to touch that perfection but, startled, snaked her hand back. The petals on the orange mum were stiff as pencils, frozen solid. She'd flicked the blossom with her forefinger: A perfumed will-o'-the-wisp sparkled above the stem as the mum shattered into dozens of tiny ice shards. And when Dad bent down to kiss her, his blond hair was wild as a field of windblown straw, his breath sweet with whiskey.

"Aw, don't worry honey," he'd said. "They'll thaw, same as fish sticks."

He'd swept up an armful of flowers from the backseat of his big car, and they'd walked to the porch. Framed in the doorway, her mother's red curls trickled to the bright green collar of her chiffon blouse. Everybody smiled as Dad presented Mom the rigid bouquet with a flourish.

"And there's lots more where those came from," he'd said.

Dad puffed up a lean chest hard with mining muscle under the yellow corduroy jacket with the leather elbow patches. Only Heidi caught the quick flash of thin grim lips on her mother's face.

"Oh, Jack," Mom had said, smiling again. "We'll use them for a centerpiece."

Dad insisted on carrying the flowers in from the car himself, armload after armload. They met him at the door, Mom's high heels clicking on the scarred wood floor until the dining room table was heaped with a bright orchard of long-stemmed flowers wrapped in red and green ribbons. They took their places at the table for the traditional ham and sweet-potato dinner, Bing Crosby crooning on the radio as they bowed their heads to say grace.

"Hm-m-m," said her father when he opened his eyes and reached for his muscatel.

It wasn't like fish sticks at all. The flowers didn't just thaw, they melted. And they didn't just melt, they dissolved between the ribbons into lumps of festive black goo. Heidi wondered what it was like in other families, because in her family nobody said a thing, as if it were the most common thing in the world to decorate with heaps of Christmas compost.

The dark stain oozed across the table like the incoming tide. The white linen tablecloth soaked up the initial flow, but the watery goo just kept coming. Finally she'd had to lift her elbows off the table so her new reindeer sweater wouldn't get wet. And Heidi remembered the hard green eyes narrowed beneath her mother's auburn eyebrows, eyes that said she'd known what was coming, and let it happen anyway.

Why? Why, why, why?

On the hippopotamus-shaped rock Heidi blinked back tears in her own green eyes, her hand rigid as a claw, the banjo dead in her fingers. She'd lost the river's tune wondering if it was true that, no matter what, we grow up to be our parents. It was so hot, even at over six thousand feet, that Heidi's light cotton tunic was plastered to her back. She set the banjo aside, stripped to the skin, and squatted on her heels alongside a deep pool between two boulders. The black river sand glimmered with fool's gold and splintered mica, a transparent face echoed back from the surface film; square chin, jolly round cheekbones, a wild hay field of unbraided hair.

Heidi rolled headfirst into her rippling reflection, the water so shockingly cold her teeth hurt, so cold she screamed with relief as she walked to shore in the waist-deep water. She air-dried on a flat boulder, belly up and arms akimbo. She bit her lip as a singing cricket crawled up the inside of her thigh, breathing faster at the six-legged tickle as the cricket scurried in and around the blond mist at the top of her legs. She let her hand drift down her belly to the shaved triangle then snatched with banjo-sharpened reflexes. One moment the cricket was pushing out a tune with its hind legs; the next it was trapped in the dark heat of Heidi's curled palm.

"Bon appétit," said Heidi, except she pronounced it "bone appetite."

"That's French," her dad had said knowingly, "for 'come and get it.'"

Heidi threw the cricket into the creek, flashing back to another bright sunny birthday. She couldn't have been more than three or four. She remembered giggling uncontrollably as her dad pounced about some streamside bunchgrass in dusty steel-toed boots. He'd been snaring yellow grasshoppers and black crickets and blue beetles in his red ball cap, then depositing the prisoner bugs into a glass jar with holes poked in the screw-on metal lid. When the jar was full enough her dad had held her to his chest and waltzed her around like a broomstick, her chubby feet dangling high in the air as he sang happily in her ear:

I love to go out fishing, in a river or a creek,
But I don't enjoy it half as much, as dancing cheek to cheek.

They'd thrown the bugs in the river, feeding the trout, clapping and shouting "Bone appetite!" as each insect disappeared in the swirl of a hungry mouth. They'd bet ice cream cones against how long the bugs would last; she'd come out one chocolate-dipped ahead. And all these years later Heidi watched the latest in a long line of bugs swimming for its life, kicking furiously through the green slot of deep water against an undercut bank held together at the top with the roots of the overlying meadow. It was the sheltered feeding water that big trout loved, and the cricket was spinning beneath a clump of purple fireweed when it vanished in a silver flash.

Salty tears ran down Heidi's cheeks and dripped onto the slope of her bare chest.

"Bone appetite," she whispered.

A hundred miles away Jack was on his stool at the Sportsman Bar, more indignant with every shot of whiskey taken neat. "A whitefish," he said. "Can you believe it? Three thousand bucks at stake, and I'm getting beat by a damn whitefish."

"Well, hell," said Nick. "You can't expect to win the fishing derby every year. It ain't realistic."

"The hell I can't," said Jack. "And besides, I gotta get Heidi that bicycle. She's my daughter, don't you know?"

Nick was so surprised he lifted an unshaven cheek off the bar to stare with bleary eyes.

"The hell you say," he said. "Heidi's a growed woman. What's she need with a bicycle?"

"It's just that I promised," groaned Jack. "I gotta get that money somehow."

"Try getting a job," said Nick. "Because you ain't gonna beat that whitefish. The lips alone weigh half a pound."

"You'll see," said Jack as he stood up. "You'll see."

"See what? You only have"—Nick peered at the clock on the wall—"five hours."

"It's enough," said Jack.

Nick dropped his cheek back to the mahogany bar. Without another word Jack vanished into the bright rectangle of lighted door that led to the intersection of Main and Iron. Standing by the stoplight he turned in slow circles, scratching furiously at his meaty red nose.

"Now where the hell," he muttered, "did I park?"

Some days Jack couldn't remember where he'd left his car, but he remembered like it was yesterday promising Heidi that bike. The relations were over for venison pot roast and potato vodka. It was eerily quiet; it always was, the first days into a new strike. The bells, the whistles that marked the days of changing shifts, the whistle of ventilator shafts, the roar of pumps and engines, it was all shut down.

So his voice sounded unnaturally loud when Jack yodeled: "Hei-dee-oh-duh-lay-hee-hee."

That was a time, then. A man's voice meant something. Heidi was with other kids, playing on the yellow ore dumps that left them stained to the skin. When Jack yelled all the cousins froze in place, barefooted marionettes on copper-colored strings. They'd lived where they still lived, in uptown Walkerville, a neutral zone in ethnic Butte. Walkerville was the kind of hardscrabble and black-tarpaper neighborhood where even a hardheaded Lutheran Swede could marry a good Catholic Irish girl.

And when Jack yodeled again the marionettes jerked and came leaping into the backyard, jumping to pluck at the clothesline as they ran past. A few squares of petunias by the back fence struggled against the blasted dirt, the only plant life in sight. All the trees had long since gone to feed the smelter. But none of it mattered when Heidi began to sing.

Uncles Sean and Mark were on the guitar and tin whistle; brother Olaf had a tuba. Jack squeezed a wheezing Hohner concertina he'd found leaking in a pawnshop and patched with a tire kit. Heidi had been swimming in the copper ponds again, her clothes hanging half in shreds as she filled her lungs and let the song begin: "Oh, Danny Boy, the pipes, the pipes are calling . . ."

The tune is the haunting "Londonderry Air," the words a poem of a woman who steadfastly awaits her one true love her whole life, and then some. In the last verse Danny kneels on her grave and says an "Ave"; it's all that girl ever wanted, and she finally sleeps in peace. The idea that someone would wait so faithfully even in death distracted Jack enough that he hit a sour note.

In the mines men died all the time. Butte was full of grieving and not-so-grieving widows. When you were four hundred feet under the ground eight hours at a time, the whistle that signaled the shift change was a bed-emptying warning all over town. Every miner who'd ever fooled around knew you couldn't trust a green-eyed girl, not really, and the old pain rang in Jack's gut as he walked circles in the hot streets in search of his car.

Jack's feet flapped in oversized slick leather shoes on the sidewalk as Heidi's song replayed like a scratchy album in his brain. When she'd gotten to the part where Danny's lover dreams warm and sweet, Jack had been so proud of his daughter he'd thrown his arms around Heidi before she even finished the verse.

"Honey," he'd promised, "anything you want, anything at all."

And Heidi had pushed herself free, staring back with her mother's green eyes.

"Sure, dad," she'd said. "How about you get my bike out of hock?"

But he never had. That much, Jack had never forgotten.

He found his car, an old yellow Bonneville with bald whitewall tires, two blocks up Iron Street. Jack was happy to discover he'd parked in the cool shade of the tall Stockman's Bank building. "Good thinking," he congratulated himself as he climbed behind the steering wheel and coasted down the hill, continuing his quest for both bicycle money and a first-place fish.

The August Fishing Derby down at the Sportsman had been going on for years, but the three thousand dollars for first place was a recent development compliments of the chamber of commerce. When the prize money changed, so did the rules. The contest was now an egalitarian affair where each fish was awarded points based on the current state record for that species. It was a matter of relative rather than absolute size: A ten-pound fish was worth fifty points if the state record for that species was twenty pounds, one hundred points if the record for that species was ten pounds, and two hundred points if the state record was five pounds.

An hour after he'd read the contest rules Jack had already pawned the television set and posted the hundred-dollar entry fee. He knew how to win. It was foolish to fish for brown trout. A fourteen-pound brown would be huge but worth less than fifty points. Browns were a sure loser. So were rainbows. The biggest cutthroats had been dead for fifty years.

But then there were brook trout. The state record was just over nine pounds, and Jack had two over seven pounds in the freezer. It was all in knowing where to look, and the deep-bellied brookie Jack brought back from a beaver pond near the Idaho border was worth eighty-six points, seemingly a sure winner until an hour ago when Merle from the Sportsman had called.

"Jack," he said, "you better get on down here. You ain't seen ugly until you seen this."

Behind the bar Merle yanked the toothpick from his mouth, the way he did usually only when he was calling your tab due. And on the last day of the contest there it was, splayed on slimy newspaper across the official scales, the biggest mountain whitefish Jack had ever seen. The fish was local to the Big Hole, but the puffy, translucent lips looked like they belonged on some goggle-eyed space creature.

"That thing's as revolting as an empty glass," said Jack. "What's it worth?"

"Ninety-six points. Damn near a new state record."

Jack had tossed back three quick shots with Nick to fortify himself against the coming trespass, then limped on his bad leg out of the Sportsman looking for his car. Now that he'd found it he headed for the highway and the recently opened Lead Works Golf Course. The links-style course was a Superfund project, turning the defunct toxic sludge of what had been the world's largest lead smelter into a playground for rich people, which Jack thought made sense especially if you believed in the Easter Bunny.

Jack liked numbers and did the math in his head. Over the years, roughly forty-eight thousand men dead in the mines; a regulation eighteen-hole course. That solved out to about twenty-six hundred souls per hole, and added up to work if you could operate a backhoe.

Jack had been employed sporadically since the beginning of the project. Last May he'd been at the edge of the pond fronting the sixteenth green, on his knees piecing sod around the base of a stout cottonwood log that stabbed out over the water like a diving board. He was sawing at a green rind of turf with a long knife when a turquoise shadow over a slab of burnt orange breast ghosted out from beneath the log.

"Jesus H. Bluegill," Jack had whispered in awe, crossing himself at the blasphemy.

Jack blinked but the fish was still there; a bluegill the size of a garbage can lid, complete with a bright eyeball shining big and round as a silver dollar. It was three times bigger than any bluegill he'd ever seen, and Jack was pretty sure radioactive landscaping was why.

The rolling hills of desolate black slag left over from a hundred years of melting the lead out of rock were about as fertile as the asteroid belt, so topsoil had been trucked in. The fill was subject to rigid quality-control specifications, but contractors being contractors, corners were sometimes cut. For instance, the sculpted fill underlying the teardrop-shaped pond at the east edge of the sixteenth green wasn't screened and washed river gravel, it was decomposed granite from the tailings piles at the Free Enterprise Radon Mine and Health Spa.

Jack knew that for a fact, since for a token finder's fee he'd brokered the deal.

Radon, a slightly radioactive gas, is found locally around Butte in veins of decomposing granite. The gas had long been hailed as more than just a snake-oil cure for everything from arthritis to vertigo. The Free Enterprise was a played-out underground hard-rock mine that had been remodeled with elevators, electric lights, and musty overstuffed furniture. Pilgrims had been flocking in since the last century to take the cure.

The guest registers two hundred feet down were thick as dictionaries, filled with glowing testimonials from cripples who hobbled in from as far away as Paris and London, believers who left singing the praises of the miracle radon cure that left them spry as born-again children. There was something to it, Jack was sure of that. Somehow hair concentrated the radiation—an hour in the mines and even a trimmed sideburn would set the Geiger counter to clacking away.

"That was a long time ago," said Jack, thinking back to when he'd had hair.

Somehow this bluegill was like hair—it concentrated the radon, then grew big like the seeds the astronauts took into space that back on earth grew pumpkins the size of Buicks. The ponds were supposedly sealed off from the slag of chemical soup with road-sized sheets of ripstop Hypalon, but the special seam glue was hugely expensive. The installation crews had been known to skimp. Maybe there was something in the water that helped the radiation along.

And so it was, in the hot afternoon sun of his sixty-third birthday, that Jack came to be standing on the cottonwood log that jutted out into the pond alongside the sixteenth green. The bluegill was still there, a faint shimmer down in the dark water. With aches in all his moving parts after a lifetime of hard labor, Jack wondered how that fish would taste; whether the intensified radon would kill him or cure him. The white sign beside the pond said in red letters, NO FISHING, VIOLATORS WILL BE PROSECUTED, so it wasn't the best of times to see the game warden come speeding over the hill.

The warden steered a collision course, veered off at the last instant, and hit the brakes so hard the soft rubber wheels of the electric golf cart fishtailed on the just-watered grass.

"Hey, Jack," said the warden suspiciously. "What are you doing out here?"

In deference to the posted waters, Jack had his bait on a string down the leg of his baggy pants. The cricket tickled as it strolled around, and Jack stifled a giggle.

"I helped build this pond," he replied. "Just out for a walk to see how it's doing."

The warden had known Jack for more than forty years. They'd gone to grade school together, wrestled in the same weight class in high school. In all that time the Warden had never known Jack to just take a little walk—unless it was to fish or hunt. And sure, the warden had looked the other way, plenty of times. Especially during the strikes. A man had to feed his family. But that was then. Now you didn't have much choice but to play it by the book.

"I heard about that whitefish," said the warden. "Should I be worried?"

Jack spread his arms to show he was clean. Another golf cart skidded to an abrupt stop.

"C'mon, Warden," said the tall man behind the wheel, "it's your shot. You gotta hit. Foursomes are getting backed up."

The warden looked at his ball in the fairway, back to Jack, back to his ball, then at the yellow flag fluttering atop the elevated green at the end of the rolling fairway. He ran his eyes over the oddly fidgeting Jack one last time, stalked to his ball, then slapped a fat five-iron into a kidney-shaped bunker full to the brim with black sand made from pulverized slag. The warden rapped himself on the forehead with the graphite club shaft, then climbed into his cart and sped down the rolling fairway.

Jack shook his head. Of all the luck. But hell, it could have been worse.

He could have been born a whitefish.

Jack's knee creaked as he shook his leg until he dislodged the cricket from the sanctuary of his boxer shorts. The cricket had been chilled on a cold beer until docile, then fixed with superglue to a number ten hook.

The eye of the hook was knotted to a spool of six-pound monofilament, and the line ran through a hole he'd sliced in the right-front pocket of the brown khakis. The pants were held up by suspenders and a couple of sizes too large for Jack's gaunt frame—leaving, he hoped, enough room between his legs to hide a record bluegill.

"Bone appetite," said Jack.

Jack stood at the end of the log on his bad leg, clutching a thick branch that jutted up for support. He dangled his good fishing leg out over the water and shook the cricket free. The cricket struggled furiously toward the log, pushing out dark rippling bull's-eye rings on the flat surface of the mirrored pond. Jack was leaning out a little bit farther so he could look to see if the fish was still under the log when the cricket disappeared in a blue hole.

"Yikes," was all Jack had time to say.

He squeezed the half-rotted branch with both hands. His knobby knee inside the baggy pants whipsawed left and right and all around as the bluegill zigged and zagged on a short leash. Jack now had two problems. First, the game warden who had just curled in a long putt for bogey and was watching from the green; second, the splintering crack of a breaking branch.

Jack belly-flopped into the tepid green pond water. He was half choking by the time he got his legs down and his head up. The fish was far easier to fight with his rod foot braced on the bottom. Once the fish came in close all those years Jack had spent on the dance floor paid off—a quick polka shuffle with a little Texas two-step thrown in and the bluegill was clamped firmly between his knees. Jack's hands were underwater, fumbling at the thrashing bluegill with a skinning knife, when the game warden skidded to another stop in his golf cart.

"What are you doing in the water?" he demanded from the padded plastic seat. "I saw you dancing on that log."

Jack smiled weakly, spitting water between the gap in his front teeth.

"A bee flew up the leg of my pants," he said.

"So you jumped in the water?" said the warden.

"I'm allergic to bees," said Jack. "It was all I could think to do."

The game warden looked at the scorecard on the dash and smiled. "I suppose so," he said absentmindedly.

The warden was three over par, playing the best golf round of his life, and contemplating his next shot. He didn't have much green to work with, and as his mind wandered so did the warden, over to check out the lie of his ball. The shot came out hot and the warden groaned, but when he drained another long putt he'd forgotten about everything except his next tee shot.

The warden disappeared down the asphalt cart path. Jack slipped the knife into the bluegill's spinal cord. He hitched up his belt, hobbled a hundred feet of open fairway to Silver Creek, then let the fish fall out of his pants in the riparian privacy of the willows. The bluegill was already fading from turquoise to black as it splatted to the stones; back at the Sportsman the fish weighed in at two pounds, eight ounces.

The bluegill was worth ninety-eight points and first place. Despite the excited clamor of fishermen comparing stories, Nick was asleep facedown on the bar. Jack put his hand on Nick's back, leaned across the bar, and pulled the chain on the brass bell from a mothballed trolley, clanging out the signal that he was buying the house yet another round.

"I'd just like to say . . ." yelled Jack, then grinned as he forgot what he was going to say.

"Congratulations," somebody yelled back.

"Where'd you get it?" somebody else yelled.

Jack's grin stretched wide enough to show the missing incisors at the back of his mouth.

"Happy birthday," yelled somebody else.

The hole of the missing teeth disappeared as Jack suddenly lost his grin. He squinted as he stared into the distance, then smacked his forehead with the palm of his hand so hard he fell backward off his stool.

"Oh, no!" he said, looking up from the floor. "The birthday party!"

Jack jumped up and ran the gauntlet of back slappers to the door, pleasantly surprised to discover the Bonneville parked right out front with one wheel up on the sidewalk. The maraschino-red mountain bike already strapped to the roof with baling twine so delighted Jack that he drove down Main Street forgetting to turn on the headlights. An hour later Heidi was waiting on the sofa, staring up at her high school tennis trophies collecting dust on the mantel, when the phone rang.

She picked up the phone and said worriedly: "Is that you, Dad?"

A hoarse whisper. "Heidi?"

"Dad? Where are you?"

"Shh-hh-hh. Don't let your mother hear."

"Dad, are you all right? What's wrong?"

"Nothing. What could possibly be wrong?"

"Well for starters," said Heidi, "dinner was five hours ago."

"Aw, honey," said Jack, "I was shopping. I got you that bike, just like I said I would."

Heidi's voice jumped an octave as a lump constricted her throat.

"What are you talking about?" she said shrilly. "What bike?"

Jack wondered what all the fuss was about, thinking maybe he'd gotten the wrong color.

"The red one," he said. "It even has the little bell on the handlebars like you asked for."

Heidi remembered how disappointed she'd been, how he'd promised.

"But Dad," she finally choked out. "That was thirty years ago. I was just a kid."

Now the lump was in Jack's throat. He didn't know what to think. Thirty years ago?

"Aw, honey," he said, "that can't be right. I've never been that late before."

The silence stretched. In the background phone hiss over her father's ragged breathing Heidi heard more phones ringing. A door slammed and two loud voices were arguing over the last jelly doughnut; the loudest voice of all was a woman demanding a lawyer.

"Dad?" said Heidi. "Are you in jail?"

"Tomorrow," said Jack. "Tomorrow, I'll see you for sure."

The Stupid Tax

THE STUPID TAX IS AS PROGRESSIVE as a tax can be. It is assessed equally on everyone, the dumb and the stupid alike, with no regard for creed, color, or credit limit. And if that isn't bad enough, the worst thing about the Stupid Tax is that there's nobody else to blame.

Whatever happened, it's your own damn fault, and you're going to pay for it in ways you never imagined. That's why it happened in the first place. You weren't thinking far enough ahead, and your debt to reality will be assessed in as many currencies as there are things that can go wrong. You might pay with Blisters if you run out of gas twenty miles up the wrong road. It could be Time if you break the law and get caught. Forget an anniversary and you'll pay with Guilt; forget enough anniversaries in a row and it's hello Loneliness.

In this case I was paying the Stupid Tax in a more conventional form: Overdraft Fees.

The seven identical envelopes on the truck seat beside me were from the Bank, and there was no need to even open them. The smudged carbon lettering behind each glassine window meant twenty bucks a pop, and as I drove the dirt canyon road to yet another day of guiding there was no telling how many more checks were bouncing through the mail.

It was stupid because I had the money, I just didn't have it in the Bank. I had it in the glove compartment, enough in uncashed checks to pay for the blown-foam insulation that would keep the winter cold where it belonged, outside the walls of my new house. But the Bank was forty miles away and I'd been too busy making the money to do anything with it.

It was the most I'd ever guided in a row, fifty days fricasseeing in the white-hot mountain sun, cooking under cloudless afternoons that came like identical blue ovens. A plume of summer dust roiled behind the truck; my hands on the steering wheel were baked brown and rough as bark. I was barbecued on the outside but inside was worse.

Inside, I'd been fried to a crisp. I turned left onto the paved county road, fighting the feeling I might scream the next time I saw a trout wiggle in the net. Catching fish with strangers is an act of will. You have to be "On" all the time, tuned to the river, locked into your client's heads. Guiding well requires an abstract concentration that takes its spiritual toll. Too much of it and you'll never want to fish again. All you'll want to do is stick your thumb in your mouth and curl up in a dark basement room with *The Flintstones*.

You can't be too careful with excess when your avocation is your vocation because you can grow to hate what you once loved, and we get too few loves in this life. It's the same with musicians. Play too many lounge chords at a Holiday Inn, you just might lay that guitar down for good. Play too many stadiums, you just might give up rock 'n' roll. Undo too many tangles and you just might take up golf. That's why I was listening to the Piano Man on the stereo in my truck as I spun the wheel to just miss the big pothole in front of the Mountain Palace.

The Piano Man, among other highlights in a fairy-tale career, played keyboards for Pink Floyd. He'd been there for *Dark Side of the Moon*. Not only that, he'd produced Michael Jackson's *Thriller* tour and a couple of

Madonna albums. Now he wrote scores for Hollywood movies and he fished only bamboo rods, preferably with dry flies.

I'd guided him a couple of years earlier. He just showed up one day. To have a rock 'n' roll star appear out of the blue and ask to go fishing—it was like a dream come true, if you were dreaming of thirty-knot winds kicking up whitecaps on the water. And then it began to sleet. We took refuge in a cave carved long ago by glacial floods where the river pushes up against the cliff at Head-Smashed-In. The sheltered arch is speckled orange with lichens, wide enough for a couple of driftboats, and there's a faint clammy echo when you speak.

"So what's she really like-like?" I asked. "Madonna, I mean-mean."

The flattened crown to the Piano Man's wide-brimmed felt outback hat scraped the damp rock of the low ceiling as we rocked in the chop. His brown eyes were dilated in the gloom; his head was cocked to the side like he listened for something he couldn't quite hear.

"Madonna's smart," he said. "And she's the boss. You do it her way and everything has to be just so. She has the whole record in her head before you start, and you don't quit until it's down the way she wants it down."

"But what's she like?" I persisted. "Is she happy?"

A tray of appetizers from the Cow Coulee Deli, "Where their meats don't lie," was open on the seat. The Piano Man smeared mustard on a circle of buffalo salami before he answered.

"The thing is," he said, "her image doesn't stop where her life begins. And she's always working an angle somewhere, so somebody's always after her for something. It's hard for her to know who to trust, so she spends a lot of time alone."

Which is just exactly what I wanted to hear. Madonna could trust me. She didn't have to be alone anymore.

"You should bring her fishing," I said seriously, but the Piano Man laughed until he cried.

"I hate to ruin your retirement plans," he said, "but forget about it. You're talking about the Material Girl here. Her idea of nature is a potted plant that somebody else waters. You'd never get her in a fishing boat. And think about it. The girl was intimate with Dennis Rodman."

The Piano Man looked more like a plumber than a rock star but that's why you never judge a book by its cover. From private jets and penthouse suites filled with naked groupies to shooting at English manors where they hauled the pheasants away with dump trucks to give to the poor, he'd done it all. Everything, that is, except play with the North Fork Nitwits. I figured it couldn't hurt to ask.

"It isn't Pink Floyd," I said, "but Friday nights there's a jam at the Mountain Palace. Some pretty good musicians show up, a lot of them fishermen. If you're still around this weekend you should come on down. You'll meet the locals, might have some fun."

The Piano Man stared at his delicate hands and replied so softly I could barely hear him.

"It's gone," he whispered. "It's all gone."

He explained in halting sentences how as a child he couldn't not play the piano. As many as fourteen hours a day he'd practice; he wouldn't even stop to eat. His mother had once threatened to remove the piano completely, to chop it up into little pieces, if he didn't go outside and play a little baseball. He tried, but too many splendid notes were lined up in his brain, impatiently waiting their turn to emerge. There were times he felt so pressurized that if it took even one instant longer to get the music out of his mind and into his fingers on the black-and-white keyboard that his head would physically burst: That's what was gone.

"It was a great gift," he finished. "I didn't earn it, I was born with it, and since it all came so easily I abused it. I made music for money, but I didn't make music for me. And I didn't do it for so long I can't remember how. It was so easy I thought it would always be easy."

He sounded not sad but surprised, peering at his hands as if they were somebody else's.

There are times you have to be Ann Landers out there.

"It's not gone," I said. "It's right where it's always been."

The downstream wind played the mouth of the cave like a flute, filling the hollow space around us with a single hypnotizing note. It was a place where rivergoing men would have long since waited out other storms. In the low, dark hum it was easy to imagine a round, willow-ribbed, buffalo-skinned bull-boat pulled onto the sandy ledge, a brown man in a bearskin tunic playing along with the cave, rattling a pair of fresh rib bones, practicing rhythms intricate enough to catch a cave-babe's eye at the next Dance to the Sun.

Music had filled that cave since the last ice age and I was betting the Piano Man could find it. He was a passionate dry-fly fisherman, a purist who would rather catch one tough fish than a bunch of easy ones. He'd set aside enough time to fish the Rockies as far as the summer took him. The next river was whatever waters happened along, and he had only the faintest of plans because he wanted to be surprised along the way.

"Keep a journal of your trip," was my advice. "I bet you'll find some music in there."

A year later a CD arrived unexpectedly in the mail. The Piano Man didn't eke out just a song or two from his journal, he found an entire album, and the fifth song was a tempestuous chronicle of our journey on the high seas of improvisational piano. The melody starts with snapping trees and gale-force winds, then waltzes through the quiet conversation in the cave. It lilts into a quiet rainy dusk with trout rising in the mist, then picks up steam at the point where I strained at the oars holding the boat against the sweeping flow of an outside river bend.

The rushing water had recently undercut a grand old giant of a newly fallen cottonwood tree. A tangled spaghetti of exposed roots hung out over the water; tucked in against the shore, a whopper trout nosed up to caddis-flies in a dinner-plate-sized eddy. The surging current was so powerful that even with gut-busting backrowing there would be time for only one or two good casts. The Piano Man's first sidearm bounce cast skipped in six inches short and was instantly snatched away as current bellied the line. The second cast shot up under five feet of overhanging root wad, bounced twice, and gently skipped *into* the trout's open mouth.

In twenty years of guiding it was the best cast I'd ever seen. The fish had no choice but to eat. A big trout on light tippet is like a shark on a thread: You can't force things. It's easier from a boat because you can follow the fish and keep the pressure steady. The song marches along triumphantly as we landed a twenty-three-inch hook-jawed brown trout in the soft rain. The finale is a mournful minor key, the piano notes as gasping and tired as the pale weak blood in the gills of the panting fish that nearly died in my hands.

The song is a reminder I can ill afford to squander the music in my own life. I pushed the button on the CD player in my truck to play it again. The storm of piano notes bounced off the bug-splattered windshield as I braked for the forty-five-mile-an-hour zone, the short canyon that leads to the high bypass around Head-Smashed-In buffalo jump. There's always a bright side, you just have to find it, and the first smile of the day crossed my sun-chapped lips.

I smiled because I was working with the Duke, guiding some of his conservation patrons. Working with the Duke is always a pleasure, and starting tomorrow, after fifty-one days in a row, I had time off, four whole days. Running power tools by the light of a headlamp is a dangerous proposition. I was contemplating the bliss of building on my house during the daylight hours when from the engine compartment there was a New Sound.

I turned up the music but it didn't help. The New Sound, a whining hiss punctuated with the occasional thwap-thwap-thwap, didn't go away. I'd been planning on trading the truck in at the end of the season so I hadn't spent the money to fix it up. The dashboard was lit up like a Christmas tree with scheduled-maintenance warning lights. I was running on borrowed time, and that morning in the cool depths of the road behind the buffalo jump my loan was called due.

The temperature gauge redlined. Prestone petro-geysers erupted in white puffs from the hood, the grille, even the wheel wells. The twisting road there was dynamited into solid rock, the narrow gravel shoulder barely wide enough for my truck. I was stranded in the shade of the cliff with my boat ten miles from where I was supposed to meet the Duke in ten minutes.

I lifted the hood and jumped back in a mushrooming burst of forehead-searing steam. Rock doves cooed from ledged perches sprouting gnarled green bitterbrush. From the road below a motor raced as someone downshifted for the steep switchback. I stood in the middle of the road waving my arms. To my surprise, dispensing mercy like a bald angel with a high forehead in a sport utility vehicle, it was the Duke who coasted to a stop.

"Hey, sailor," he said, leaning on one thick arm out through the open window.

"Man am I glad to see you," I replied.

"I'll bet," he said.

"What are you doing here?" I said. "I thought you'd be with the clients."

The Duke pretended to wipe a tear from his eye and said in a sad voice: "Do you want the good news first or the bad news first?"

"The bad news," I said. "I've had about all the good news I can take for one day."

"The clients canceled. Their plane was late. You don't have to guide today."

It took a moment to sink in. I felt like Fate had decided not to press charges.

"So what's the good news?" I asked.

"You're getting paid anyway."

There was more good news under the hood. It was only a broken fan belt, and I had a serpentine spare under the seat. The Duke pried while I tugged, and half an hour later we were wiping our greasy hands on the T-shirt I'd taken from the laundry behind the seat. I folded the shirt oily-side in and tossed it into my boat.

The Duke looked at his watch.

"Do you know what time it is?" he asked.

The sun was still well below the jagged rim of the canyon depths.

"Yeah," I said, "it's time to buy a new truck."

"Not even close," he said, "It's time to go fishing."

The Duke was right. A day fishing—not guiding—was exactly what my spirit required.

"Nope," I said. "I just can't."

I could think only of my undone chores. The lack of a toilet spoke for itself, particularly when dating. The overdrafts remained on the seat beside me, sliding into the sheaf of unopened bills. The laundry was so rank burning might be the only cure. My boat was long overdue for a good scrubbing, if I didn't tie flies I'd have to buy them, and the last time I'd checked a dozen messages waited impatiently on voice mail. I viewed the morning's reprieve complete with a day's pay as a warning, a sign from the celestial soothsayer of the Absurd, and the sign said it was time for a new truck.

Next time I wouldn't be so lucky.

The rubber checks presented a special problem that required immediate attention as I U-turned at the top of the canyon. I'd need unblemished credit to buy a new truck. And for sure I'd need money—all I could get. Used-car salesmen will go low if you flash cash. They can't stand to watch that money walk out the door.

The Kingfish owed me for eight days. I stopped at Trout World to bolster my haggling reserves. He was leaning back on both elbows against the split-log railing that surrounded the elevated deck out over the river, head back to the shafts of sunlight that pierced the spaces between the cotton-wood branches. Pinpoint yellow lasers reflected from his mirrored sunglasses as he glanced down toward the opening squeak of the door hinges on my truck. A green handblown quart bottle stoppered with an oversized cork hung limply in his right hand. The Kingfish hadn't had a drink in seven years but he still remembered how it was done. As I climbed the stairs that led to the deck the Kingfish was already into what appeared to be a bottle of very old Scotch as far as rhyming couplets.

"Genie in the bottle," he quoted, "Genie in the sky, Genie is Coyote, he's coming by-and-by."

The Kingfish on whiskey was unpredictable. I walked across the deck one slow step at a time. He extended the bottle with a weary grin, but when he pulled the cork his eyes were drawn as if by smoke up from the fluted neck of the green bottle. The smoking bottle must have been hot because the Kingfish dropped it to the wooden deck and crouched in mock surprise.

"Coyote?" he said, his eyes focused ten feet in the air. "Is that you?"

The Kingfish jumped across the bottle and stood tall, peering down at the spot where he'd just been. It was the beginning of a one-act play with the Kingfish taking the parts of both himself and Coyote the Trickster, alternating personalities as he jumped back and forth across the bottle, and now he squeezed his skull like it was no picnic shooting headfirst from a bottle.

"Oh, wow," said the Kingfish as Coyote, "right in the middle of Oprah."

The Kingfish went back to being himself, looking up suspiciously at tall Coyote.

"TV?" he said. "Your bottle comes with TV?"

"It's good work if you can get it," said Coyote as he adjusted the air over his head.

"What's with the turban?" said the Kingfish. "You pawn your feathers?"

"Moonlighting," shrugged Coyote. "I'm filling in for Kazaam. Okay, now you know the drill. One wish, then I'm back in the bottle."

The Kingfish looked surprised. "One wish?" he said. "It's three wishes. It's always been three wishes. What kind of racket are you running? Did you get a job with the BIA?"

"It's a new policy," said Coyote. "Comes right from the top. Something to do with the liability insurance is what I heard. What do you want? Money? A new boat? One wish, and make it snappy. I'm missing 'Girls who love their boyfriends' mothers too much.'"

"Money's too easy," said the Kingfish. "I want to understand women."

Coyote scratched his balls and stared over the parking lot, looking perplexed.

"Well, cousin," he finally said, "a long time ago there were only two people on the earth, Old Man and Old Woman. They could never agree on anything, but they had to decide on how to bring other people to this earth. Finally one day they were swimming at the river and Old Woman said to Old Man, 'We can't put this off anymore. We have to agree on how people are going to live when they come to this world.'

"'All right,' said Old Man, 'as long as I have first say in everything.'

"'That's fine,' said Old Woman, 'as long as I have final say in everything.'

"This was in the days before bathing suits. Old Man had no choice but to agree.

"'All right then,' he said. 'Women will have the work of tanning the hides, rubbing in the brains of the animals to make them soft, and scraping out the hair with tools sharpened from certain rocks. And the work should be easy, so the women will have time to braid their hair, and lie on the beach.'

"And Old Man drew a picture of what he meant in the mud, just so there would be no confusion, but Old Woman rubbed it out with her foot.

"'No, no, no,' she said. 'Women will tan hides as you say, but the work will be hard. That way the good workers can be found out and honored.'

"'Well, then,' said Old Man, 'the hunters will have their eyes in their hands, so that they may hold up their arms and see around corners.'

"'No, no, no,' said Old Woman. 'The eyes will go with the mouth, in the face.'

"'All right then,' said Old Man. 'I think ten fingers on each hand will be enough.'

"'No, no, no,' said Old Woman. 'Ten fingers is like ten snakes, way too many. Each hand will have four fingers and one thumb for grabbing.'

"And so it went as Old Man and Old Woman decided how people would live on earth.

"'And what about life and death?' asked Old Woman. 'Will the people live forever, or is it better that they die sometime?'

"It was the toughest question yet and they just couldn't agree. Finally Old Man said, 'We will settle it this way. I will throw a buffalo chip in the water. If it floats then the people will die for four days and come back to life; if it sinks, the people will stay dead.'

"'No, no, *no*,' said Old Woman. 'We *won't* settle it like that. We'll throw a stone in the river, and if the stone floats the people will come back to earth after four days, but if the stone sinks the people will stay dead.'

"And when Old Woman threw the stone in the river it fell to the bottom.

"'It is better like this,' she said, 'because if people didn't die they wouldn't feel sorry for each other. This way there will be sympathy in the earth.'

"'Well, then,' said Old Man, 'you have chosen. So it shall be.'

"But then Old Woman had a baby daughter who became sick and died. Old Woman was sorry they'd agreed that people wouldn't live forever. 'Let's talk this over,' she said.

"But Old Man shook his head. 'No,' he answered. 'What is made law must be law. What is done is done and cannot be undone.' "

The Kingfish had been pantomiming out all the parts as he told the story. Now he leaned back against the railing, panting with the effort of leaping out the parts of Old Man and Old Woman. Throwing stones, tanning hides, and especially giving birth had really taken it out of him; he was back to being himself as the Kingfish looked up at Coyote and said: "I didn't ask why people die, I asked to understand women."

Coyote looked troubled. "It was as close as I could come," he said and disappeared.

The Kingfish sank to his knees on the deck like a gut-shot Hollywood gunslinger.

"It's Heidi," I said. "Isn't it?"

I squeezed his shoulder but the Kingfish immediately moved away to grope for the bottle between his legs. He held it upside down over his open mouth. When nothing came out he said: "The Seventh Cavalry was nothing compared to that Greek prick Oedipus."

There isn't much you can say except you're sorry.

"Yeah," he said. "Me, too."

The Kingfish stood up, lit a cigarette, smoked it, stabbed it out in a rusty can full of sand, then lit another cigarette, muttering to himself the whole time.

"Me," he said. "A father figure. What a crock of chicken shit. I didn't even know my father. There are good reasons Indians don't touch."

It had been an issue from day one. Tactile Heidi couldn't talk without touching, and the Kingfish couldn't stand to be touched. There are reasons people reared in tribal societies prefer not to shake hands. A hundred and fifty years ago the customary response between people meeting for the first time was to try to kill each other. The truth was, there wasn't much the Kingfish could have done. Heidi had taken her fortieth birthday hard. After that her expression toward the Kingfish had gone from merely annoyed to something a whole lot worse: pity.

"Don't blame yourself," I said. "People change."

"All I can say," he said, "is, don't believe everything you read at the checkout counter."

His face had always shown time like the mountains, changing with the seasons but not the years. I'd never thought of the Kingfish as old until that moment. Bare-chested, his sagging bones and loose flesh exposed each of his sixty-two years as he fingered the leather pouch that hung on a raw-hide string at his hollow neck.

"Do you know what time it is?" I asked.

The Kingfish squinted at the sun hanging in the upper branches of the trees.

"About quarter after nine," he replied.

It seemed like about a month had passed since the fan belt had broken.

"No," I said. "It's time to go fishing."

The Kingfish turned a slow circle on the deck, studying the pale blue sticky-hot sky.

"Beaver Head Rock down to Prairie Dog," he decided, "We might see the *Ephoron*."

It was a long shot. The giant white *Ephoron* is a rare burrowing mayfly that favors silt bottoms and hatches only on the hottest and muggiest of August nights. In twenty years I'd never encountered the hatch, but it was something I'd always wanted to see.

"Let's take your boat," I said. "My truck has issues."

The Kingfish nodded as he opened the propane barbecue and produced another bottle.

"And I'll drive," I added.

I threw my fishing bag and double-rod case into the Kingfish's wood-en boat, climbed behind the wheel of Mister Dead, and drove the fifteen miles to the concrete boat ramp across from Beaver Head Rock. There was a line. I parked behind an old Ford pickup with a blue canoe strapped to a welded angle-iron rack that belonged to a nonpracticing Buddhist named Road Kill who never combed his frizzy hair.

Road Kill made his living tying flies. He believed that even in death life should not be wasted, and took his name from his favored source of fly-tying materials. Road Kill's patterns were always cutting edge; if I bought his flies I wouldn't have to tie my own. I could cross it off my list of undone chores.

"Is the candy store open?" I asked as I walked up to the window of his truck.

Road Kill opened a small plastic box of samples and handed me a tiny yellow fly.

"Check out this new cripple," he said. "It's part of the Highway Twelve series. I call it the Jaws of Life."

Cripples are emerging mayflies that don't quite make it. Their wings get stuck in the shuck, and since they can't escape there are days selective trout won't eat anything else. The bugs drift downstream hanging from the surface film, writhing furiously in a life-or-death struggle to extricate those trapped bent wings, and feeding trout will key on that wiggling motion. The Jaws of Life was tied with a soft-hackled feather; Road Kill fluffed it with his finger to demonstrate how it would pulsate with the currents.

"Look at that feather," he enthused, "look at that bright yellow. The only place you'll find that color is the breast of spring meadowlark, and those birds are fast. The only way you ever find one is combing the fence line on the paved straightaways."

I examined the Jaws of Life. Road Kill held out a gray extended-body mayfly dun.

"The body is porcupine quill," he said. "It's hollow, guaranteed to float."

Trout, especially when they've seen a lot of flies, are selective to size first and pattern second. Most fishermen change patterns when they should be changing size.

"What I really need," I said, "is five dozen number twenty beadhead nymphs."

Road Kill began dumping flies into a plastic container, I pulled out my checkbook and wrote yet another rubber check.

"Don't cash this until the day after tomorrow," I said. "I need to get to the bank."

Road Kill looked up over my shoulder and whistled with half-closed eyes. "Hey," he said, "what happened to him?"

My stiff neck cracked as I turned my head. The Kingfish was fancy-dancing a circle around the green bottle he'd placed on the faded double yellow centerline of the frontage road.

"It's Heidi," I said. "She's gone."

It wasn't the first time she'd left, but it seemed like it might be the last. It was hard to tell what Road Kill was thinking. Over the years Heidi had been the object of more Apikuni fantasies than a ten-pound brown trout. On the crumbling asphalt the Kingfish danced so hard his braids wiggled like snakes.

"Well," I said, "we'd better get him out of the road."

"Although," said Road Kill, "those braids would make some good black caddis wings."

The heat reflected off the pavement in rippling curtains. It was an entirely different climate zone on the water. Thousands of launches later I still tingle like a virgin in that magical instant the boat rocks free in the waves. All the water that's you has finally come home to roost. The fishing would be slow until the sun lowered a couple of hours to the west. We pulled in under a pair of low-leaning cottonwoods. Twenty feet away prickly pear cactus yellowed in the stifling alpine desert. On the water under the leafy green shade it was that perfect temperature where you couldn't feel your skin.

Of course, it might have been the Scotch. Having decided to take the whole day off, the next step was an easy one as I leaned back in the padded high-backed seats in the Kingfish's wooden boat. There was compartment after compartment of built-in waterproof storage, and in twenty years he'd never completely cleaned everything out. We finally found the worn crib-bage board behind a propane-powered hand warmer in the duck-hunting compartment; at a quarter a point I was down seven dollars when bright, cheery words rang in from upstream: "Hi guys, is any of that shade for sale?"

It was Prozac, the happiest guide on this or any other river. He eased his boat close, dropped the anchor, shipped the oars. Both his clients were holding nasty tangles, but Prozac was beaming like Santa Claus on a high-protein diet above his prematurely white beard.

"We're down for the count with a technical knot-out." He smiled.

Some guides would run screaming into the parched yellow-brown hills, but not Prozac. He was seemingly imperturbable. Most of the other guides suspect pharmaceuticals, but Prozac assured us it was just the way he was born.

"What a life," he continued. "I wish I had your job. I think I could get good at sitting in the shade sipping iced drinks. Don't you guys ever work? You got any cigars?"

"Sure," I said. "Let me get my humidor."

Lots of river guides do tobacco. The habit is rampant because it helps kill the standing-around time.

Prozac wrung his hands in delight as I opened my fishing bag. "Bless you, my son," he said, crossing the thin air over his black graphite oars.

The paying customer sitting in the front of Prozac's boat had a sun-burned face and wore monogrammed neoprene waders despite the heat. He introduced himself as Bill, and was highly amused as I produced my stash of cigars.

"I like your humidor," said Bill. "I see that it's waterproof."

"Thank you," I said. "I don't often encounter an epicurean with such a discerning eye."

With the notable exception of women I opt for Function over Form. My humidor was a Rubbermaid plastic box with an airtight lid. A damp chunk of kitchen sponge controlled the humidity. The system worked so well I was down to my last cigar.

"Dude," said Prozac, "I can't take your last one."

"You're right," I said, "but you can take the last half."

My humidor was complete with single-edged razor blades because it's the only way to get a clean cut. First you slit the wrapper all the way around, then guillotine the filler in a single angled slice.

Bill quit chuckling so he'd have time to be mildly horrified. "Do you know what you're doing?" he said. "Do you have any idea?"

The Cuban cigar was compliments of Bernie the Billionaire and larger than a lot of cucumbers. You knew it had to be pretty special.

"Sure I know," I said. "I know if I smoke a whole one I turn green."

"That's right," said Prozac. "Friends don't let friends smoke cheap cigars."

"I'm giving you the top end," I said. "Leave the label here near the cut. That way the wrapper won't unravel."

My lips burned with potent nicotine as I moistened my half of the cigar. Prozac puffed away as he opened the surgery ward on his client's tangles. A striped abdomen swelled red with blood on the Kingfish's neck. Too drunk to fly, the mosquito crashed with a full load into the side of the boat. The air was thick with humidity and carried sound like water. An engine whined then died half a mile away as a Jet-Boat waked to a stop in front of a row of four fishermen.

"They're checking licenses," I said idly. "You'd think it would be too hot for the cops."

Bill dug through one ironed pocket after another. His level of agitation increased visibly, and when you show weakness on the reservation you're no longer a predator, you're prey.

"They're checking licenses," said the Kingfish, "and they've been really strict."

Dark stains spread from under the arms of Bill's salmon-colored shirt.

"Geez," he said, "I left my fishing license back at the motel. What's going to happen?"

"It's not the fine that's so bad," said the Kingfish. "It's the mandatory night in jail."

Then he turned to me and asked sadly: "You remember what happened to the last guy that showed up at the reservation drunk tank wearing rubber pants?"

I tapped my cigar, half an inch of blunt gray ash sizzling as it hit the water.

"And him not wearing underwear," I said sadly.

"Especially on a Friday night," said the Kingfish. "It'll be a full house."

"I'm wearing underwear," Bill said anxiously.

Bill snugged up his waders even though he was wet with sweat. Prozac just grinned.

"Don't believe a word these guys say," he said. "The only way you can tell for sure that they're lying is when their lips are moving. Don't worry, nobody's going to jail."

Just to make sure Prozac handed Bill his newly rigged rod and weighed anchor. The boat hadn't gone ten feet before the new flies were irretrievably snarled in the shade tree. His head was still in the branches, he was about to be checked for a license he didn't have, and Bill had still tried to cast in the midst of the foliage. That's how insane the mere possibility of catching a fish makes otherwise normal people feel.

"Nice tree," said Prozac as the leader snapped. "That's the biggest one so far."

They disappeared downstream. The Kingfish shuffled the cards. I pegged a sixteen-point hand and an eight-point crib to surge into the lead. I stirred my drink with my thumb, the Scotch burning at the web of thin trout-tooth cuts in the fleshy pad. Turkey vultures circled on the thermals, soaring black V's in the thin blue sky, and when the Jet-Boat again whined to life up the river a cold chill of déjà vu settled in the bones and muscles between my shoulder blades.

There is a theory, Determinism, that says every particle in the universe is where it is because it can't be anywhere else. Every particle interacts with every other particle in predictable ways according to laws like Gravity and Magnetism: Once you know where a particle is, then you can calculate where it was, and where it will be. Determinism says the fabric of a preordained universe unfolds the only way it can; that the stage for the absurd theater of our lives was set at the moment of the Big Bang; and when the time comes the actors don their costumes because they can't do anything else. The show must go on.

Of course it would be Black Drum. Of course it would be the Kingfish.

The shiny new aluminum tribal Jet-Boat roostertailed up the river, straight for us, kicking up a wake that rocked our boat hard enough to knock the cards off the cooler. Black Drum is a big man, but it's all dough-nuts-in-the-patrol-car. His spongy bulk jiggled the space–time fabric under the tightly stretched green short-sleeved shirt of his uniform as he kicked out an anchor and stepped off the boat.

"Well," said Black Drum, smiling with a full set of crooked yellow teeth. "What a happy coincidence. The Council Elders tell me I'm sup-posed to write as many tickets as I can today, and then I see your driftboat tied up in the trees."

"A ticket?" I said. "For what, playing cribbage?"

The Blackfoot had recently traded in their hatchets for lawyers. Invoking eighteenth-century treaty rights, they now controlled the pol-itics of the Apikuni, including law enforcement. Black Drum splashed over in black dress shoes and green pants wet to the knees, reeking of sour body odor as he tapped the guide number decal stuck to the side of the Kingfish's boat.

"If you're not guiding," said Black Drum, "the law says you have to remove these numbers. We don't want to be deceiving the public now, do we? John Q. has a right to know who's guiding and who isn't, doesn't he?"

"But anybody can see this isn't a guide trip," I protested. "We aren't even fishing."

"And it's a discretionary offense," continued Black Drum like I wasn't there, "which in this case I figure is worth five hundred dollars."

"Five hundred dollars!" I said.

Black Drum heard me that time. "Did I say five?" he said. "I meant six."

A red-tailed hawk screamed in the distance as Black Drum wrote out a ticket. He tore off the blue carbon copy for the Kingfish, who took the paper, folded it in half, spiced it with salt and pepper from the cooler, and then put the ticket in his mouth.

"That's a pretty nice boat you're driving," the Kingfish said as he chewed with his mouth open, "especially since the Bureau of Indian Affairs cut your budget. What are you doing for cash, dumping commodity cheese on the black market? And maybe storing it overnight in your office? That would explain your problem with pack rats."

His hands on his hips, Black Drum bellied out his round stomach. His shirt lost the battle of the bulge. Two overmatched buttons popped off in the same instant, plinking into the water. You could have hidden a ketchup bottle in the hairless dark maw of his freshly exposed navel.

"Rats," said Black Drum. "What do you know about pack rats?"

"Not much," replied the Kingfish. "But I've read that they'll nest in filing cabinets."

"You son-of-a-bitch," said Black Drum.

"And everybody," continued the Kingfish, "knows a pack rat will foul its own nest."

"You're a dead man," grunted Black Drum. "That's what I know."

Then the portable radio in the Jet-Boat squawked.

"Hey, cousin," said a slow voice full of static, "you got any more of them forms? We been busting white guys right and left. Twelve more and we can take tomorrow off."

It was a way out and Black Drum took it, splashing back to the boat.

"Roger that," he said into the microphone. "Where you at?"

"Head-Smashed-In," said the mechanical voice.

"Ten minutes," said Black Drum, then he pointed a finger at the Kingfish.

"This isn't over," he said.

Black Drum disappeared downstream. Now it was my turn to point a finger at the Kingfish. I'd already fulfilled my role in the unfolding drama.

"My rats?" I said. "You put my rats in his office?"

The Kingfish smiled back, his lips and tongue dark carbon-blue from eating the ticket.

"Eddie flew away," he said. "I wanted the rats to have a good home."

The blue lips, the cool shade, the soaring vultures; it wasn't just a feeling of déjà vu. It was more like rewatching a movie I'd seen often enough to memorize. I wasn't experiencing the moment, I was remembering it, like not only had this happened before, but it would happen again. That feeling of repetitive inevitability—it's at least possible in a circular universe that collapses and expands upon itself in a paradigm of infinity.

The show must go on. And on and on and on.

Of course Black Drum would be back. Of course the Kingfish would have a gun.

And not just any old gun, either.

For close-range demolition work, it's hard to beat the Road Warrior.

The Road Warrior is a sawed-off, double-barreled, small-caliber shotgun equipped with a pistol grip. It's a fierce-looking weapon, like something you might use to shoot an alien, but you can buy it over the counter at Joe's Guns-n-Ammo in downtown Cow Coulee. When loaded with number eight shot the Road Warrior is an ideal brush gun for the dropping of grouse; when loaded with solid lead slugs it's a handheld cannon perfectly suited for the dropping of small motorized craft.

The yellow sun was hanging over the western mountains when the curtain rose on the final act in the day's play. I was hanging neck-deep in the river, spent mayflies stuck to my chin, holding the boat so the Kingfish could fish the Slot where the river channels to the left of Martha's Island just above Beaver Head Rock. The boat rocked slightly with each cast; lifted and dipped, lifted and dipped. I'd been lifted and dipped until I was as contented as a wick in warm beeswax. Complacency should be one of the seven deadly sins. My premonition of impending doom was a flatline of lost electrical impulse that was soldered back together in a shower of sparks as a silver Jet-Boat skimmed around the bend behind Beaver Head Rock.

Black Drum could have taken the main channel but he knew his part by heart: He rammed the Jet-Boat straight for the narrow Slot. A one-burner stove and a coffeepot clunked into the bottom of the driftboat as the Kingfish dug through the same cold-weather bird-hunting compartment that held the cribbage board. He stood up with the Road Warrior hidden in the crook of his leg. It wasn't my fight and I swam to shore, the same as I'd always done.

Black Drum zoomed in pumping his fist. He was about ten feet out and thirty feet away when his smile turned to dust. The Kingfish had just drawn the Road Warrior and leveled a bead with both hands. Black Drum yanked the wheel in a hard turn away, but all the maneuver did was expose more hull below the waterline. Two shots came half a second apart, and the mushrooming lead slugs tore the bottom half off the prow of the boat.

The hole in the nose planed down and stopped dead in the water. The back of the boat kept pivoting up and over at thirty-five miles an hour. Black Drum and his big round belly were catapulted in a slow-motion flip out of the boat and up the river, the Jet-Boat landing upside down behind him. Black Drum struggled atop the overturned hull, then boat and rider disappeared the way they had come, back downstream around the corner below Beaver Head Rock.

Except for the oil slick and the birds not singing, it was like nothing had happened.

"Nice shot," I said.

The Kingfish blew across both smoking barrels. "The name is Tonto," he said in a British accent. "Tonto Bond."

Laughter is the only Band-Aid big enough for life on the reservation—that much I do understand about the Kingfish. Now he hung his head, feigning chastised.

"I'm sorry," he said. "I didn't mean to put the fish down."

"No problem," I said, which was about as far from the truth as you could get.

It was over in moments but things had changed forever. The Stupid Tax would be oppressive and we drifted down as slow as the river allowed. It was dark by the time we arrived at the Prairie Dog Put-in. The parking lot was ablaze with flashing red and blue lights. A dozen jurisdictions were represented, and a helicopter was just landing. Villainy had been slow that year, and every agency from the Border Patrol to the National Guard wanted in on what was being reported as a "cop shooting."

A local news crew from Channel Seven in Cow Coulee peeled up in a white van. The various authorities eagerly displayed the Kingfish like a head on the wall. He was handcuffed, spread-eagled, and blinded by halogen lights arranged so close to his face that his braids were smoking when a blond reporter with perfect bangs stuck a microphone in his mouth.

"Do you have anything to say?" she demanded.

"Well," mused the Kingfish, "at least I won't have to worry about finding work this winter."

Entropy's Amusement Park

BUGS AT NIGHT SWARM TOWARD beacons of bright light because all those concentrated photons overload an insect's primitive navigational systems. Fishing guides have much the same problem with neon beer signs, and the green Spuds MacKenzie in the big front window at the Mountain Palace is widely regarded as a mecca among experienced saloon entomologists.

It's the perfect place to examine the current entrées at the Trout Café, and about a month after the Kingfish shot the Jet-Boat I was standing at the window. A seething mat of insects was stacked up three-deep. Through the water-spotted glass I saw the same thing a trout sees: the bottom of the bug. Stomach color, motion, silhouette—it was all there and more. In the garish neon glow I watched wide-eyed as bugs did things to each other you wouldn't think bugs could do to each other. For a fishing guide it was like having an ant farm, only better; refreshments were mandatory and therefore tax deductible.

"Here you go, Sherlock," said Squatty, the owner of the Mountain Palace.

I was studying the bugs with a brass-bound magnifying glass the size of a Ping-Pong paddle. The optics were phenomenal. I spun with the glass still pasted to my eye. Up close Squatty's nose looked like pink cottage cheese. If I was Sherlock Holmes, this was the Case of the Abused Capillaries. I hastily lowered the lens and set it on the table. Squatty handed me a pint of cold ale.

"The game's about to start," he said, pulling a remote control from his pocket.

Squatty aimed at the television niched back into the granite fireplace. The screen flared with a blue buzz, then the Giants were at Denver in the first Monday-night football game of the regular season. I pulled a wad of crumpled bills from the pocket of my grass-stained fishing shorts and dropped them on the table. Squatty picked up the magnifying glass.

"What did this little beauty set you back?" he asked. He sighted down the oversized hickory handle like it was a gun barrel, drawing a bead on the stuffed grizzly bear wearing a New Year's Eve party hat in the corner.

"It was a gift from the river Gods," I said. "I found it lying on Martha's Island."

Squatty hooked a thumb in a greasy red suspender and glanced at the window. "Anything interesting?" he asked.

"Check it out," I said. "These bugs won't take no for an answer."

The window was XXX all the way. Adult mayflies exist with only one thought in mind, and with only a few minutes to live they completely forgo niceties like foreplay and candlelit dinners. The mayflies couldn't eat if they wanted to. They've just lost their mouths, stomachs, and most of the rest of their insides. It all goes into the production of vital juices, so much juice the crazed insects on the dirty glass couldn't help but beat their skinny chests while engaging in random acts of shameless sex. In the evening's most startling act, gangs of wild tricos were doing their best to jump a beetle's bones. Or at least its horny exoskeleton.

"This is great," said Squatty, peering through the lens. "I could charge admission."

"Bikers would pay double," I said. "You'll be in Disney World before you know it."

Squatty loved theme parks and went as often as he could afford. Mickey the Mouse grinned out between the suspenders on the back of his shirt. "Talk about Mister Toad and his Wild Ride," he said.

I leaned against the pool table watching the game. The Broncos had drawn first blood with a touchdown on a touch pass from the one when the Duke slouched up. His eyes usually spun in different directions but now they were as lifeless and puddled as spilled gray paint.

"Republicans," he said forlornly.

After three years of drought the Apikuni was so low you could walk across it. The Duke had been lobbying that what little water was left belonged in the river first and irrigating the hay fields second, but the conservative ranchers who controlled the Montana State Senate weren't about to put trout ahead of their cash cows.

"There's something here for everybody," said Squatty from the window. "Even the ones that are into mostly dead bodies."

The Duke's eyes sparked with interest then went dead again. Saving the world can be a depressing business. I just feel lucky to have been born at a time on the face of the planet when there are both jet airplanes and a few remaining bastions of worldwide wilderness.

"We saw it when it was good," I said. "Never forget that."

It really is the Golden Age, especially when it comes to beer. The Blackfoot Brewery in Cow Coulee was pumping out a new microbrew, Woolly Bugger Wheat. Served frosty cold with a slice of lemon, it was the perfect libation to celebrate a sixteen-yard touchdown pass to Ed McCaffrey. The Broncos were up by a touchdown when the whirlwind arrived in a lime-green cotton T-shirt with the hems cut away at the arms and neck.

"God it's hot," gasped Heidi and grabbed the Duke's mixed drink from his hand.

She started to sip, then took a good look at his sad face and handed back the glass.

"Whatever you had," she said, "I don't want any."

Then she grabbed the Duke by the nippers, fly floatant, and forceps that dangled from a leather thong around his neck and pulled his face so close his breath fogged her dark glasses.

"What happened," she said. "Did ZZ Top break up?"

The Duke's bald head gleamed in the light of the lamp hanging over the pool table. "It was so crowded out there today," he said, "I'm thinking of taking up golf."

The collar on Heidi's baggy shirt fell open as she grabbed the Duke's glass. "Poor baby," she said, forcing the drink to his lips until the Duke sputtered.

"I don't feel sorry for me," he said, "I feel sorry for my kids."

In the low water the fish had nowhere to hide. Some trout had been hooked and released so many times their mouths were purple with blood blisters. It was to the point where we weren't catching fish so much as torturing them, but I still had to work. I couldn't whine about the crowds, not when I was recruiting them for profit. Some days it was hard to look in the mirror, especially since I didn't have a mirror. What all those fishermen meant to me was that someday I'd be able to afford carpet for my new house.

"You know what I've been doing with clients," I said, "is, after they've caught some fish, then I bend out their hooks. The trout stay on for a jump or three. That's enough to count."

The Duke's eyes started spinning again. "And nobody complains?" he said.

"They hook so many," I replied, "hardly anyone even notices."

Heidi sat on the pool table beside me in cutoff jeans. A patch of thin blue veins showed on her upper thigh, our bare knees not quite but so close to touching that I could feel her heat.

"The real problem," she said, "is how to limit use. How about this: Sell fishing licenses that are good for the morning or the evening, but not both. A blue license is good until two in the afternoon, a red license is good after two. Everybody still gets to fish, and the quality of the experience goes way up because just like that the river is half as crowded."

It was an interesting idea. The color scheme would be at least somewhat enforceable.

"The same concept as a car pool lane," I said. "I like it."

Heidi had been talking with her hands, holding up two fingers to indicate the hour that shifts would change, slicing the air with an open palm to illustrate how the river would be half as crowded. She smiled at my carpool analogy and rested her hand on my thigh. Her fingernails were painted with black crickets on a silver flake background.

"And the chamber of commerce would love it," mused the Duke. "All those fishermen would have to spend that other half a day doing something: playing golf, whitewater rafting, digging sapphires, eating at restaurants. There would be some support for that idea."

"It'll fly," said Heidi, "if you limit it to out-of-state licenses and then give back . . ."

Her husky voice faded and the crickets dropped to her side as I hopped up.

"Time for a pit stop," I said. "Anybody need a beer while I'm up?"

"Gin-and-tonic," said the Duke. "Double lime."

"Organic pale ale," said Heidi.

I'd leapt up because Heidi's fingers had squeezed my thigh and when it comes to matters of moral turpitude I have one steadfast rule. It's all Ten Commandments and the Golden Rule balled up together into the following caveat: You don't fuck your friends, and you especially don't fuck your friends' wives. Heidi was always massaging hands and rubbing arms when she talked. It had never bothered me before, but lately a curious tingle when we touched was making me frog-jumpy every time it happened.

Out of respect for my water I pee outside whenever possible. White-winged nighthawks swooped in the silver moonlight above the river. With each deep breath of cool air I could see how wrong I'd been. Heidi wasn't flirting. We were like brother and sister. It was all in my head. If I said anything I'd just make a fool of myself. It was easy to choose a path of reticence; not knowing what to say to women is a course of inaction I've followed most of my life.

Back in the bar the Broncos were up fourteen to seven at the half. The preseason pundits had Denver as a team that could go all the way to the Super Bowl. Heidi and the Duke were scheming at an oval table made from a slab of whole tree. Their foreheads were pressed together, her corn-silk bangs against his wrinkled shining dome; they both looked up and Heidi grabbed my arm as I set their drinks on the table.

"How long has it been since you climbed Napi Peak?" she asked.

Heidi rubbed the inside of my elbow with the backs of her fingernails. Just the thought of the high country was enough to make me grin.

"Too long," I said. "And there's some good fishing, too. Wind Maker Lake in the south bowl holds some nice cutthroats. At least it did back in the good old days."

"Nice?" said the Duke. "What's 'nice'?"

"Six pounds," I said, holding my hands a good two feet apart.

Heidi's thick braid slapped from shoulder to shoulder as she shook her head. "That's giving the good old days the benefit of the doubt," she said.

I pressed my tongue against my front teeth, letting that long-ago trip come back. "And there's a waterfall," I said. "Down the cliffs at the back of the lake. The biggest fish I caught was in the plunge pool, on a little green Woolly Bugger."

"Big?" said the Duke. "What's 'big'?"

"Ten pounds," I said, holding my hands a good three feet apart.

Heidi put a hand on her hip burlesque style and said in a husky Mae West voice: "They're getting bigger, boys, I like that."

The Duke rubbed his hands together. "Let's go," he said.

My house was complete as far as hanging and taping the Sheetrock, jobs that I was contracting out. And it had been far too long since I'd gone fishing with the Duke.

"I have a couple of days off," I said. "I can go."

"I have a three-person tent in case it rains," said Heidi. "Otherwise we can just sleep under the stars."

Stove, fuel, aluminum pot with a lid, a stout rope to hang the food bag out of the reach of the backcountry bears. First-aid kit, flashlights, sleeping bags—over the years we've planned hundreds of late-night fishing trips. We've circumnavigated the globe in our minds, and once in a while we actually go. At six-thirty the following morning I'd just flipped the switch on the coffeemaker and was rolling up my inflatable blue sleeping pad when the phone rang.

"My DTI needs some work," was all the Duke said.

DTI is short for "Domestic Tranquility Index." In the background the Duchess was discussing lawn mowers and chicken barbecue.

"Yes, dear," said the Duke in a faint voice as the connection clicked dead.

I'd no sooner hung up than the phone rang again.

"Are you ready?" said Heidi.

"Duke backed out," I said. "He . . ."

"Already called me," interrupted Heidi. "I'll pick you up in half an hour."

"But . . ." was as far as I got before that connection clicked dead too.

Three days alone in the mountains with Heidi. I thought about her hand on my thigh as the coffee dripped. The hot plate sizzled with stray drops as I pulled out the glass carafe and slid in a cup for more immediate caffeine gratification. Two cups later I was out front lashing a fly-rod tube to my old orange backpack at a table made out of a piece of plywood and two sawhorses when Heidi rumbled down the rock-cobbled driveway in her yellow pickup truck. She backed up to the porch that had a roof but still no floor. The September morning was crisp enough on the shady side of the mountain that goose bumps puckered in the sun-bleached hair on my bare arms and legs as Heidi climbed down from behind the wheel.

"I brought you something," she said. "A housewarming present."

"You shouldn't have," I said. "What is it?"

"Yes, I should have," she replied, throwing back a canvas tarp to uncover two cardboard boxes in the bed of the truck.

"Wow," I said. "A toilet!"

It was almost enough to make me want to stay home and plumb. Behind us the vertical fir siding on the house glowed yellow in the morning sun, the green metal roof blending with the needles on the tall fir. The home I'd built with my own hands from trees bandsawed from my own land looked like it belonged, and Heidi wrapped me in a knee-to-shoulder hug.

"You should be so proud," she said, "so very, very proud."

My goose bumps grew goose bumps. Heidi was warm across the front, so very, very warm. I exhaled for wiggling room and took a quick step backward. We stood slightly apart, listening to the chickadees fighting over sunflower seeds in the tray of the birdfeeder.

"So," I finally said. "What do you hear from the Kingfish?"

The chickadees flocked off as a squirrel jumped in from an overhanging branch.

"Not too much," Heidi said. "Just that he agreed to sign the divorce papers."

I've seen it before, too many times. With women, when they quit loving, it's like turning off a faucet. And men, they didn't even know the water was running until the tap runs dry.

"Is he talking to anyone yet?" I asked.

The Kingfish had drawn eighteen months with time off for good behavior. It could have been worse; the original charge was attempted homicide. I'd gone with a contingent of Nitwits to say hello. The Kingfish wouldn't even leave his cell to come to the scratched bulletproof window at the yellow-green greeting-visitor area.

"Nobody yet," she said. "But he asked for his guitar."

Chattering furiously at the feeder, two gray jays chased the squirrel back into the trees.

"We should get going," I said. "It's a long hike, and I told Harry I'd stop by and sign some books down at the Fly Shop this morning."

Heidi bit her lip and crossed her arms like bandoliers on her chest, white-knuckled hands clenching opposite shoulders. She needed a hug so bad that she was hugging herself but Butte girls grow up tough. Before I could make up my mind to help, Heidi reached over and grabbed a cardboard box by the cutout handles. The tendons in her forearms flexed as she easily swung half the packaged toilet out over the dented bed of her truck.

"Hey, Mac," she said like a Jersey longshoreman, "where you want dis t'ing?"

The toilet went on top of a stack of two-by-sixes against the wall, my old backpack went in the back of Heidi's truck, and we were ready to roll. I didn't even lock the door since I'd only be gone for a couple of days.

The Fly Shop was on the drive to the trailhead that led to Napi Peak. Inside the low-ceilinged room full of feathers and fleece a small television in the corner was tuned to CNN. It was unusual because nobody watches television in a trout shop. On the screen a jet airplane had just flown in an orange ball of flame into the side of the World Trade Center.

"Why is everybody watching a movie?" said Heidi.

It was my thought exactly: *It can't be real*. But every person in the room stared at the television as the hypnotizing footage ran again. The exact same airplane again burst into the exact same orange ball of flame against the exact same side of the South Tower. A chubby man in a Yankees hat held a cell phone to his ear, tears coursing down his face.

"If Jimmy left at six-thirty," he said, "then he must have already been at work."

The screen on the television changed to a live picture and both towers of the World Trade Center were on fire. The banner of words beneath the picture said the Pentagon had been attacked, the White House was being evacuated, and Arab terrorists were suspected. Black columns of smoke billowed into the blue sky above the World Trade Center. A harried reporter's voice came over the tinny speaker.

"Here's what we think we know so far," he said, "At about eight forty-five Eastern Time—"

I checked the clock. It was five minutes after eight, Mountain Time.

"—the first of two what appear to be commercial airliners cra—"

The voice stopped midsyllable in obvious shock. I looked from the clock back to the television set as the South Tower of the World Trade Center collapsed in a heap of dust. It happened so fast I almost missed it. Where there had been a building, there was only blue sky and white smoke; a cell phone clattered to the floor as the man in the Yankees hat rubbed both eyes with the heels of his pudgy hands.

"The bastards," he said. "The dirty bastards."

His son Jimmy worked in the North Tower, which twenty-three minutes later peeled apart from the top down in a white cloud with a black mushroom top. The Pentagon was on fire, and another airliner had crashed southeast of Pittsburgh. Commercial air traffic was suspended indefinitely.

A dark-haired woman in brown nylon chest waders was renting a mid-sized car, her voice shrill as she shouted into her cell phone. "That's right. Something with a CD player," she said. "I'll pick it up this afternoon. It's imperative that I'm back in Nebraska by Thursday morning."

Bernie hadn't gotten the World Trade Center; I wondered who had. Somebody had just lost a whole boatload of money and it was the merest tip of a financial iceberg. The Fly Shop phones were ringing and the computer had mail. Cancellations were arriving in a steady stream. The Twin Towers fell for what could have been the hundredth time and I wondered how long Heidi had been nestled under my arm. The silver barracudas on my black silk shirt were dripping wet with her tears. In ten years it was the first time I'd seen her cry.

"We have to leave," she said.

Two men stood at the oak table grid of compartmentalized flies discussing the relative merits of crippled mayfly imitations. Above their heads the scrolling letters on the glowing screen said five warships and two carriers had just been launched.

"We can't leave," I said. "There's too many—"

Heidi slapped my cheek hard enough to leave a red palm print.

"Snap out of it," she said. "It's sadistic showing this over and over like that."

Of course, Heidi was right. I'd never been so glad to get away from anything in my life as I was glad to get away from that endless loop of television suffering.

The road to Napi Peak led to a gravel parking lot, then became a single-file dirt trail that grew fainter until it finally dissolved in a storm-tossed stand of lodgepole pine. The trees were four inches around, eighty feet long, and jackstrawed everywhere. Bushwhacking through was like crawling through a maze of giant gray, brown, and yellow Pick Up Sticks.

You'd be tempted to tightrope over the top rather than clamber through the middle, but if you did, beware the yellow trees. Those shiny trunks of sap-covered pine had just lost their bark and were as slippery as soap. A patch of soggy moss only partially cushioned my fall into the cool, dark ravine; I lay on my back, feeling the ache of the day in every bone.

"What's going to happen?" I said.

Heidi's somber face appeared in a hole between the crossed trees above my head.

"War," she replied.

Back at the Fly Shop I'd been ravenously thirsty for hot Arab blood, all in favor of lashing back with a blast of America's technological might. But here in the quiet of the forest history did not propose a war on the other side of the planet as a viable solution.

"Before they do anything crazy," I said, "I hope they remember Vietnam."

I'd fallen into a patch of ripe huckleberries, and Heidi pulled a Ziploc bag from her pack. "They'll remember all right," she said. "Especially the guys that sell the bullets."

We talked in bits and bursts, between bites as we filled both our mouths and the bag with tart purple berries. The problem with smart bombs is that no bomb is that smart. If you kill somebody's mother or brother it's not something they're going to forget.

"A war is just going to create a whole new generation of suicide martyrs," I said.

And you had to give Muhammad credit. He'd recruited a holy army by convincing his warriors that if they died in battle a bevy of virgins would be anxiously awaiting their arrival in heaven. Fifteen hundred years later that promise was enough that Muslims were still willing to make the ultimate sacrifice by flying planes into buildings as Heidi flipped a huckleberry in the air and caught it between her teeth.

"Men," she said with a purple tongue. "What is it about that Y chromosome?"

It was an issue I'd often contemplated. I'd read that men think about sex every couple of minutes, but the data seemed flawed. It wasn't nearly that long for me. Now that I'd reached my fourth decade I still thought about sex more than any other single thing, I just didn't think about it more than everything else combined. If that wasn't a sign of maturity I didn't know what was.

"I don't know," I said, "Maybe it's just that in the libido hope springs eternal."

We talked as we walked until at last we broke through into the boulder-studded meadows above the pencil-sharp timberline. Columns of jagged peaks carved by the icy snow-blue remnants of once mighty glaciers marched to the horizon. The air tasted thin, impossibly clear, the mountains sharp-edged as cardboard cutouts against the azure sky as we strolled through crackly brown bunchgrass speckled red and yellow and blue with dried wildflowers.

The solitude, the majesty, the sense of insignificance—the high country was healing, not in the way of forgetting, but in the way of letting go. By the time all those plodding steps added up to Wind Maker Lake it was hard to think of anything except being tired. Climbing mountains was a lot harder than I remembered it, and I remembered it as being pretty hard.

My pack crashed to the pebble beach like fifty pounds of liposuction. When you drop that pack you feel so light and springy it's like you can fly. For about five minutes. Then all you're good for is falling over. With the backpack for a pillow and the stony beach for a bed, my body burst into song. Then the snap, crackle, and pop of my shifting ligaments, tendons, and bones was drowned out by a roll of rattling thunder.

Heidi groaned. "We'd better set up the tent," she said.

She sat up toward the lake, but only got as far as resting back on her elbows.

"Holy shit!" she said.

Rigging a rod never seems to take so long as when fish are jumping, and huge silver torpedoes were leaping through the calm air before the storm. Responsible adult trout that should have known better were cavorting about like foolish minnows. The mirrored surface of the lake dribbled with a hatch of so many speckle-winged mayflies, it looked like rain. You couldn't keep the fish off the hook. They hit anything that moved as the thunder reverberated closer and closer until the ground shook like steel tracks under a runaway train.

The storm cloud billowed in over Napi Peak so quickly that the sky turned black between casts. I barely had time to reel in my line before a solid wall of pelting rain drove us to the meager shelter of stunted subalpine fir etched into curious bonsai shapes by ice crystals driven on the winter winds. We hunkered with our backs to the wind in the lee of a tree shaped like a goat's face. Heidi punched my arm then held her hands a good three feet apart. "Ten pounds!" she shouted, her lips to my ear. "You weren't kidding."

Fifteen minutes later the sun was out and you would have sworn there wasn't a fish in the whole lake. We tried everything on those big trout. Nothing worked. I was twitching a couple of weighted nymphs beside a logjam when a distant crack of thunder again flipped nature's switch. As quickly as that, the water dimpled with mayflies and I had a pair of fish on the line, which jumped in opposite directions and just as quickly broke off.

We built camp between tempests and fished the thunderheads until the cool of evening stars toppled the towering black clouds. Making fire was a cinch with parchment-dry driftwood; a foil-wrapped trout stuffed with onions, fresh parsley, and sliced lemons roasted in the orange coals. Butter-browned peppers-and-potatoes sizzled in an aluminum skillet. Heidi stretched her bare feet toward the flames, wiggling toenails done up in black beetles on shiny red flake.

"So," she said, "All these years you've just been pretending you couldn't cook."

"Sauce du jour?" I said, handing her a bottle of ketchup.

The instant cheesecake was chilling at the edge of the lake, outlined with the silhouette of the Twin Towers in purple huckleberries. The two-liter bota bag of white wine was growing limp. Half an hour later the fish was a picked-over skeleton in the yellow ring of firelight as I heaped on a fresh armload of gnarled driftwood. It was going to happen, I knew it, and my leg started to cramp I was so tensed up.

"Sit down over here," said Heidi, patting the beach at her hip, "and keep me warm."

I was surprised at how much I wanted to do exactly that. The day's events had the effect on me of reinforcing the essential hedonism of Reduced Humanism. If there's something you want to do, do it, because you might not get another chance. I closed my eyes but Heidi obviously didn't because we were locked up to our tonsils in a kiss when her warm hands fell from my cheeks. She leaned back on her knees, squinting over my shoulder at the fire.

"Do you believe in God?" she said.

If there is a God, He needs his prescription changed. When I turned around to look an unmistakable image of a fire-nosed Kingfish crackled in the head-high flames. The Kingfish brandished a flickering hatchet in his hand as Heidi plucked a fire-warmed rock off the beach and walked toward the lake. I was left alone with one huckleberry tower still standing on the half-eaten cheesecake.

Heidi said: "You never answered my question."

Any concept of God has to explain pervasive human suffering. "There's lots of Gods," I said. "It's just that they couldn't care less."

It is possible to view the universe as an amusement park and the earth as the Tilt-A-Whirl of Life. We get to ride the Tilt-A-Whirl until we run out of tokens; meanwhile Gravity, Fusion, Magnetism, Electricity, and all the other Gods watch us the way we watch Shakespeare in the Park. All these various Gods are both uncaring and half crazy. Electricity especially could stand to double His dose of lithium. The Amusement Park stays open until a state of maximum disorder is reached, which makes Entropy the Boss God, because He wins in the end.

"What about you?" I said. "What do you think? Is there a God?"

A stone splashed in the darkness. Heidi's voice came from the same place. "She's a Catholic."

Talk about a mood killer: That face in the fire was definitely it. Unrequited guilt made for a restless night in the tent. Heidi's blue sleeping bag tossed and turned alongside my red one. It was easy to rise with the sun. Boiled coffee and instant oatmeal didn't have the liberating effect of two liters of white wine; breakfast was a quick and silent affair.

Twin plumes of white breath condensed on the chill morning air as we started side by side up the South Face of Napi Peak. Talus, the heap of broken rock that piles up at the base of mountains, is a task most Odor-Eaters aren't up to. The boulders settle out over the centuries, leaving pebbles at the surface. Climbing is like scrambling up a steep roof shingled with ball bearings. For every three steps up you slide two steps back. Blinded with stinging sweat, you keep surging forward, because every time you stop you begin sliding right back to the bottom. The stones in that half a mile of diagonal talus below Napi Peak had been accumulating for eons, and that's how long it seemed to take before we cliffed out at a soaring escarpment of black diorite.

The cliffs, an ancient flow of lava from a chain of extinct volcanoes, are all that stand between you and the summit, and present an entirely new set of problems. First of all, you can fall off. Some places it's no harder than climbing a ladder, but others it's four thousand feet straight down. The route leads around to the sheer North Face where you concentrate on one thing and one thing only: never moving more than one hand or one foot at a time, because when you're hanging by a thread there's no room for mistakes.

There is a euphoria in climbing mountains because it isn't arbitrary. You either do it or you don't, and from the summit you can't do any better. You will be giddy because there isn't as much oxygen up high. For once in your life, you've done everything possible. You can relax because there's nothing left to do but enjoy the view.

At the top of Napi Peak there's a flat spot about the size of a living room with a hundred-mile view in every direction. To the east the Great Plains faded into purple haze past the khaki green of the Sweet Grass Hills. Far below, the tent was a tiny red speck alongside the blue oval dot of Wind Maker Lake. Striated rock tables were strewn haphazardly about the summit, sculpted glacial remnants of pure sun-baked lounging pleasure.

It was warm enough even at ten thousand feet that Heidi sprawled flat on her back in a black sports bra, using her yellow cotton shirt as a pillow. She was snoring lightly, her curves joining with the long line of hard-capped peaks rising off to the north. I tugged boots and socks off aching feet, then settled into a rock with the smooth curves of a reclining Barcalounger. The slightest of breezes rustled the coarse black hair on my toes. There might never have ever been a yesterday except for the clear, blue sky.

I'd climbed dozens of mountains but had never seen a sky without a white contrail. The planes were still grounded. I wondered how long it would last. September and October are two of my busiest months, and I stood to lose a bunch of work. At least there would be time to finish my house. I'd have to do something for money but the thought of a real job just put me to sleep. The next thing I knew Heidi was shaking me awake.

"Get up," she said. "Get up!"

I shivered, my throat dry as sand. It had gotten colder. The thunder boomed before I'd even opened my eyes. The top of a mountain is no place to be during an electrical storm. There would be no dillydallying in the lava cliffs. The hard part is a North Face ledge that's thirty feet long and a little narrower than a telephone book. With your nose scraping the sheer black stone, you crab-walk, heels hanging out in space behind you, fingers searching above you for the tiny cracks that serve as handholds. Below the ledge it's a couple of thousand feet straight down. Even so I'm not convinced a slip that afternoon would have been fatal.

That's how many insects we encountered, a cloud thick enough to cushion a fall. The drop in barometric pressure ahead of the storm instigated a monumental hatch of pale purple-blue army cutworm moths that smothered us in a viscous lavender haze. A swirling blue mist of rustling wings enveloped us as we worked our way off the ledge and down the giant rock staircase that opened out onto the top of the talus slope. Bugs clogged the air, tickled our cheeks, plugged my ears. A swooping flock of gray-crowned rosy finches worked a fog of moths so thick I smelled the trouble before I saw it. The sour, nitrogen-rich, piglike stench was unmistakable. When I turned to warn Heidi, her nostrils were already flared so wide she'd lost the freckles on her nose as she pulled a bleeding forefinger from her mouth.

"Bear," we whispered together.

I'd seen the feathery blue-gray scat of undigested wings on a dozen different mountains, but never watched it happen until a moaning gust of wind raised the hair on the back of my head and parted the purple cloud. Cutworm moths hatch so prodigiously in the harsh land above timberline that even five-hundred-pound bears will feed selectively. The monster grizzly was fifty feet away, a silver-tipped hump of muscle the size of a wheelbarrow swaying between his shoulders.

It would have been an easy cast. I've fair-hooked everything from alligators to chickens on a fly rod, and a grizzly would raise the bar of wildlife casting to new heights. I'd be the envy of Montana natives everywhere. The bear swallowed without chewing, bugs disappearing down the black hole of his throat like water swirling down a three-inch drain. Then he stopped, sat up, and squinted our way. With the rising wind coming down the mountain he had our scent.

Ropes of chunky blue drool spilled between long yellow fangs as the grizzly made up his mind to charge. The first charge is nearly always a bluff; all you can do is hold your ground. If you panic and run, you're dead. Bears can't resist chasing down their food, and over the first hundred yards they're faster than racehorses. Two mighty talus-scattering bounds later the roaring silver-tipped bear pulled up fifteen feet away, eight feet tall on his hind legs, clawing at the air with both front feet, spraying streams of moth husks with every barking grunt.

At this point you have two choices. You can curl up in a fetal ball on the ground, or you can act like the predator you are and not the prey you might become. I opened my Swiss Army knife and waved both hands over my head, putting up as formidable a front as possible. Grizzlies have notoriously poor eyesight; all he'd see was a blurry silhouette. If I looked tougher than I really was, the bear might be satisfied with just showing us he could have eaten us instead of actually eating us. It's also a good idea to either talk or sing.

"Hey Mister Bear," I said quietly. "Don't do anything we're both going to regret."

The bear's rheumy eyes narrowed to angry bloodshot slits. All I could think of was "Turkey in the Straw." When I began to sing the bear's hairy brown snout wrinkled into an expression every bit as human as the horrible surprise of a boy's first taste of chewing tobacco. The bear's eyes blossomed like frightened red cherries as he dropped to all fours, turned, and bounded down the talus in a skidding avalanche of miniature rockslides.

Heidi squeezed my arm hard enough to leave fingerprints.

"My hero," she said in her shaky Mae West voice.

I looked at my knife. Something had scared that bear. It sure wasn't me.

"My voice is bad," I said, "but not that bad."

The wind came up so quickly it knocked us to our knees in the same instant that the cliff behind our heads exploded in a blinding flare of white light. Thunder rolled out a two-count later, and a hailstone the size of a radish shattered five feet away. Thirty seconds after that the torrential hail could have flayed the hide from a cow.

The only available shelter was a small cave formed beneath a leaning slab of fallen rock at the bottom of the rock staircase. The ground quivered as pile-driving concussions of light and sound flashed in and out as regular as a strobe, painting the blackness with alternating instants of electron-blue. The air buzzed with electricity that crawled like snakes on my skin and caterpillars in my beard. Heidi's braid stood up and danced to the calypso beat of the lightning barrage, a green ball of phosphorescence gleaming at the knotted blond tip.

The glow is called Saint Elmo's fire, and it's usually the last thing you see before you poke a fork into the celestial toaster. Heidi's hair was wiggling toward the roof because the lightning wanted to bypass the insulating resistance of the air in the cave by arcing down the path of least resistance through our ionized bodies. We could be reduced to cinders at any instant, fifty-watt filaments in a six-million-volt cave.

It's one thing to have electricity; it's another to Be Electricity. It was like sharing skin as we embraced in a slippery lip-lock of cold green fire. Adrenaline and testosterone formed a potent cocktail. Heidi was naked except for socks and boots as she straddled my thighs; I still had on my shirt, although the buttons had been torn asunder. For whatever reason her nipples and my ears glowed with the same green flame that still fluoresced at the end of her hair.

You'd think for one day that would be enough entertainment to satisfy even the most voyeuristic cabal of deities, but once the Gods saw how much fun Electricity was having, Gravity decided He'd play along, too. Sunshine splashed down on the wet gleaming rocks and the rain quit as quickly as it had begun, which was about how long it took Heidi to get dressed.

An (unfortunately) short lived side-effect of having been electrified was that twenty years seemed to have been removed from my eyesight. I could read the writing on the wall; I could see the tiny letters on Heidi's blue backpack as she undid the red-and-white-striped bungee cords holding down her ice ax even though she was a good hundred feet away.

"Last one to the bottom is a rotten egg," she called out, then disappeared.

Scrambled egg was more like it. The possibility of pain is the price of trust, and too many times I'd paid with my soul. Because whatever we'd just done, I'd give anything to do it again.

By the time I'd gathered myself Heidi was already halfway down the long snowfield that stretches nearly to the waterfalls at the northeast end of Wind Maker Lake, trailing a linked string of symmetrical S-turns carved into the snow. It was Nature's Escalator and I started my own glissade, stomach to the sky, leaning back on the ice ax that served as both rudder and brake. The afternoon snow was bright even behind sunglasses and soft as mashed potatoes. The heels of my boots cut sparkling twin troughs flanked by curling white waves.

The towering, sharp-edged thunderhead had blown out to the east. A dark tendril fell off to the south like a long black braid; a broken ski slope of a nose was forming to the north. Maybe it was my imagination but maybe it was all-but-forgotten Plains Indian medicine. The face in last night's fire had been vivid enough to chill the spine. I was so engrossed watching the transforming cloud that I'd never noticed as the soft white snow became hard black ice.

A spring rockslide had disintegrated as it rolled down the field of snow, leaving a trail of dark debris to soak up the sun's heat. For weeks the dirty snow had been thawing and settling during the day, then refreezing at night, until it had built into an enormous half-pipe of glare ice. In the time it took my pupils to dilate I was plunging down the fall line, the red palm trees on my buttonless blue shirt flapping in the wind of my descent.

I angled my feet hard left, braced like a taut wire against the chattering ice ax, but the concave chute was forty feet wide and five feet deep. I stalled out on the steep lip and slid hard back for the middle, building lateral momentum that I hoped would carry me up and out the other side. The tip of the aluminum ice ax screeched like fingernails on an icy blackboard. I was descending at a good thirty miles an hour when I smashed into a basketball-sized hunk of diorite and flipped into the air.

The half-pipe dropped away. It was a hawk's-eye view, eerily quiet in the calm air, and when I dropped back out of the sky I was down to the last trick of a dying mountaineer. It's the simple self-arrest: Sliding feetfirst on your belly, you jab the pointed ice ax into anything you can find except you. Keep your elbows in; otherwise the sudden jerk as the tip bites can rip your shoulders right out of their sockets.

I didn't stop completely until the hard ice of the half-pipe petered out in the spreading base at the bottom of the slope. I'd fallen farther than the World Trade Center, and the smoking images of devastation burned like melting film in my mind. Another hundred feet and I'd have been smeared on the craggy rocks below. I tried to open the white knuckles clenched to the blue metal shaft by my shoulder but my fingers wouldn't move. I remained welded to my ice ax until Heidi arrived to pry me loose and relay the judge's award for my fall.

"Out of a possible ten points," she said, "that ride was worth a thousand."

It was an astronomical score, unheard of, and that's what worried me.

Change begets change. What I've noticed about life is that once things start to happen, they tend to keep right on happening. It's momentum, mass times velocity, and it wasn't just me. The human race is accelerating at an exponential rate. Overdosed with leftover adrenaline I quivered like a shocked fish as blood from my flayed chest stained the white snow beneath me red, wondering what Entropy had planned next.

The Testicle Festival

THIRTEEN MONTHS LATER I BLINKED, cleaving apart eyelashes stuck together with the crusty yellow stuff that grows of its own volition in the fertile night. It was Halloween morning, a day I'd been dreading every one of those last thirteen months. At least it was still dark outside as I curled in bed listening to the staccato rattle of rain against the green metal roof. I didn't have to get up yet. There was time to just lie there, snug against the storm.

The rumpled goose-down quilt was warm and comforting but nowhere near as warm as jalapeño Heidi. We were fused together in the flannel sheets like hot glued spoons, her back to my front, Heidi whimpering softly in the bad dreams that chase her through the dark. Supple skin stretched then popped as I peeled my forearm from her sticky chest. I felt for her temple, massaging the soft crease in slow circles with my thumb until her breathing slowed.

My upstairs bedroom has a lofted ceiling that angles down toward the pillows. The gusting tempest was in my ear, ten inches of insulation away. The east window that opens toward the rising sun was as black as the rest of the wall. There wasn't even the faintest glimmer of coming dawn. It was far too early to be so wide awake after such a late night.

A moment or two generally passes before I think of girls in the morning, and I moved my thumb from Heidi's head to the pale cherry gumdrop that rose from her fist-sized breast. That the next orgasm is the best orgasm had been a guiding precept, all my life, but if that was true I was about to go up in smoke. Last night I'd arrived home soon after dusk following a long day of guiding in a cold wind, the glowing windows in my house grinning like a face at the end of the driveway. A box of mail-order Godiva chocolates in my hand, I'd knocked on the door.

"Trick or tree . . ."

The traditional Halloween greeting died in my mouth as the door swung open.

"Since it's All Hallows' Eve," said Heidi, "I thought something pagan might be in order."

Hand on a high round hip, lean calf muscles stretched tight to the tendons above four-inch stiletto heels, she posed in the golden rectangle of the exposed doorway. The see-through lace of her lingerie was emerald green to match her eyes and shoes. Below the fringed silk hem her oiled legs were bare, rising to a patch of curly hair that hung like a squirrel's tail in the light of hundreds of candles arranged to burn in the shape of a giant pentagram on the newly varnished white-oak floor.

"Champagne?" she said sweetly.

A raised altar of scarlet throw pillows flickered in the candlelight at the center of the pentagram. At the foot of the altar a knobbed bottle was iced down in a recycled drywall bucket. I untwisted the wire basket, then shot the cork into the vaulted ceiling, where it bounced off a wood beam and pruned a small branch from the top of the fifteen-foot ficus in the corner.

The first glass of champagne we shared with a kiss, slow dancing to Van Morrison on the stereo. The second glass of champagne I held in my shaking fingers as Heidi wiggled into the throne of oversized pillows for a good fit, like she expected to be there a while. The fantasy express roared down the tracks as Heidi's slender fingers lifted a mounded black square of silk fabric from what it covered on the floor alongside the altar.

"You're kidding?" I said. "Right?"

"I'm kidding?" she replied. "Never."

Heidi had pulled back the cloth to reveal a blue ceramic bowl of freshly whipped cream, a jar of jasmine-scented oil, and a double-edged Lady Gillette razor. It had been twenty-five years since I'd shaved anything even as innocent as my face and I knocked back the champagne in one gulp. No matter how pagan the ceremony, drawing blood was out of the question.

"Do you have any helpful hints?" I asked.

Heidi settled back into the pillows, licking her glossy green lips, knees up and slightly spread. Her emerald eyes locked on my sapphire eyes and the world turned to diamonds as my lungs dried up. The spell was broken as Heidi blindfolded herself with the square of black silk.

"It's just like building a house," she replied. "Start at the bottom and work your way up."

I squeezed her thigh, the skin as hot and brown as sizzling butter under my clammy palm. Right off the bat I ruled out the ankle bones; they would be trickier than an Adam's apple, which was mostly why I'd quit shaving in the first place.

The cream was cool on the oiled skin, sweet to the touch of the tip of my tongue. The long, tapered muscle in Heidi's calf hung loose, then tightened at the first touch of steel. I placed each of her feet in turn on my shoulder to get at the meaty underside. Heidi's soft moans were running together as I worked my way ever upward against the grain of the fine blond mist. The smooth calves were clear sailing, the thighs a breeze after the tricky knees, and finally I was kneeling wide-eyed at the forest surrounding the slippery wet gates to the Promised Land.

The lump in my throat was jumping around like a barking dog. I could barely speak.

"Huh-huh-how high?" I croaked.

The sharply defined tendons on the inside of her upper thighs twitched continuously as Heidi slipped two pillows under her hips to improve the angle.

"Huh-huh-high," she said.

Sex researchers say men on average contemplate an erotic act every eight minutes. Since puberty that meant I'd been the conduit of more than two million fantasies, none of which remotely involved shaving a woman's legs. I don't have many regrets but that was one. The libido-boiling intimacy of the short, clean razor strokes was off the charts. Just lying behind Heidi remembering it, my penis was swollen like a blimp in a blast furnace. The mattress barely contained the three of us, and I have a queen-sized bed. The rest of the previous night replayed itself scene by scene and only then, as I lay back on Halloween morning with blood gushing through every organ except my brain, did it dawn on me.

It wasn't early, it was late. It wasn't dark, I was blindfolded.

The room filled with gray, stormy light as I pulled the square of rolled silk up over the top of my head. The wrong digits glowed red on the alarm clock that hadn't been set. I poked a finger through the jumble of blond hair on the pillow and tickled Heidi's sensitive earlobe.

"M-m-m-m," she said, pulling the covers up over her head.

"It's ten," I said, shaking the highest round lump under the curled ball of quilt.

"Ten-n-m-m," she mumbled.

Then her entire body went stiff. I cleared the runway just in time. Heidi windmills out of bed in the morning like a weed whacker on jet fuel. She was in the air, on the floor, and singing in the shower in the time it took me to put bare feet on the unfinished plywood floor.

I pulled on jeans and sheepskin slippers, then went down the oak quarter-turn staircase to start the coffee. The front room that overlooked the river looked like an exploded duckling. At some point in the bacchanalia a couple of the throw pillows had blown seams. Tiny white feathers were everywhere. A brassiere trailed flapping straps from the ceiling fan over the kitchen island counter, the billowing C-cups slightly sordid in the cold light of the cloudy day.

As light and airy as congealed ether, that's how Heidi filled the void. Her steps on the stairs after showering were gentle as falling leaves. Her hair, darker when wet, was still the straight yellow of sun-bleached wheat, and she smiled as she brushed past where I was kneeling on the floor picking up feathers fossilized in lumps of candle wax.

"How's your hand?" I asked.

Heidi had been dancing on the kitchen counter. In those spiked heels she was plenty tall enough to stick her hand in the twirling mahogany blades of the fan. The bra she'd been twirling over her head was snatched away, and now Heidi rolled her eyes as she rubbed ruefully at the purple bruise in the shape of the ace of spades that had formed on the back of her hand.

"Being blond," she said. "Somebody has to do it."

I smiled back and said: "You make it look so easy."

I went back to picking up feathers so Heidi grabbed the phone when it rang. The receiver clamped between her ear and shoulder, Heidi listened a few moments as she filled an insulated go-cup with coffee, then said loudly: "Elk meat? You want elk meat? Of course our elk meat is guaranteed raw."

Heidi listened a moment more, and was almost shouting as she said: "Well, if you don't want raw elk meat then what the hell are you calling here for?"

She hung up hard and gave the phone the finger.

"Telemarketers," she explained.

It was funny but I didn't laugh. I stared without focusing at the rain through the window, wondering what came next. I was lost enough in melancholy to be startled by the twin press of Heidi's chest as she hugged me lightly from behind.

"You're awfully quiet this morning," she said.

I leaned into her the way a plant grows toward the sun, her hair damp against my cheek. "I'm just wondering what to say this afternoon," I said. "Got any ideas?"

I'd been dreading the day because Halloween marked the Kingfish's last day in jail. I was picking him up at two, wondering what words to use to tell him his ex-wife had moved some of her clothes into my closet, thinking maybe those words just don't exist.

"People gossip," Heidi finally said. "He probably already knows."

I wasn't sure whether that made me feel better or not.

"Can I ask you something?" I said. "Something personal?"

I hadn't noticed Heidi's warm breath on my ear until it stopped.

"Sure," she whispered.

Congealed ether travels randomly at the speed of light. I wasn't sure I could keep up.

"Do you think you'll ever get bored with me?" I asked.

Heidi stepped away so quickly I stumbled backward and nearly fell.

"Hell," she said, "I get bored with myself."

Then she swept up her coffee along with an armload of papers and books.

"Whoops," she said, "look at the time."

She backed through the front door, her dandelion-yellow parka disappearing through the empty rain-splattered window down the stone walkway in the gray spitting drizzle. The engine on her truck whined and finally caught, then Heidi's square-jawed face was back at the window, puckering sloppy, red kisses on the wet glass.

You'll be fine, she mouthed.

Heidi took her caffeine on the run. I took mine to the fly-tying vise at the table by the bookshelves. Wise women knit for a reason. Busy hands liberate the brain. The repetitive nature of tying flies is a soothing finger mantra that sets the mind free to roam. I let my mind go, hoping for inspiration, since in a little more than three hours I was picking the Kingfish up in Cow Coulee, and still didn't know what to say to him.

I wrapped waxed olive thread on a hook, thinking how your average male had no chance with your average female. And Heidi was far from average. She'd set me up on the Napi Peak trip. The Duke told me afterward she'd volunteered to staff the phone banks at the next Trout Unlimited fund-raising drive if he'd pretend he wanted to climb the mountain, and then back out. My gut churned with strong coffee thinking how Heidi had connived to get me alone.

Because once she had me where she wanted me she let me go.

Four forces are generally acknowledged to hold the universe together. The strong and weak nuclear forces bind atoms and electrons, gravity spins the planets, the electromagnetic force brings us light and sound. That's as far as science takes it but I'd add a fifth force, the power of human love. Love may be the most powerful force of all, because without gravity all you do is fly off into space. It's love that has the power to hurt.

I spun up the scissors hanging off my right forefinger and cut the thread. A relationship without physical attraction, no thanks. Whatever it is that makes one person catch their breath when they catch a glimpse of another person in a crowded room, I can't live without it. At least that's what I'd told myself all those years, but in a quarter century of trying I'd had every kind of relationship there was except one that lasted. I dropped another completed fly into the pile wondering if somehow I'd gotten it all wrong.

Old and Home Alone wasn't a movie I cared to star in. After a ridiculously healthy life last spring I'd been in the hospital with kidney stones; it was a grim realization that I had nobody's name to write in the space where they ask for somebody to contact in case you don't wake up. Heidi had appeared unexpectedly next to the aluminum pole that held my morphine pump, and for the last six months we'd been on again. But more than any woman I'd ever known Heidi ran all the way hot or all the way cold, like I needed her more than she needed me, like it was only a question of time until I'd wake up one morning and she'd be gone.

Again.

I tried to think about the Kingfish but all I could remember was Heidi. I picked up the flies and put on my coat, but even driving into Cow Coulee she still ricocheted around in my skull like an obsessive bullet that kept the rest of my thoughts ducking for cover in obscure synapses. I drove slow enough that I was late and still couldn't come up with any ideas, so when the time came to break the news, I didn't.

"Kingfish," I lied. "You're looking good."

The Kingfish cackled as he stomped barefoot circles in the dead grass. His cracked leather cowboy boots had been cast aside on the splintered sidewalk.

"Yeah," he said, "it's been like living in a spa."

The Kingfish was so gaunt I hardly recognized him. His face was more yellow than brown, and he was wheezing as he danced on the frozen brown lawn below the concrete lions that flanked the courthouse steps. His red flannel shirt hung gunnysack-loose as he chanted a medicine song, and on every eighth beat he raised both hands to the heavy stratus clouds that weren't quite raining out here on the lower elevation of the plains.

"Here," I said, after a couple more revolutions. "This is for you."

The Kingfish stopped dancing, his black eyes as piercing as they'd ever been.

"Dynamite?" he panted. "It's a clear violation of my parole."

I held out the red crepe paper cylinder complete with an oversized fuse.

"Open it."

The Kingfish reached for the cartoon explosive with his left hand, catching me off guard as he stepped in with an uppercut right to the solar plexus behind the heavy-duty zipper on the belly of my rain jacket. It was a good punch for an emaciated old man. The Kingfish licked blood from his knuckles, then reached down to help me up. I slapped the jaundiced hand away. The Kingfish cackled again.

"I knew how guilty you'd feel," he said. "That was more for you than me."

The cold air burned in my lungs as I took deep, calming breaths. He knew.

"It just happened," I said. "The whole thing, it came as a complete surprise."

In the silence I had quick vision of green nipples erect with Saint Elmo's fire.

"Yeah," the Kingfish finally replied. "To nobody but you."

The north wind briefly trembled in the naked limbs of elm trees stripped for winter, then died down as I stood up. The Kingfish lit a cigarette, shooting smoke down both nostrils like he'd just touched off a side-by-side shotgun. He opened the soft leather of the doe-skin pouch that hung from his neck, felt inside with nicotine-stained fingers, and produced an odd-looking oversized dry fly he cupped reverently in his palm.

"Meet the Jailbird," he said. "Everything in that fly, it came from my cell."

I bent down for a closer look, balanced on the balls of my feet, not expecting another punch but ready just the same. The Jailbird had a bright pink wing, the kind of pink that causes cancer in laboratory animals, and the hook was far too thick and shiny.

"Did you tie it on a paper clip?" I asked.

"Feel how sharp I got it," the Kingfish said proudly.

Then he smiled like a fast lizard surrounded by slow bugs.

"And you're gonna love this," he said. "The dubbing is bushy-tailed wood rat fur."

Transplanted rats from the double-long still had the run of the jailhouse ventilation system. To mark his territory the Kingfish had speared one with a fork. The feathers were from the mattress, the thread from a sweater; the Kingfish lightly tapped the upright parachute wing he'd unraveled from government-issue socks.

"One hundred percent polyester," he said. "It'll float like a cork."

A little color in the wing is good (especially if your eyes are over forty) because it helps you see the fly out there on the water. But this wing wasn't just pink, it evanesced with its own fire, like a fringe fluorescent on a prodigal visit to the ordinary spectrum of visible light.

"Bright pink socks?" I said. "In jail?"

He shook his head as he replaced the Jailbird in the leather medicine pouch. "The socks come white," he said. "But I dyed them in the cherry cobbler they serve Sunday nights. I got the idea from what it did to my shits."

He'd been laughing since the day I'd met him, but now his rumbling chuckle rasped into a dry, wracking cough. I wondered how many packs a day the Kingfish was up to in jail.

"That sounds great," I said. "You should probably have another cigarette."

It had been a sore point, the way she lectured him.

"Thank you, Heidi," he wheezed back.

The Kingfish had always seemed impervious to the cigarettes he smoked. Singing, he had the lungs of a pearl diver; hiking, he was the first one there; now he waved a hand sagging with loose, wrinkled flesh in dismissal.

"The cough is nothing," he said. "Inside it's called prisoner's hack. Even the guards get it. It's what happens when you're surrounded by cold, damp concrete twenty-four hours a day."

I was done nagging the Kingfish but the Heidi crack was still hanging in the air.

"So," I said, "what about it? Are we okay now?"

"Unless you think you'd feel better if I knocked you on your butt again," he replied.

It goes against everything the Y chromosome stands for to let another man hit you without hitting back, friend or no friend, circumstances or no circumstances. "The first punch was free," I said. "After that the price goes up."

The Kingfish smiled but didn't laugh as he rubbed his still-bleeding knuckles. "Well, then," he said, "I guess it's time you handed over that dynamite."

I was still holding the cartoon explosive and extended it again with my open palm. The Kingfish tore off the red crepe paper and ate the black licorice fuse, rubbing at the corner of his eye as he studied the parchment invitation that had been rolled up inside:

27TH ANNUAL MOUNTAIN PALACE

TESTICLE FESTIVAL AND HALLOWEEN BALL

COSTUMES, AS ALWAYS, ARE OPTIONAL BUT REQUIRED

THIS YEAR'S THEME, BECAUSE THE KINGFISH IS BUSTING OUT:

IT'S A BALL-AND-CHAIN PARTY

MUSIC BY THE NORTH FORK NITWITS.

FOLKS, YOU'VE NEVER SEEN ANYTHING LIKE IT,

SO COME ON OUT AND WELCOME HOME

AS GOOD A FRIEND AS A RIVER EVER HAD.

"Squatty did the art work," I said. "He got a new computer."

The annual Halloween Ball at the Mountain Palace is invariably the ultimate shindig of the year. It's a theme party; over the years there had been a Beach-Ball, a Sleaze-Ball, a Screw-Ball, even a Hanni-Ball Crosses

235

the Alps (in honor of elephants). You can just imagine the costumes; well, no, maybe you can't, and this year's Ball-and-Chain Party promised to be extra special.

"It could be the best Testicle Festival ever," I said.

We'd sent hundreds of invitations to thirty years of the Kingfish's friends celebrating his release from prison. Fishermen, musicians, and other one-celled organisms had been arriving in droves. Dwight Scrotum with his electric white Telecaster and Ball McCartney with his upright bass had been hanging around all week; His Holiness Pope John Ball II was expected later that afternoon. It was an overwhelming show of support and the Kingfish was all choked up.

Of course, he could have been thinking about dinner.

The Testicle Festival is a hallowed western tradition. It begins at spring branding when a calf is thrown, a knife flashes, and the difference between a bull and a steer is tossed into a galvanized washtub. A few hundred cas-trations later the tub will be heaped high with what could be racquetballs, if racquetballs came green and slimy with meandering blue veins.

Frugal ranchers view dumping the tub in the hog pen as a waste of good meat. They freeze their collections to serve later with plenty of alcohol, since that's the only sure way to get people to eat. In traditional western cookery testicles are batter-fried in boiling grease; this makes for food both hot and durable.

The first time I tried one it scalded the roof of my mouth, so I clenched it between my front teeth until it cooled, pushed it to one side with my tongue, and began to chew. And chew. And chew. The meat was tough as steel-belted radials. I looked around, observing the Festival rites, still chewing. The frail man in the green John Deere cap on the bench beside me had to be at least sixty, and he'd been worrying the same bite since before I'd sat down. His jaws finally stopped working; he lowered then lift-ed his head as he swallowed, wiggling his butt like a goose to help things settle.

"Ah-h-h-h," he sighed, plucking the next course from the heaping brown pile on the platter of grease-splattered napkins in the middle of the picnic table.

"U leally like flench-flied balls?" I said through my own mouthful.

He nodded his head vigorously up and down while squirting ketchup on a big one. "Why be a colt," he said, "when you can be a stallion?"

And then he winked so hard his horn-rimmed glasses slid down his nose. "Who knows why," he whispered, "but it works for my wife, too."

Nobody who has tried them denies the holistic health benefits; the problem is consuming statistically significant quantities of such an unpalatable aphrodisiac. The potential of the resource remained relatively untapped until Chef Jeff arrived and transformed an abandoned farmhouse into the Hilly Chili Café. If anybody could do it, Jeff could; he'd cooked all over the world supporting a fly-fishing habit for exotic species.

"Can you make them at least edible?" we pleaded. "Is there any hope at all?"

"Edible," he scoffed. "I can make those balls walk on water."

Calamari is an art form in Greece. Chef Jeff figured a testicle was nothing but squid in cow's clothing. He put on his high white hat and began by slicing the translucent green meat thin as quarters. Following a saltwater rinse the round wafers were patted dry, soaked for ten minutes in buttermilk and black pepper to break down the proteins, plunged into an ice-water bath, dipped into a tempura batter mixed with enough cornstarch to make it stick, and flash-fried in a sesame-flavored oil. The plunge into the ice-water bath is the secret step.

It's essential because the meat cooks faster than the batter, and chilled meat won't turn rubbery before the batter is crisp. If this sounds simple, it isn't. Not with a couple of heaping bushels staring you in the eye. Out of the shell they're nothing if not slippery. There are no edges to grab, and the thin bone-white scar on the fleshy pad of my index finger is a testament to Jeff's stiletto-sharp knives.

Just remembering how close I'd been to losing the tip of my finger was enough to make me shiver. I turned up the hood on my faded red rain jacket as a flurry of rain mixed with sleet raked the courthouse lawn. The Kingfish tilted his creased face up to a gray sky tarnished with clouds of streaming black ink. Raindrops trickled from the folds of yellowed skin hanging off his chin. Soaking-wet plaid flannel plastered the thin parallel chines of his jutting ribs as he raised his arms to the black storm in celebration.

"The blue-wings will be coming," he said. "It's time we ought to be going."

Blue-winged olives are the first and last mayfly hatch of the year. The inside riffle below Head-Smashed-In Pishkun is a thousand feet higher than the courthouse lions, and the gravel bar was white with three inches of wet snow by the time we arrived. It's weather blue-wings crave, their genetic niche, and one of the last good gluttonies of the year for trout.

Emerging blue-winged duns are easy pickings because they can float fifty yards or more before their wings are dry enough to fly away in the cold air, and even ten feet is a daunting gauntlet when every fish in the river is up and chomping. On the other evolutionary hand, once the bugs have made it past the navy they don't have to worry about the air force; by the time winter sets in most of the fly-catching birds are already long gone to southern climes. Walking to the river, sticky snow built up on the felt soles of my wading boots until I teetered on three-inch platform heels. I kicked the clumps free as the Kingfish rigged a rod.

"Are you sure you remember how to do this?" I asked.

"Some things you don't forget," he said.

"Then why are you using 7X?" I said. "The trout won't be leader-shy in this storm."

Seven-X tippet is thin as gossamer and too weak to be of practical use on big fish. I never use the stuff, but the Kingfish ignored my advice. He whistled the Beatles' "Norwegian Wood" between his teeth as he tied on the Jailbird, then lifted his aviator sunglasses to release a blue-wing that had flown in.

"It all depends on what you're trying to do," he said.

Forty feet away a hot-tub-sized pod of rainbows nosed up through the falling snowflakes. I stomped my feet to keep warm. The Kingfish was still whistling as he stripped off line and threw his first cast in more than a year. Theoretically the Jailbird was too big to work—a dozen times larger than any real bug on the water—and way too pink for the natural order. But at least one fish in that school had been playing hooky the day they studied selective trout.

The pink glowing fly disappeared in a black mouth. A silver rainbow tumbled through the air at the bite of the paper clip. The Kingfish yanked back as the fish jumped; the leader twanged as the tippet broke. Down in that icy water the color of cold forged steel a trout was already rubbing its hooked jaw against the gravel bottom. The barbless paper clip would pop free in moments, and the Jailbird would assume its place in the eons of accumulated river sediment. The pod was still rising and the Kingfish looked better already. Some of the color was back in his cheeks, and a little meat had filled in the cavities between the stringy tendons in his wrist as he turned with his big hand out. "Got any flies?" he said.

Snowflakes melted on his hairless skin as I reached for the plastic box in my pocket. "Hungry fish like this." I said, "You want to feed them a Half-a-Chicken."

The Half-a-Chicken is actually a duck in disguise. The fly lands light as feathers because it is feathers: CDC, an acronym for "cul de canard," which is French for the naturally oiled feathers surrounding the preen gland on a duck's butt.

Left-handed Larry at the Fly Shop named the fluffy white fly because it's so easy to see on the water—as in, "That looks like half-a-chicken floating out there." There's a reason ducks float and preen-gland oil is it.

Tied with the squared tips of four webbed feathers on a dubbed hook, the Half-a-Chicken lies so wispily on the water that the fly barely dents the surface film. For a trout looking up, that dent appears as a mirrored-silver bowl, a tiny dimple of light. Seen from below it's the same flat, bright dimple of light that a helpless mayfly drying its wings pushes into the surface film.

In terms of catching fish, think of CDC as Trout Magic.

Trout won't refuse Half-a-Chicken, not if it's over their heads. The airy-white fly is easy to see, even if the muscles in your eyes have gone the same way as the muscles in your waistline, even if you're trying to find it in a snowstorm. We went to thicker tippet and the Kingfish was hooking fish every couple of casts as the Half-a-Chicken rode the dark currents through a barrage of flakes twirling down as fat as crystal nickels.

The cliffs of Head-Smashed-In disappeared as the gloomy clouds settled in for the approaching night. Visibility was down to a couple of hundred yards. Snow fell so fast it piled up on my wool hat, and fresh snow is filled with billions of sound-absorbing air pockets. It was so quiet you could hear the snowflakes dissolve, hissing as they released the energy of their formation to a river that was greasy-silver with the force of surface tension. Even the cartwheeling trout were quiet and ripple-free as they sliced back into the river with exquisitely executed half gainers at the end of the light green fly line. The catching was as good as it ever gets but, standing there in the blizzard, snug in my multiple layers of fleece, Capilene, and Gore-Tex, it was an easy decision not to take off my warm gloves to fish.

"Aren't your hands cold?" I asked the Kingfish.

His fingertips were rimed with ice. His blue thumb appeared frozen to the cork handle. "After an eight-by-ten cell," he replied, "there's no such thing as cold."

I could appreciate the sentiment but still draw the line at fishing when the fly line freezes in the rod guides. It helps keep the line free if you dip the

the rod in the water, but that's why the Kingfish's hand was covered with ice. If it's cold enough the line freezes anyway, and dipping the rod in the river just makes the problem worse. The temperature had been dropping steadily all day. It was nearly dark and couldn't have been much more than ten degrees above zero when the Kingfish saw what he'd been looking for all along.

"One more trout," he said, holding up a blue index finger, "then we can go."

The trout was rising behind us only a couple of feet from the snow-covered shore in water so shallow the fish's flowing golden dorsal showed. It was a big brown, and when the Kingfish was a kid he practiced casting by running down Badger Creek dropping his fly into a toy wooden canoe as it bobbed through the riffles. His first cast was perfect. The white Half-a-Chicken vanished in a dark ring centered on a bulging nose.

The Kingfish set the hook and four or five pounds of heavy yellow-bellied trout flopped in silhouette against the white snow. The trout jumped again then tried to run, but it was now so cold the line had frozen solid in the rod guides. Something had to give and it wasn't the fish; the iced graphite rod shattered with a muted crack like a distant gunshot in the falling snow. The fly ripped free but the fish was still jumping somersaults as it vanished in the gloom.

I looked at the Kingfish, he looked at me, then we both looked down at the broken rod.

And we laughed and laughed.

I'd laughed enough that my stomach hurt as the Kingfish dropped to his knees in a foot and a half of water. That sharp Roman nose, those piercing black eyes, the high cheekbones; all he needed was a feathered headdress. It was easy to see he'd descended from chiefs as the Kingfish scooped a double handful of river and held it up as an offering to the sky.

"It's a good day to die," he said happily. "It's such a good day to die."

That tenet of Blackfoot philosophy is echoed in the live-for-the-moment theology of the Church of the Reduced Humanist; all it means is that a fully lived life isn't something that death can take away. That's what you get to keep.

"You can't die yet," I replied. "We still have a party to go to."

Two miles up the river the yellow neon sign advertising beer, food, and ice flickered on the roof above the Mountain Palace. Snow melted on the warm hoods of recently parked cars and trucks as we left the blizzard in the parking for the steaming debauchery of a full-blown Testicle Festival. The Ball-and-Chain Party was at Mach One and climbing, led by an all-star cast of musicians assembled from the Ghost of Nitwits past.

Jake and Elwood, the Balls Brothers, were fronting the band, moon-walking on the wooden stage in slick black shoes and short blue suits that showed two inches of hairy leg above six inches of white sock. In keeping with the evening's jailhouse theme, drinks were half price for anyone in criminal's garb. With a $250 first prize for best costume on the line, competition was fierce.

Jesse James was there with a bullet in his back, tearing it up on the scuffed maple dance floor. Robin Hood, Al Capone, and Leona Helmsley knocked back half-price shots at the bar. O. J. searched frantically for his missing glove. Bonnie and Clyde slam-danced alongside a papier-mâché Packard riddled with bullet holes. Six bald bikers in orange county work-suits were bound together with leg irons, but it looked to me like everybody was fighting it out for second place. Hanni-Ball the Canni-Ball Lector was a shoo-in for the big money.

Up on the stage, Jake was strangling the skinny microphone stand with both hands as he growled out the chorus to "Bartender Blues."

Elwood put down his beer and tried a running cartwheel as a lead-in to his harmonica break, but in real life Elwood was a 250-pound logger who hadn't cartwheeled since grade school. He missed the stage entirely and landed on the dance floor, his fall cushioned by the twirling tassels of two fat biker babes dressed up as hookers in black rayon mini skirts and shiny thigh-high boots.

Pope John Ball II, in a touching ceremony at a mock pulpit just inside the front doors, anointed the Kingfish the Patron Saint of Sunken Ships. The Kingfish, now clad in a regal purple bathrobe and a wide cardboard hat that looked like an exploding Jet-Boat, turned at the touch of a hand on his shoulder. The bow of the spinning boat whacked the pope's tall white pointed hat right into Heidi's arms. She'd snuck up from behind in a clinging white body-stocking written all over in black Magic Marker with the formula: $C^{19}H^{28}O^2$.

Heidi gave the pope back his hat. The Kingfish sniffed at the air.

"Let me guess," he said, "You're formaldehyde."

Heidi folded her arms under her breasts. "Testosterone," she replied.

The Kingfish leaned down with an exaggerated squint at the numbers. "It doesn't seem like nearly enough oxygen," he said.

Heidi blinked hard several times as she looked the Kingfish up and down. "So," she said quietly, taking him by the hand, "how was it?"

"Hey," he said as they walked away, "it sucked."

This left me alone, which wasn't the same as being by myself. I needed a drink. Even slipping sideways it was tough to squirt through the dense crowd to the bar. At any given conversational knot you were as likely to overhear tales of piranha and pike as trout. A Styrofoam effigy of Osama bin Laden hung by a horsehair noose in the corner; people were using him for a dartboard. The visual mayhem continued as Jake and Elwood made way on the stage for Heidi in her white facepaint and the Kingfish with his long black braids.

"We're going to do one—" said Heidi, her husky voice rumbling through the speakers.

"—about growing up poor," finished the Kingfish.

Butte Girl and Reservation Indian, they leaned into the same micro-phone, her sloping shoulder burrowed beneath his lean biceps. The Kingfish bore no resemblance to the wizened old man I'd picked up at the jail. A couple of hours on the water had rejuvenated him. There must have been a logical chiropractic explanation, like his spine straightening, but it was more like he was swelling with the music; filling out before my eyes. His hacking cough was gone, and arm in arm the Kingfish and Heidi sang a dust bowl ballad to life.

The haunting minor melody described a succession of disasters: drought, pestilence, tornadoes, the death of children; by the time the town dried up and blew away the raucous Mountain Palace had gone quiet as church. The two of them up on the stage, the way they sang, it may be as close as human beings ever get. Tears slid down my cheeks and splashed into my red wine. No matter what else I had with Heidi, I'd never have that.

The torment was that I knew what I was missing.

One time, and one time only, I'd known that joy they shared. I was leaning against a hot rock in the pine forest, half asleep, doodling a guitar, thinking about nothing in particular when a mule deer doe walked up with wet, yellow eyes. The deer stood so close I could smell the juniper on her breath. The coarse white hairs inside her long gray ears were directed like antennae toward the round sound hole on the guitar; after a time I realized I'd just ripped note for note through half a dozen rollicking fiddle tunes I'd never played before.

I was the music and the music was me. But as soon as I knew it was happening I lost it. The music was gone, and it's never come back. Not like that, and what I wonder is this: Where did it go?

It can't just disappear. Nothing, not matter or energy, not music or marmalade, just disappears. Cutting-edge physicists describe a universe made up at its most fundamental level of tiny vibrating strings, and where strings vibrate, there must be music. The aborigines may have gotten religion right with their belief that the world was sung into existence.

You were there for the Big Bang and so was I. So were the rivers and all the stars in the sky; all the strings in the universe were there, performing the opening note in an ongoing concert that is now spread out over fifteen billion light years of space. It's the music of creation, the hum before the Big Bang, the bottom line of harmonic vibration that binds the universe together. The music doesn't go anywhere because it's the one thing that's already everywhere. You just have to know where to look, and as Heidi and the Kingfish let the last lingering note float away, the hushed Mountain Palace erupted in a turgid roar of spontaneous applause.

"Another one!" The throng screamed for more. "Do another one!"

The Kingfish turned to the Nitwits, a smear of Heidi's white facepaint on his cheek. "Jailhouse Rock," he said. "In G."

The Ball-and-Chain Party went late. The next day, the first of November, began far too early with the jangling of the telephone on the overturned milk crate beside the bed.

"M-m-mph," said Heidi, pulling the pillow over her head. "It's for you."

I picked up the phone, dropped it with wine-deadened fingers, picked it up off the down comforter. The day was blue and bright. The big round thermometer outside the bedroom window read eighteen degrees below zero as I lay back in bed with the receiver to my ear.

"This is the coroner's office," said a somber voice. "The note had your number on it."

The Kingfish had known since the physical they'd given him before they'd let him out of jail; he just hadn't told anybody. Three packs a day had finally caught up with him. It was cancer, riddling his lymph nodes. The doctors gave him six months but the Kingfish decided not to wait; for a warrior a hospital might be the only punishment worse than jail. He'd left a message with 911; they found him in the cottonwood grove by the old wagon at Trout World, covered with snow, frozen solid in the front seat of his driftboat.

The note specified cremation, the dust to be spread in the Apikuni at the Prairie Dog Put-in at midnight of the next full moon. He'd asked that his hair be tied into flies, a box of Black Wulffs on a rock at the edge of the parking lot for mourners to grab. Cremation is an imperfect process with bones and especially teeth; at the appointed hour the Kingfish splashed like a handful of pebbles. The rest of him rose in a mushroom cloud of ash toward the far shore on the slightest of following breezes. I knelt on wet knees on the cold ground, Heidi warm at my side, trying to forget how jealous I'd been, the two of them singing that last night together.

How can you ever really know another person? And what did it matter? Everybody leaves you in the end. You come in alone, you go out alone. I'd tried so hard for so long to give meaning to existence but the Church of the Reduced Humanist had failed me, which was the same as saying I'd failed myself. The specter of the waiting void choked off the windpipe in my constricted throat. I couldn't imagine ever breathing again when Heidi squeezed my hand hard enough to grind the knuckles together.

From rippling water to Heidi, my eyes followed her locked gaze across the river.

And there, through the smeared wedge of ash glowing golden in the moonlight, a beefed-up hot-rod convertible was towing a wood-strip driftboat down the frontage road. Chrome carburetors stuck up through the hood of the car, and the backseat was full of five-gallon gas cans, but the engine was so quiet it could have been magnetic. A man and a woman, young Blackfoot Indians, laughed in the front seat, unbraided hair blowing straight back in the wind. Car and boat streaked through the silvery moon-shadows fast enough to skim the potholes, then vanished around the corner of the cliff. I looked back at Heidi but she was already looking at me, crow's feet wrinkling the corners of her bright green eyes.

"Did you see that?" we said together.